IMAGES
of America

Lakota Sioux Missions
South Dakota

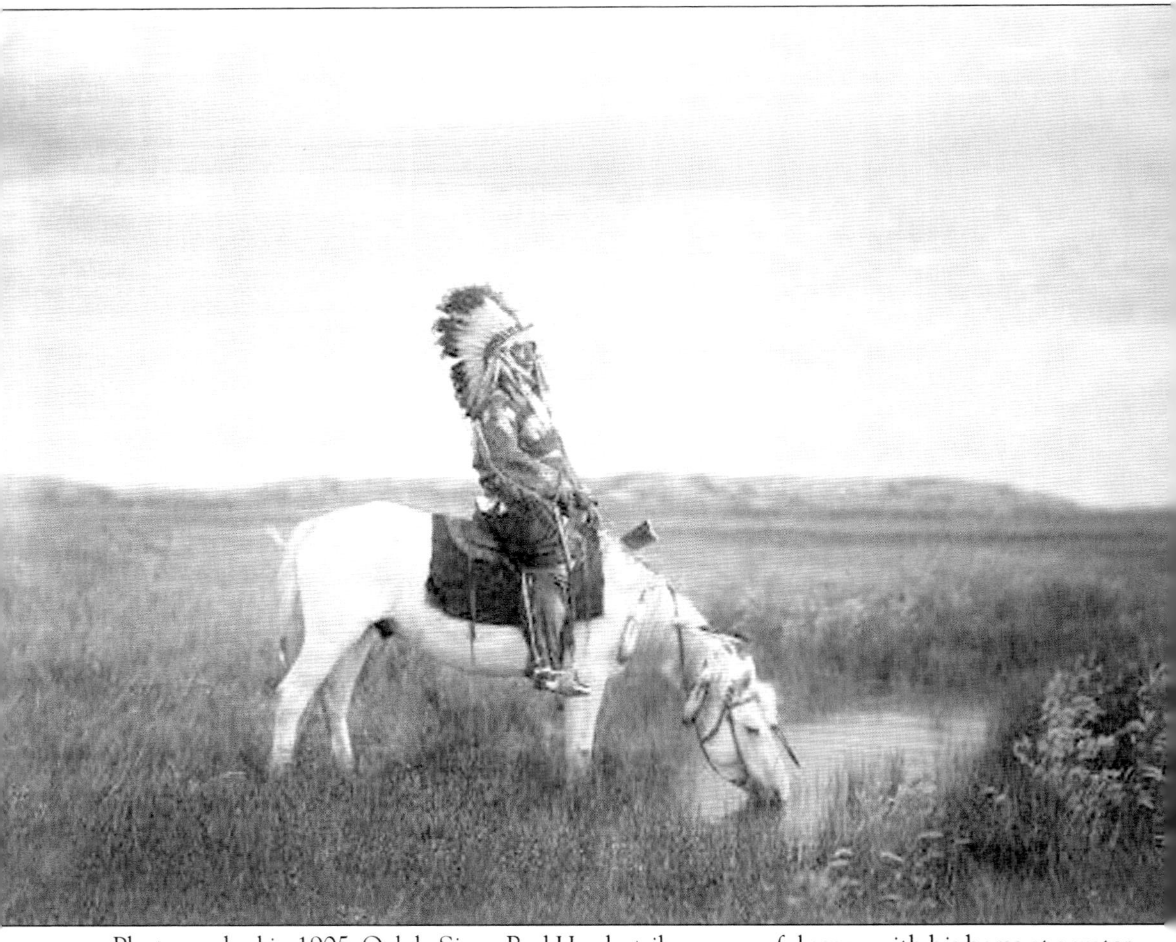

Photographed in 1905, Oglala Sioux Red Hawk strikes a peaceful scene with his horse at a water hole on the Pine Ridge Reservation. (Library of Congress Prints and Photographs Division; Edward Curtis Collection. LC-USZ62-107914.)

Chronology of Events

1840 Father Christian Hoecken administered the first sacrament of baptism west of the Missouri River in South Dakota
1849 DeSmet ministered to the Sioux along the Missouri River
1862 Sioux uprising in Minnesota
1868 Ft. Laramie Treaty created the Great Sioux Reservation
1869 President Grant instituted the Peace Policy
1872 Thomas Riggs established Hope Mission on Cheyenne River Reservation
1873 Bishop Hare came West
1875 Hare sent Rev. Cleveland to organize a mission on Spotted Tail Agency
1876 Bureau of Catholic Missions assigned Bishop Marty to the Standing Rock
1877 Hare assigned Luke Walker Pine Ridge
1881 Restrictions of Grant's Peace Policy lifted
1885 St. Francis founded by Jesuits
1888 Holy Rosary founded
1890 Mission established at St. Elizabeth's, Wakpala

IMAGES
of America

LAKOTA SIOUX MISSIONS SOUTH DAKOTA

Jan Cerney

ARCADIA
PUBLISHING

ISBN 978-0-7385-3393-3

Published by Arcadia Publishing
Charleston, South Carolina

Printed in the United States of America

Library of Congress Catalog Card Number: 2005920675

For all general information contact Arcadia Publishing at:
Telephone 843-853-2070
Fax 843-853-0044
E-mail sales@arcadiapublishing.com
For customer service and orders:
Toll-Free 1-888-313-2665

Visit us on the Internet at www.arcadiapublishing.com

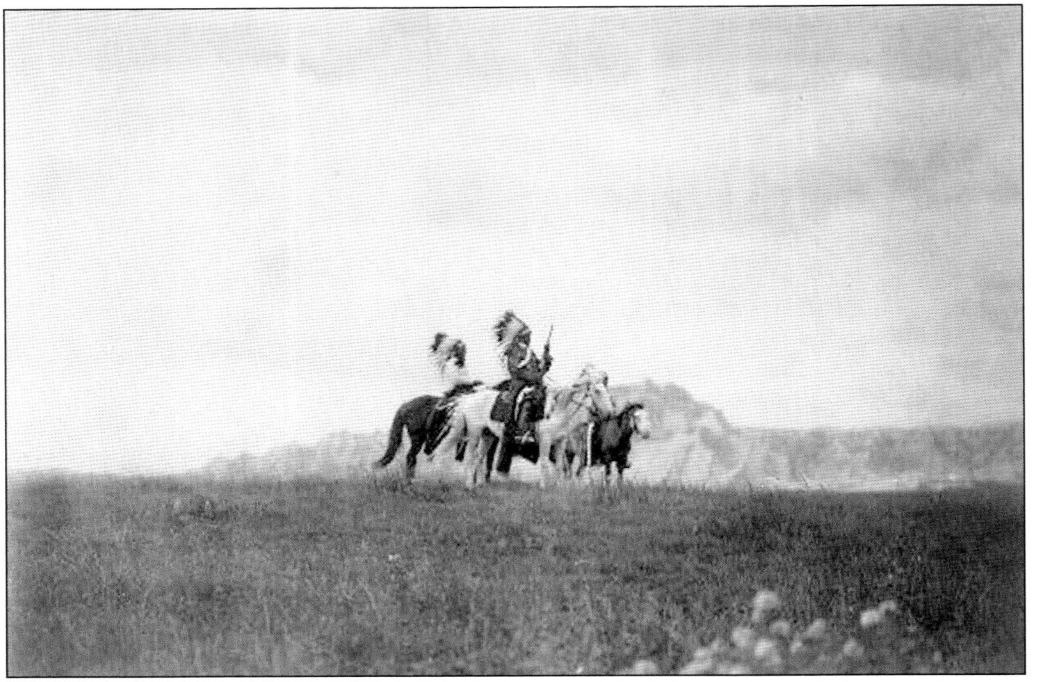

The Land of the Sioux is the title of this 1905 photograph by Edward Curtis. (Library of Congress Prints and Photographs Division; Edward Curtis Collection. LC-USZ62-105379.)

Contents

ACKNOWLEDGMENTS

I owe special thanks to Amy Duxbury of St Joseph's Indian School for permitting me access to the school's photo archives. I also extend appreciation to Diane Kindt of the Klein Museum in Mobridge, Jim Nelson of the Timber Lake and Area Historical Society, the South Dakota State Archives, Mark Hertig of Agate Fossil Beds National Monument, Penny Gerling, and Mike Marshall of Buechel Memorial Museum, St. Francis Mission, for their assistance in locating photographs and providing information.

I am grateful to the authors of the following books. Without them, research of the Lakota religion and identification of churches and sites would have been difficult.

Black Elk, Nicholas. *The Gift of the Sacred Pipe.* Norman: University of Oklahoma Press, 1982.

Eastman, Elaine Goodale. *Sister to the Sioux.* Lincoln and London: University of Nebraska Press, 1978.

Sneve, Virginia Driving Hawk. *That They May Live, The* Episcopal *Church in South Dakota.* New York: Seabury Press, 1977.

Solon OSB, Sister Eleanor. *We Walk By Faith, The Growth of the Catholic Faith in Western South Dakota.* Strasbourg, France: Editions du Signe, 2002.

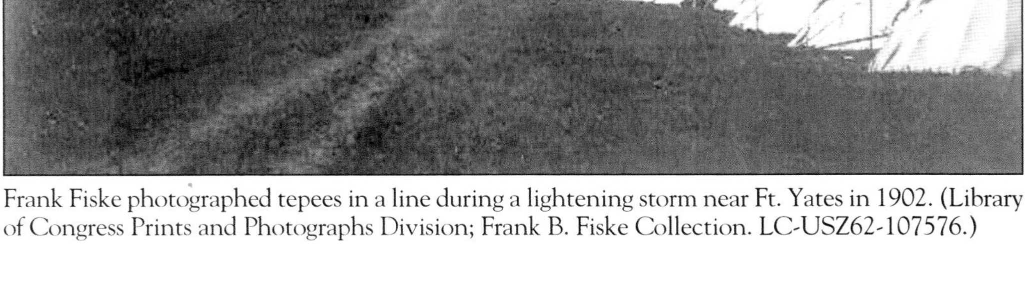

Frank Fiske photographed tepees in a line during a lightening storm near Ft. Yates in 1902. (Library of Congress Prints and Photographs Division; Frank B. Fiske Collection. LC-USZ62-107576.)

INTRODUCTION

By the time President Grant issued his peacekeeping policy of 1869, relations between the non-Native Americans and the Sioux were strained. White intrusion threatened the Native American way of life. Wars had been fought, hunting lands had been restricted, and with each new treaty the Sioux were more dependent on the U.S. government for survival. In order to maintain peace, the Fort Laramie Treaty of 1868 designated western South Dakota as the Great Sioux Reservation. No white man was to intrude. With the 1874 discovery of gold in the Black Hills, peace again was threatened.

Grant's peacekeeping policy assigned one specific religious denomination to each reservation with the task of "civilizing" the Indian. In the region of Dakota, the government determined Catholics would administer to the Standing Rock and Devil's Lake Reservations, the Episcopalians were given the Rosebud, Pine Ridge, and Cheyenne Reservations, and the Congregational Church was granted Lower Brule. The government promised to provide food, clothing, and a small amount of money to the various sects who would build schools and educate the Indian.

Prior to this time, Pierre DeSmet of the Society of Jesus had been a missionary to the Sioux who were free to roam the prairie near the Missouri River, unhindered by the reservation system. DeSmet won the trust and respect of his converts and laid the groundwork for the Catholic faith among the Sioux. The various religious denominations first sent missionaries into the region of Minnesota. These missionaries ministered here, east of the Missouri River, before they came west. When the Santee Sioux revolted in Minnesota in 1862, the Santee were imprisoned and then deported to the Crow Creek Reservation, just east of the Missouri River. The missionaries followed them and assisted them in their adjustments; first to Crow Creek and then to Santee Agency in Nebraska. They also established missions at the Yankton Agency.

The mission goal, regardless of denomination, was to convert, educate, and train their new charges in vocational occupations so they would ideally assimilate into white culture more readily. Many denominations joined in to civilize and acculturate the Native American. Some of those involved were the Hicksite Friends, Orthodox Friends, Baptists, Presbyterians, Methodists, Catholics, Reformed Dutch, Congregationalists, Episcopalians, Unitarians, and Lutherans. The late 19th century viewpoint supported the belief that to civilize the Native American was to Christianize him. Reformers felt they were pursuing their destined objective and consequently would become the Native American's friend. They also believed that if Native Americans were separated from their culture and language, they would become like the whites. Little did they realize how ingrained the native culture was, and how important it was to their very being.

When the government withdrew funding in the early 1900s, the missions and churches struggled for existence. The missions that survived, found resources elsewhere. Well over 100 years have passed since the first missions were established. Fires, tornadoes, and the ravages of time have destroyed much of the physical evidence of the early mission era. However, the achievements of the dedicated missionaries live on. The missionaries helped to preserve the Lakota language by translating prayer books, Bibles, hymnals, and dictionaries into the Lakota language. Many missionaries photographed tribal members and daily events on the reservations and collected artifacts that are now displayed in museums. Many missionaries, who spent their entire life with the Sioux, became very knowledgeable in their culture and wrote about their experiences. Schools and churches still thrive in the reservation communities, although the number has dwindled. The tribes have taken over the responsibility and decision-making in organizing and administrating schools and churches. A growing number of Lakota Sioux still hold to their time-honored religion. Those who embrace the traditional customs still observe the Sun Dances and other rituals. Others have retained the religion that the missionaries brought to their ancestors. Still others have merged beliefs of the two religions.

Even though this book is written about the Lakota who primarily inhabited western South Dakota, other Sioux communities are included. To clarify the various divisions of the Sioux people, I have included the following classification of the Sioux, or Dakota.

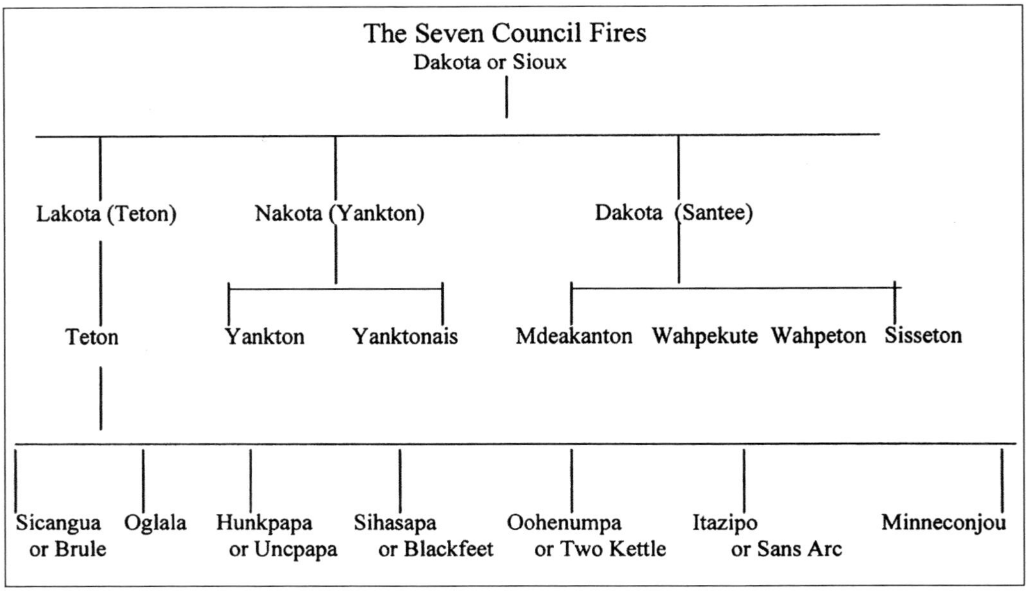

One

IN THE BEGINNING

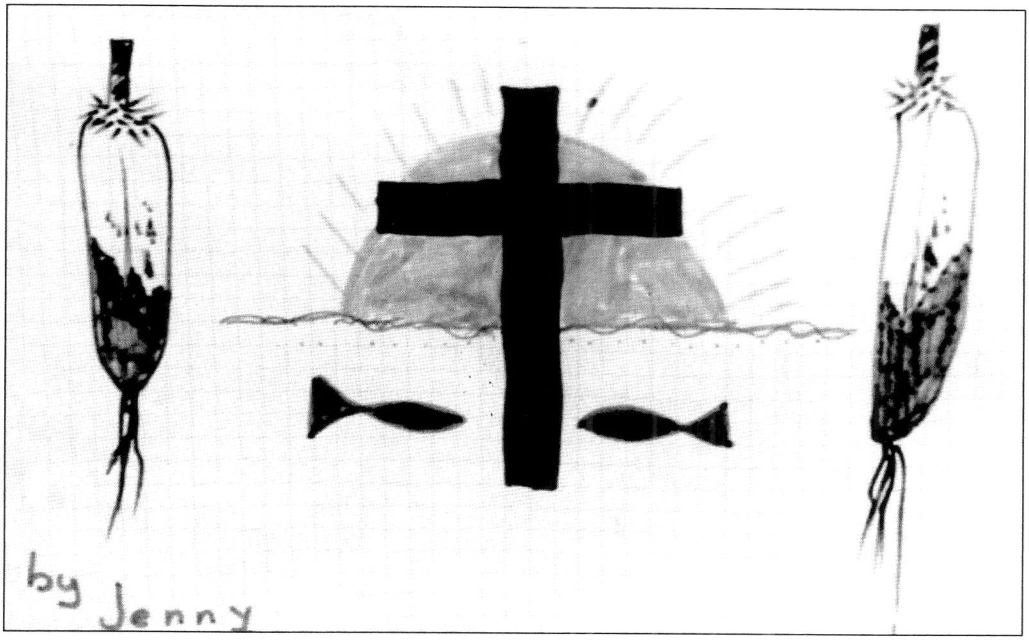

When the native children came to mission schools, they had their own religion and culture. At first the Sioux people were forbidden to practice their culture, but later they were permitted to incorporate their heritage and traditional beliefs, as illustrated in this drawing by a St. Joseph's Indian School student. (St. Joseph's Indian School, Chamberlain.)

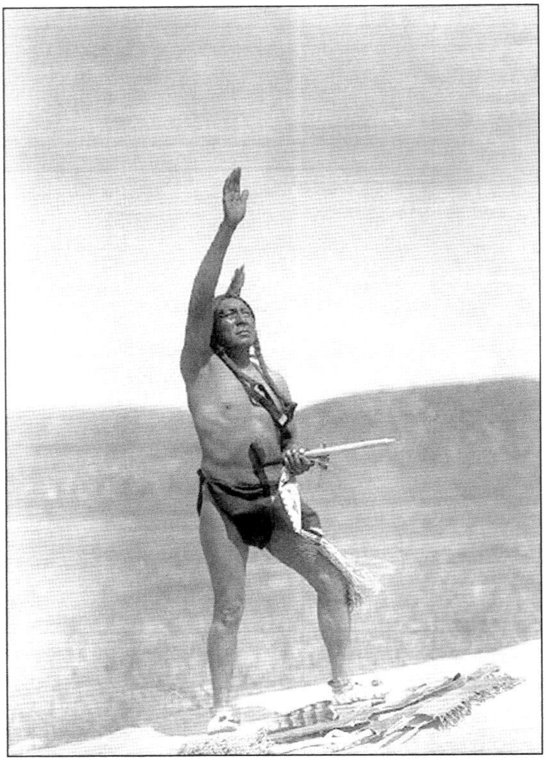

A Sioux man wears a buffalo headdress and holds a peace pipe. The pipe was an important part of Sioux tradition and was used to communicate with the Great Spirit. (Library of Congress Prints and Photographs Division. LC-USZ62-54813.)

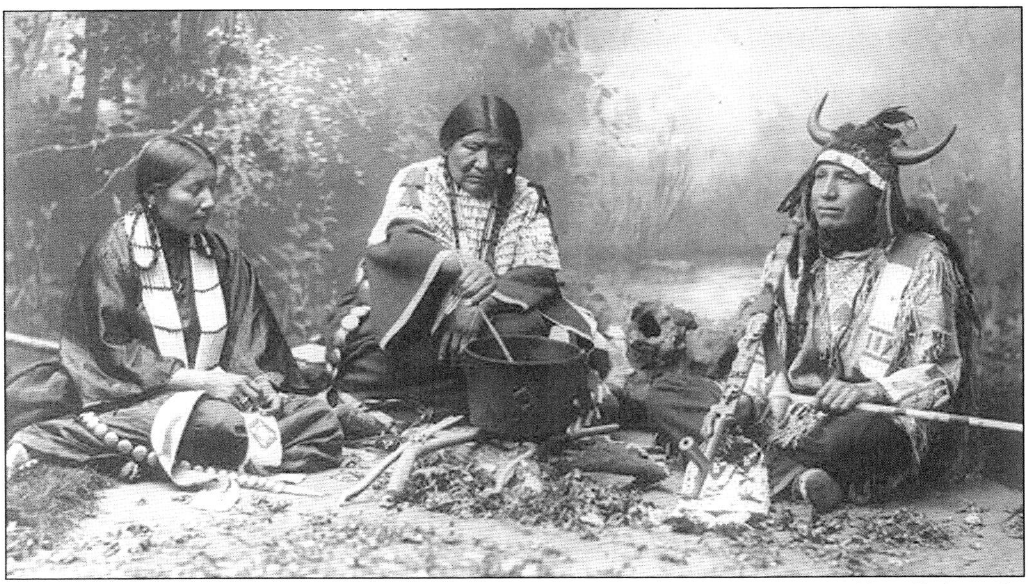

According to Sioux tradition, a woman clad in white buckskin and carrying a sacred bundle brought the gift of the Sacred Pipe to the people. With the pipe, they would be able to send their voices to Wakan-Tanka, the Great Spirit. She took from the bundle the pipe and a small round stone. Upon the stone were seven round circles representing the seven sacred rites. (Library of Congress Prints and Photographs Division; Ed Curtis Collection. LC-USZ62-51434.)

Our Lady of the Sioux Chapel's interior, St. Joseph's Indian School, was refurbished in 1985. Ron Zeilinger created the following stained glass windows representing the seven sacred rites. This stained glass window represents Crying for a Vision. The vision quest was sought after a purification rite. Those who were of good character and were the most qualified received the greatest visions. A Holy Man often instructed the vision seeker as to the correct method in seeking a vision. A great vision would bring strength to the nation. (St. Joseph's Indian School, Chamberlain; David Meyer, photographer.)

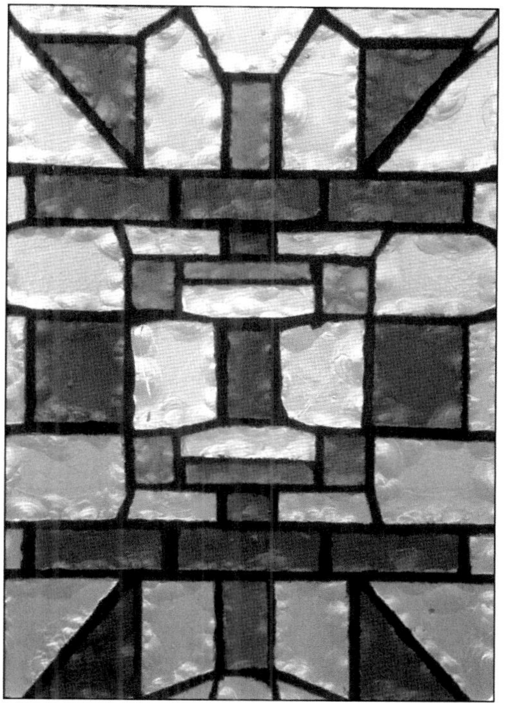

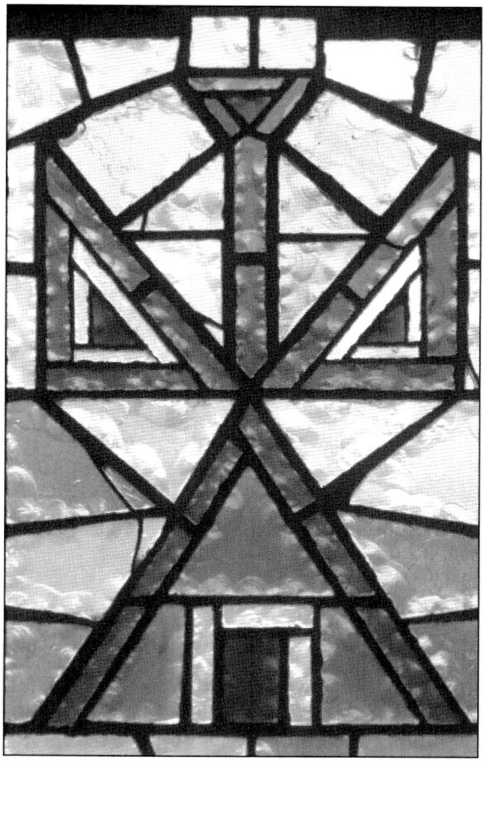

The sweat lodge used in the rite of purification was made of a willow frame, marking the four quarters of the universe. The lodge represented the entire universe. All people and things required purification before their voices could be sent to Wakan-Tanka. (St. Joseph's Indian School, Chamberlain; David Meyer, photographer.)

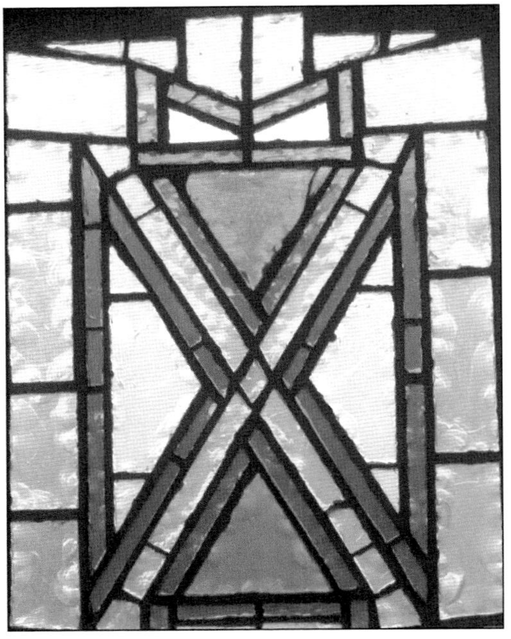

The rite of the Sun Dance, held in June or July when the moon was full, symbolized the offering of body and soul to Wakan-Tanka. The sacred cottonwood placed in the center of the circle, stretched from heaven to earth, sending the voices of the people to the Great Spirit. Dancers pierced their skin and attached leather thongs. As they danced, the thong broke loose from the flesh, symbolizing breaking the bond of ignorance. (St. Joseph's Indian School, Chamberlain; David Meyer, photographer.)

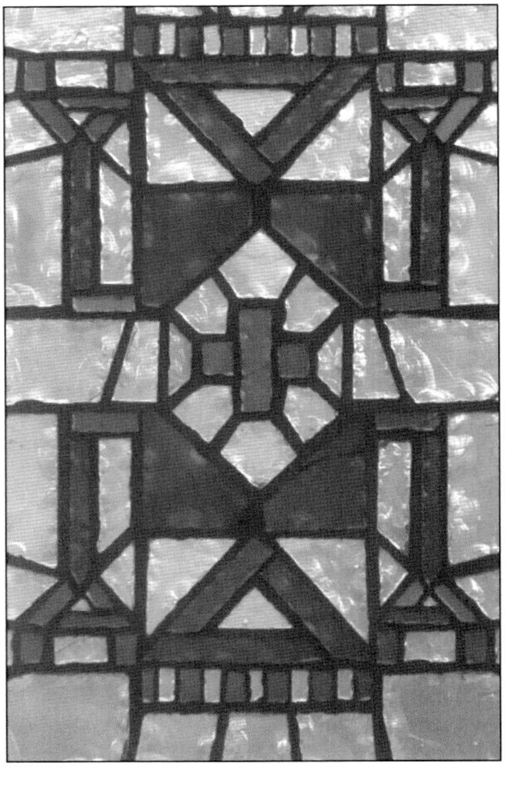

The Keeping of the Soul ritual purifies the souls of the dead so they may travel the sacred path. The person designated as keeper of the soul and the sacred bundle follows ritualistic instructions until the soul is released, usually after about one year. The government prohibited this rite, as well as that of the Sun Dance. (St. Joseph's Indian School, Chamberlain; David Meyer, photographer.)

In this rite, The Making of Relatives, the people strive for a closer relationship with their fellow man. The necessary items needed for this rite are: a pipe, tobacco, four stalks of corn with ears, one cornstalk without ears, a buffalo skull, three sticks for a rack, dried buffalo meat, red and dark blue paint, eagle plumes, a knife, sweet grass, and dried buffalo bladder. (St. Joseph's Indian School, Chamberlain; David Meyer, photographer.)

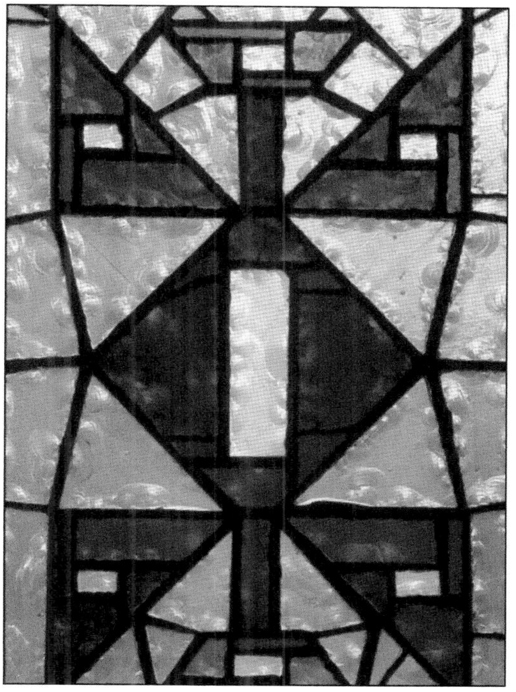

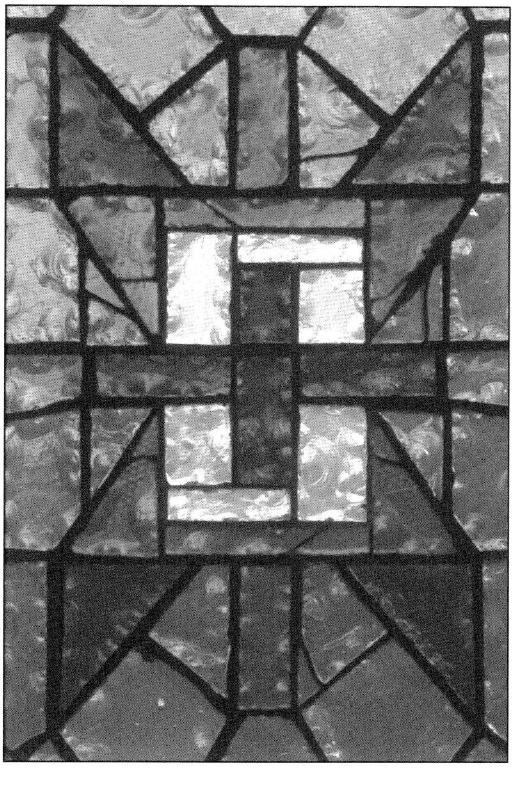

Not only was a girl purified during the Preparing a Girl for Womanhood rite, but an entire generation would be purified as well. Prayers were offered that she, her children, and children's children would walk the sacred path. (St. Joseph's Indian School, Chamberlain; David Meyer, photographer.)

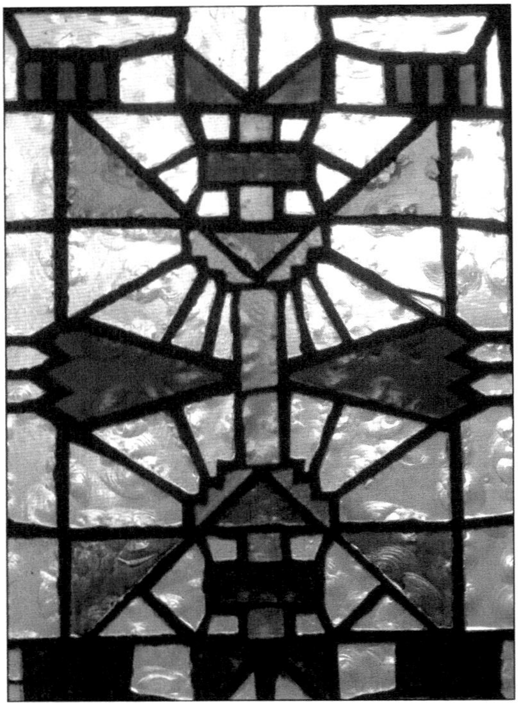

The Throwing of the Ball, the seventh and last rite, was a game in which a ball represented Wakan-Tanka, or the universe. A little girl stands in the circle and throws the ball symbolizing the youth and purity of Wakan-Tanka. She throws the ball from the center to the four quarters where it descends on the people and is received by few. (St. Joseph's Indian School, Chamberlain; David Meyer, photographer.)

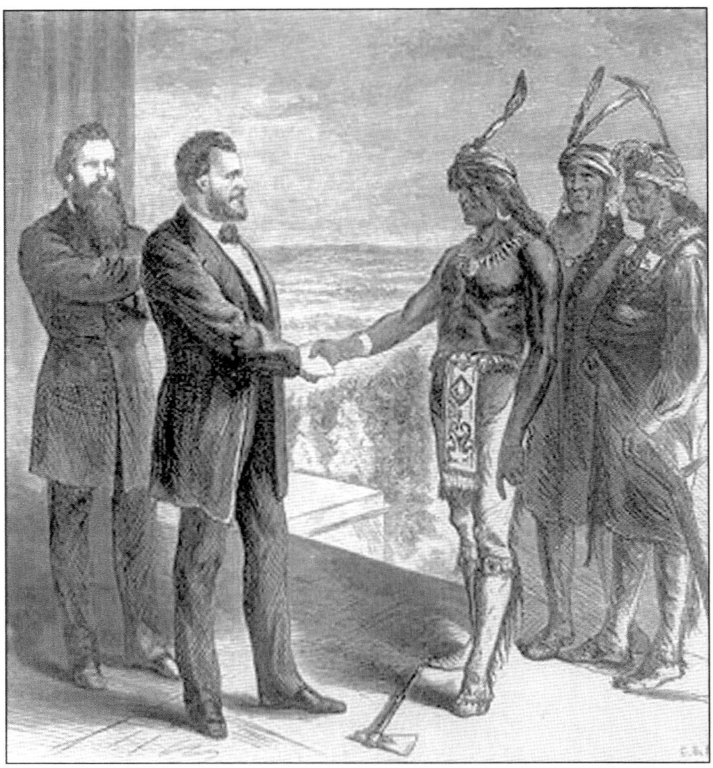

C.S. Reinhart drew this image, entitled *Let Us Have Peace*, for the June 18, 1870 edition of *Harper's Weekly*. Ulysses S. Grant, not absolutely identified, and another man greet Red Cloud, Spotted Tail, and Swift Bear during a visit of an Indian delegation with Commissioner of Indian Affairs, Ely S. Parker. Grant initiated the 1869 Peace Plan that would send missionaries to the reservations to educate and civilize the Native American. (Library of Congress Prints and Photographs Division. LC-USZ62-96533.)

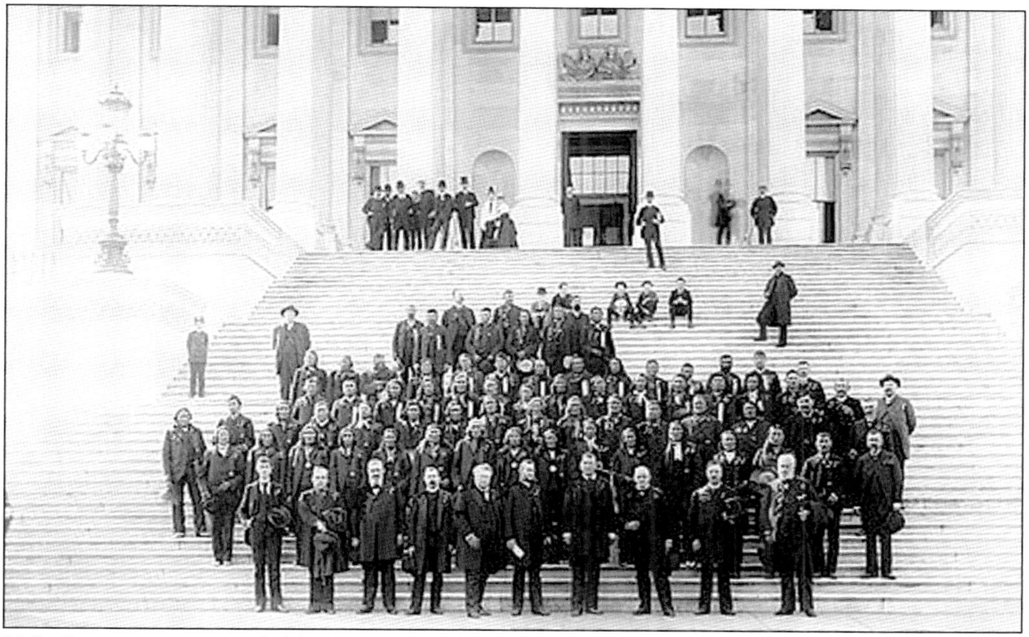

U.S. Commissioners and delegations of Sioux chiefs visiting Washington, on October 13, 1888, stand on the steps of the U.S. Capitol building. Sioux delegations negotiated treaties and other policies affecting their tribes. Many of the major chiefs are included in this photograph. Sitting Bull, to the left, stands apart from the group. (Library of Congress Prints and Photographs Division; C.M. Bell Collection. LC-USZ62-92959.)

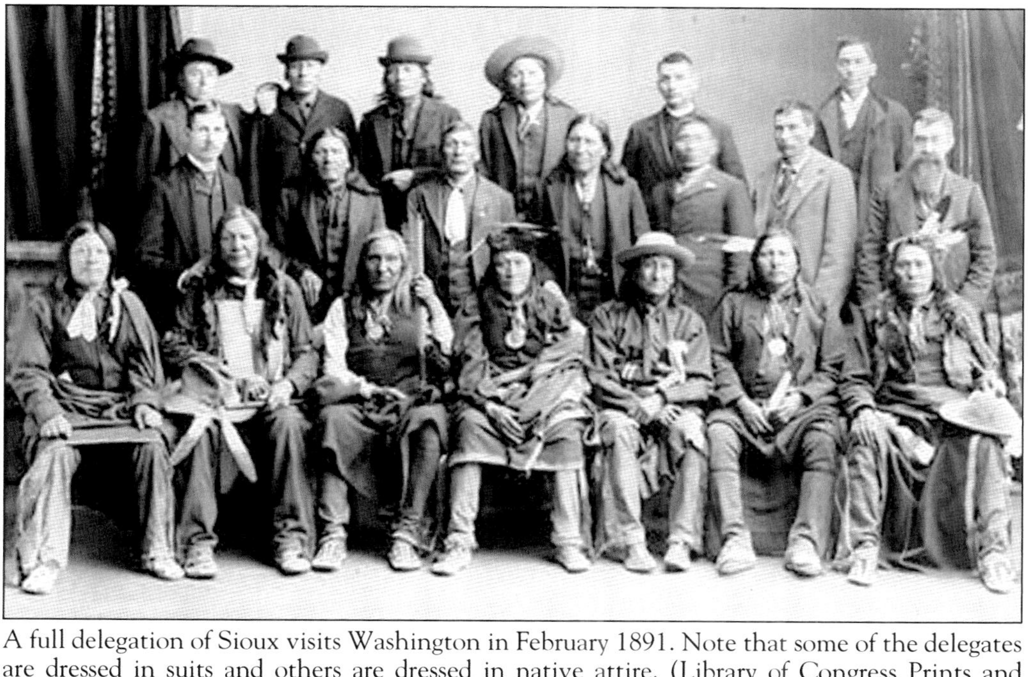

A full delegation of Sioux visits Washington in February 1891. Note that some of the delegates are dressed in suits and others are dressed in native attire. (Library of Congress Prints and Photographs Division; C.M. Bell Collection. LC-USZ62-4536.)

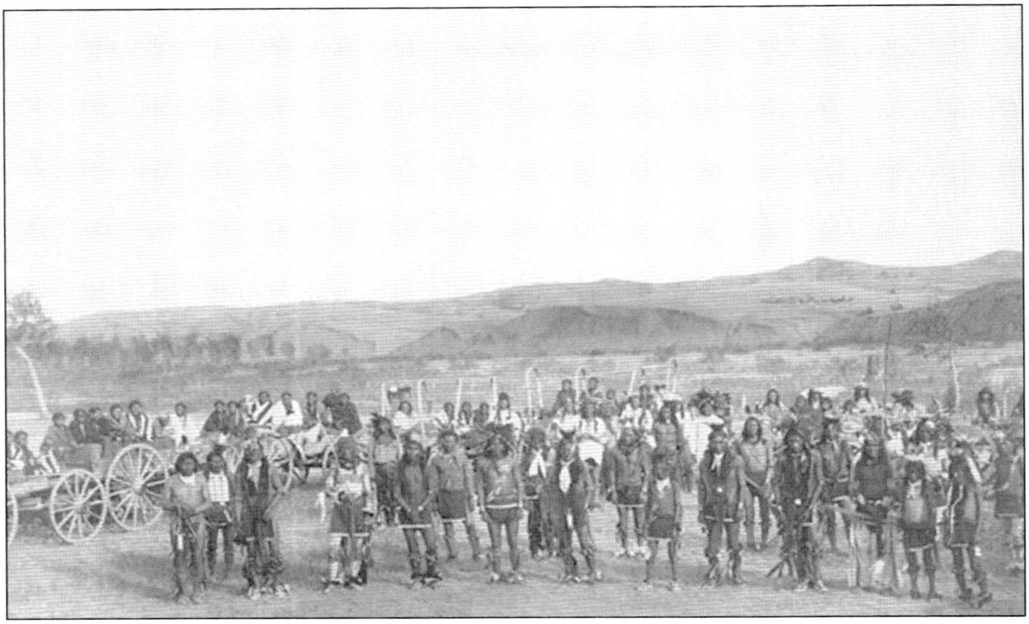

Although the government forbade the practice of some of the rituals, the Lakota continued to dance. This photograph is of Big Foot's band at a grass dance in 1890. The government felt threatened by the grass dance and forbid its practice. Part of the 8th U.S. Cavalry and 3rd Infantry were present at this dance on the Cheyenne River Reservation. (Library of Congress Prints and Photographs Division; John C. Grabill Collection. LC-USZ62-22968.)

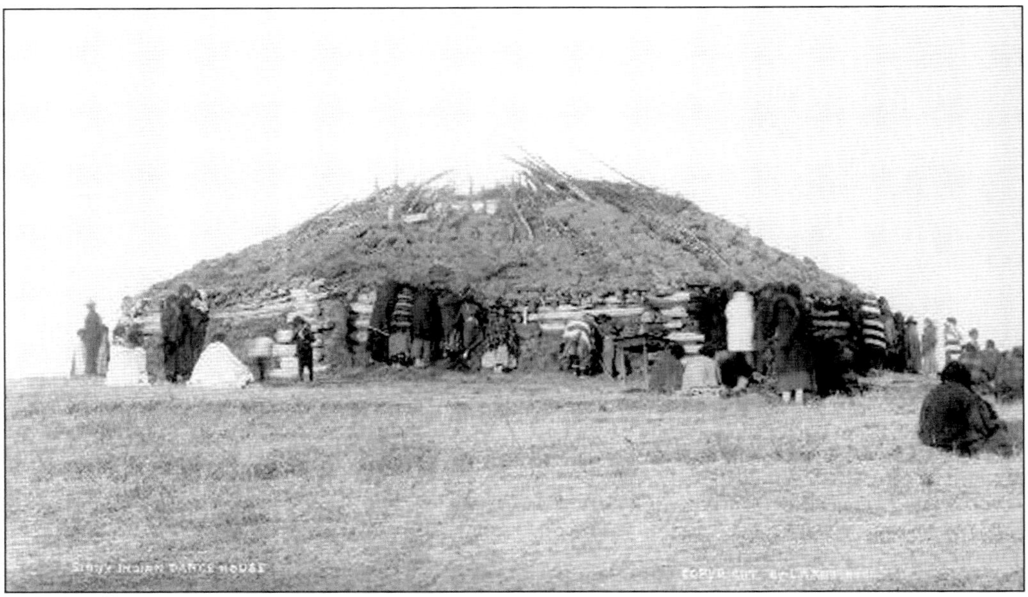

This 1911 dance house was made of logs with a sod roof. (Library of Congress Prints and Photographs Division; John A. Anderson. LC-USZ62-101270.)

The powwow tradition has always been observed, even through turbulent times. Dancing at powwows today has become competitive with various categories in which to enter. The men's Fancy Dance, a relatively new dance, is very colorful. The men wear feather bustles and vivid regalia. The dance requires increased speed and intricate footwork. (St. Joseph's Indian School, Chamberlain; David Meyer, photographer.)

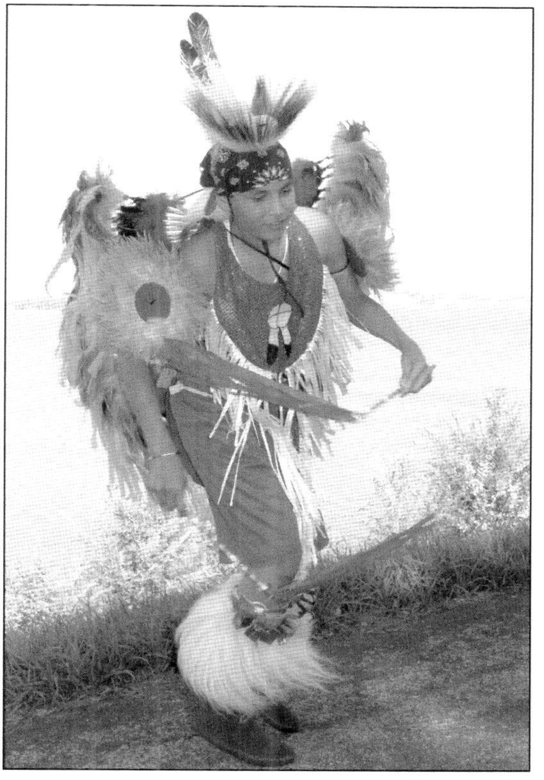

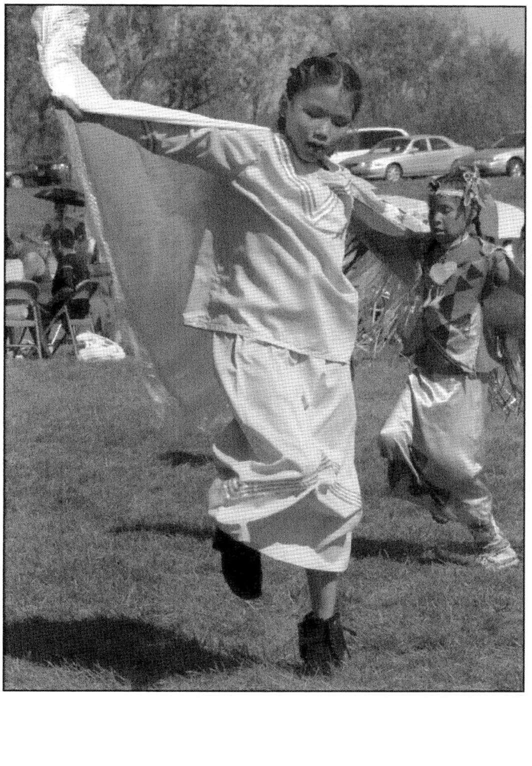

In the 1930s and 1940s, the women began to show off the fancy shawls they made by dancing what became known as the Fancy Shawl Dance. The dance evolved into a fast spinning movement incorporating fancy footwork. (St. Joseph's Indian School, Chamberlain; David Meyer, photographer.)

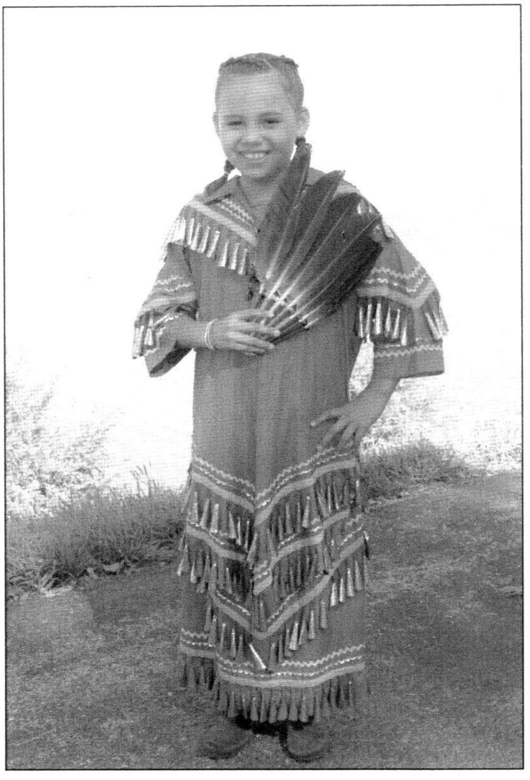

The Jingle Dance originated in Mile Lacs, Minnesota, and made its way to the Lakota in 1920. Metal cone jingles are sewn in a pattern on cloth dresses. Graceful movements keep the jingles moving in time to the music. (St. Joseph's Indian School, Chamberlain; David Meyer, photographer.)

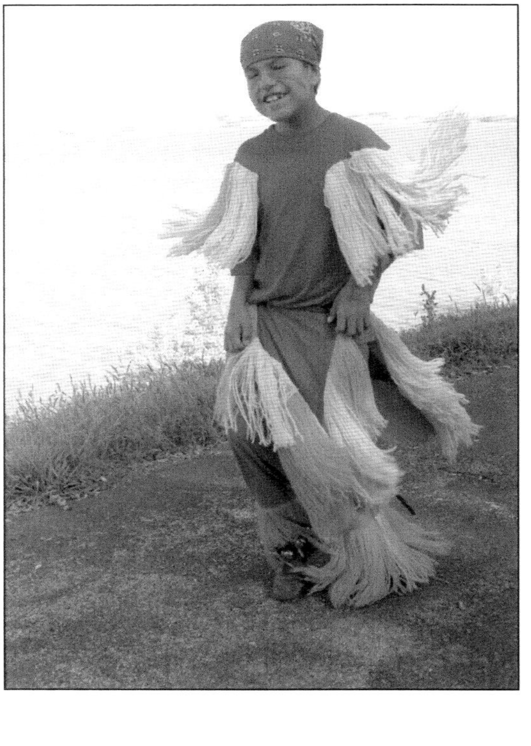

One of the oldest surviving dances is the Omaha or Grass Dance, borrowed from the Omaha tribe in the 1860s. The fringe on the dancer's regalia represents the long, flowing grass of the prairie. (St. Joseph's Indian School, Chamberlain; David Meyer, photographer.)

The Men's Fancy Dance may have originated in Oklahoma in the early 1900s when dancers were asked to beautify their regalia for the spectators. (St. Joseph's Indian School, Chamberlain; David Meyer, photographer.)

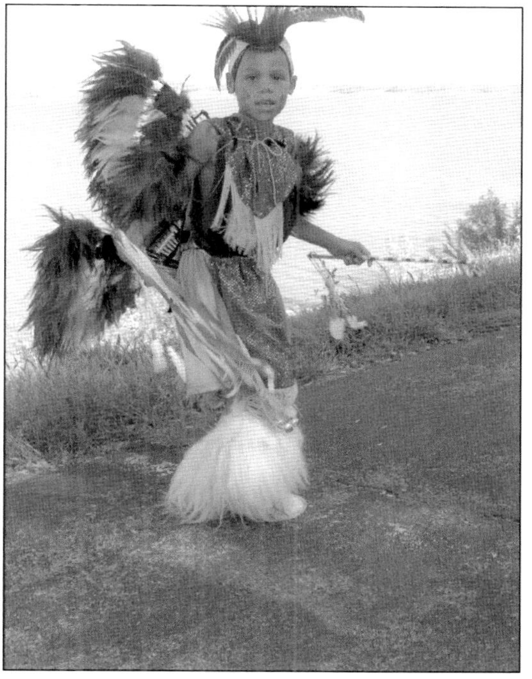

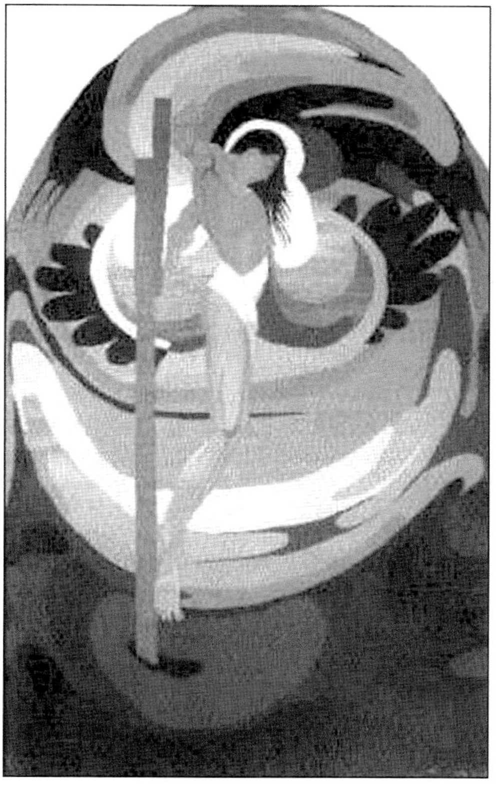

Oscar Howe, the noted Crow Creek Sioux artist, painted the Indian Christ, which Greta Heikes wove into this tapestry. The seven-feet by ten-feet six-inch tapestry occupies a place of honor behind the altar in Our Lady of the Sioux Chapel at St. Josephs' Indian School. The Oscar Howe Indian Christ painting is part of the Akta Lakota Museum Collection at St. Joseph's Indian School. (St. Joseph's Indian School, Chamberlain; David Meyer, photographer.)

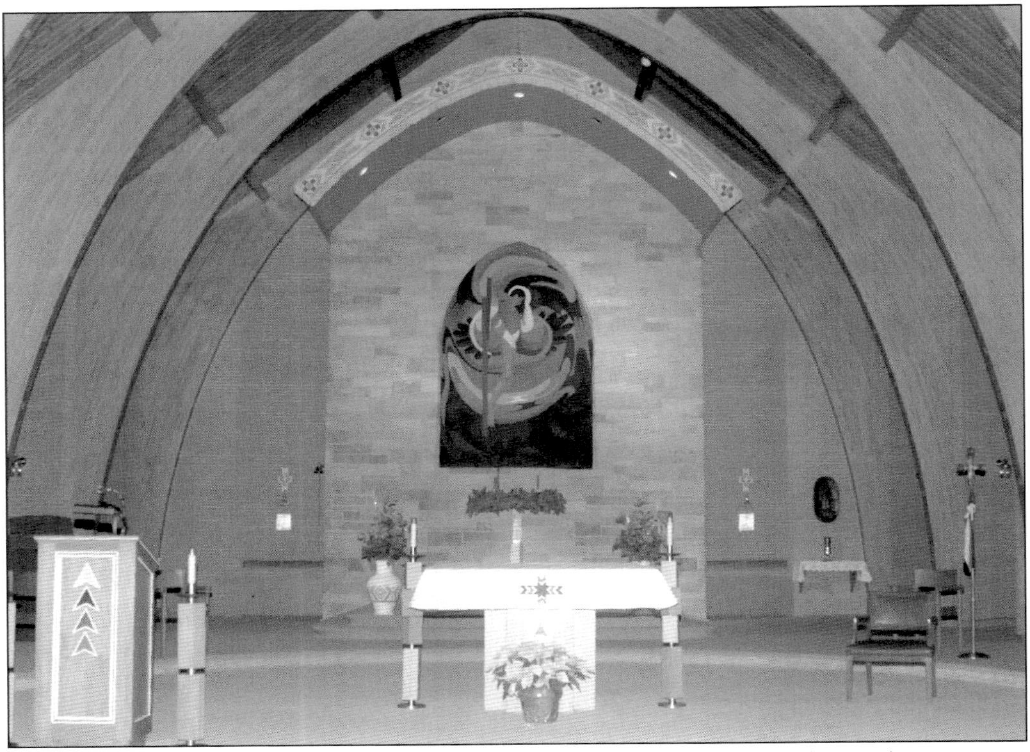

The Indian Christ tapestry is the focal point behind the altar. Two hand carved statues, not shown, stand on either side of the altar. Lakota volunteers stenciled the woodwork and crafted the beadwork arched over the tapestry and statues. (St. Joseph's Indian School, Chamberlain; David Meyer, photographer.)

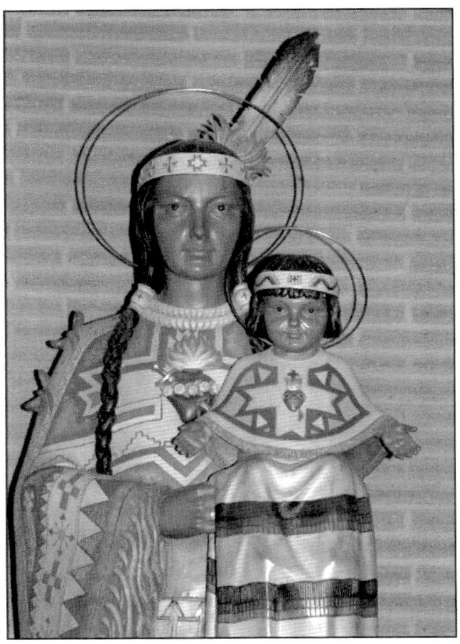

Brother Bonoventure, SCJ, hand carved this statue, *Our Lady of the Sioux*, out of one piece of wood. He also carved the statue *Joseph the Worker*, not shown. Both statues are housed in Our Lady of the Sioux Chapel. (St. Joseph's Indian School, Chamberlain; David Meyer, photographer.)

Two

Cheyenne River

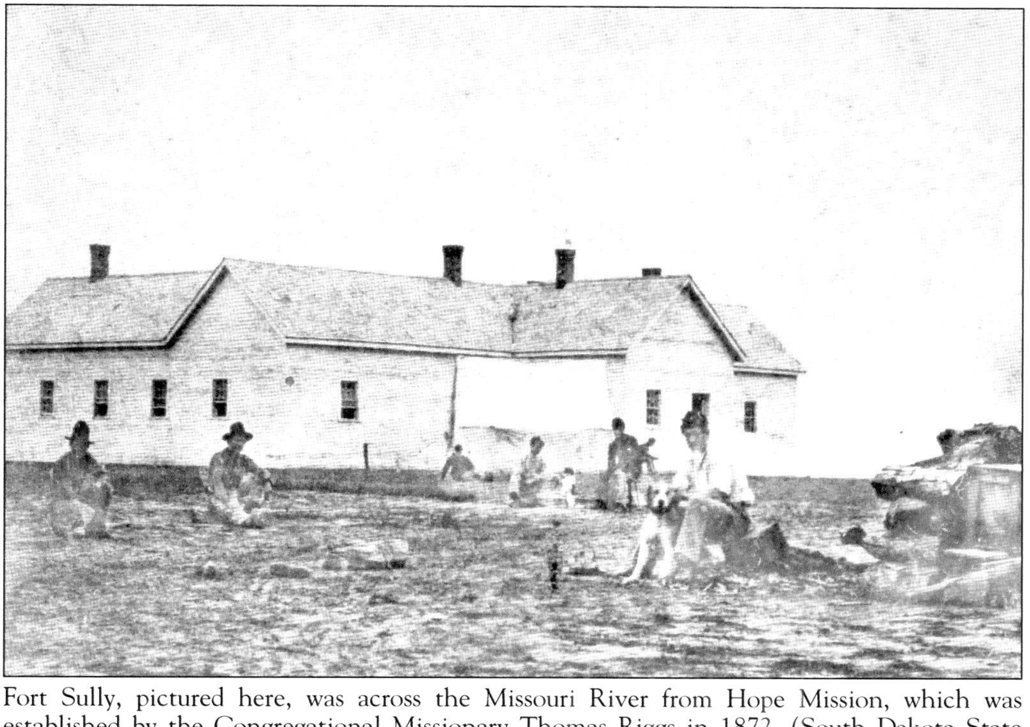

Fort Sully, pictured here, was across the Missouri River from Hope Mission, which was established by the Congregational Missionary Thomas Riggs in 1872. (South Dakota State Historical Society Archives and O.H. Over Museum; Morrow Collection.)

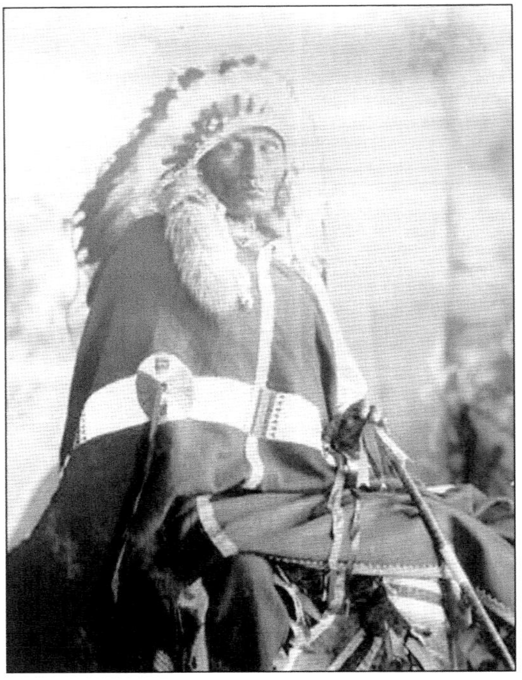

The Cheyenne River Sioux, descendants of the Teton Sioux, are divided into four bands: the Minneconjou, Itazipco (Sans Arc), Sihasapa (Blackfoot), and the Oohenumpa (Two Kettle). Yellow Hawk, pictured in this photograph, was a Chief of the Itazipco band. (Library of Congress Prints and Photographs Division; Frank B. Fiske Collection. LC-USZ62-104389.)

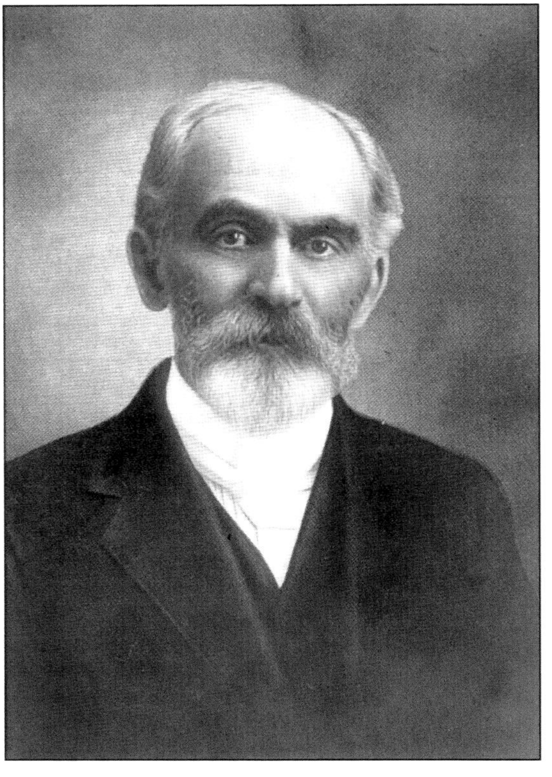

Thomas Riggs, the son of the noted missionary Stephen Riggs, was sent to Dakota Territory in 1872, where he established Hope Mission. Two years later, he moved the mission to the east side of the Missouri River at Peoria Bottom where he began the Bogue, later called Oahe Mission and Industrial School. Thomas Riggs became the Superintendent of Congregational Indian Missions on the Cheyenne River, Standing Rock, and Rosebud Reservations. (South Dakota State Historical Society Archives.)

Nina Riggs accompanied her husband, Thomas, to Dakota Territory. Nina died in childbirth in 1878 leaving behind a four-year-old son, Theodore. Mary Collins, another missionary, with the help of Elizabeth Winyan, cared for Theodore and kept up the work of the mission. (South Dakota State Historical Society Archives.)

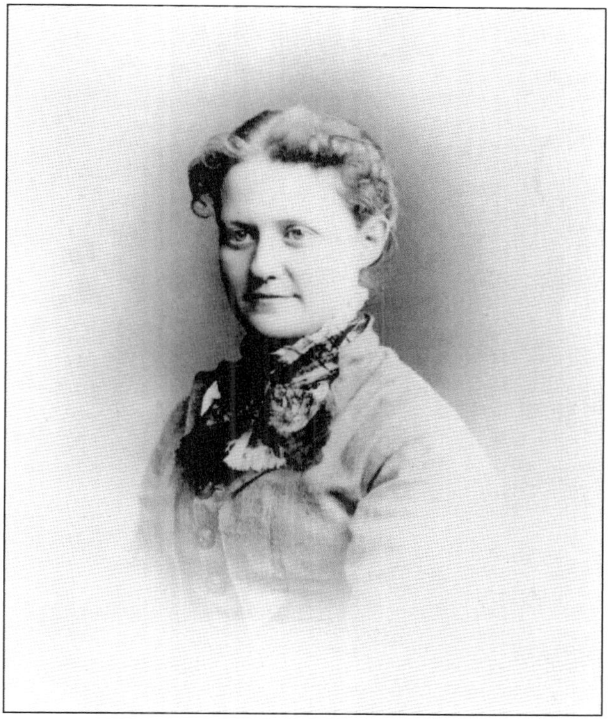

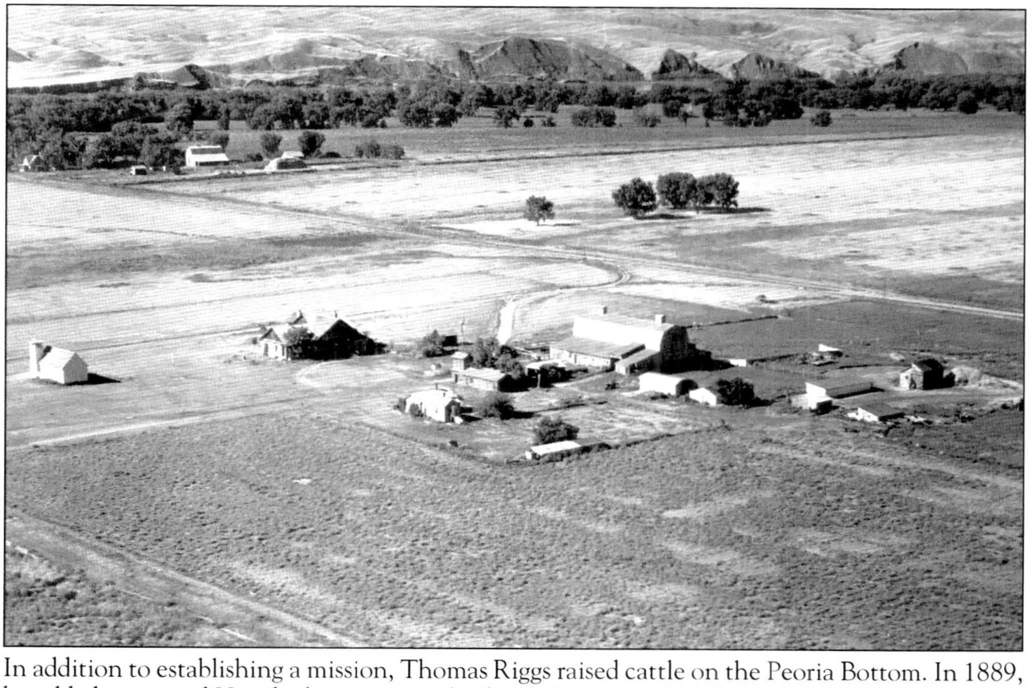

In addition to establishing a mission, Thomas Riggs raised cattle on the Peoria Bottom. In 1889, he added registered Herefords to improve his herd. Prominent ranchers, including Scotty Philip and Tom Jones, bought registered Hereford bulls from the Riggs's ranch. Notice the chapel to the far left of the photograph. (South Dakota State Historical Society Archives.)

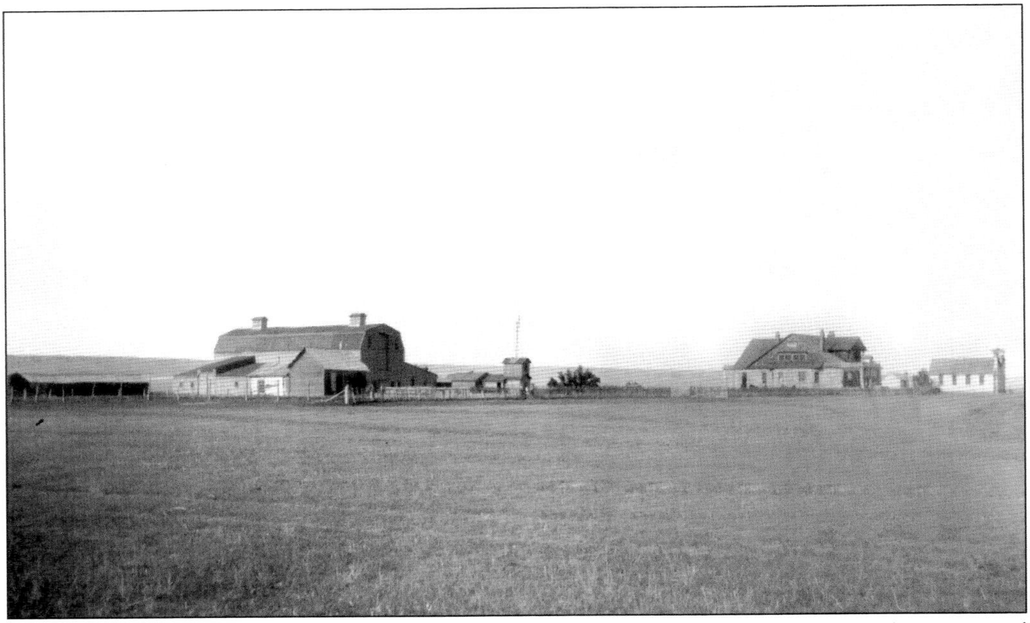

Originally, Thomas Riggs and his family lived in a log home, built in 1874-1875 of cottonwood logs. One winter, it burned to the ground, requiring the family to live in temporary quarters until the rock house was built four years later. (South Dakota State Historical Society Archives.)

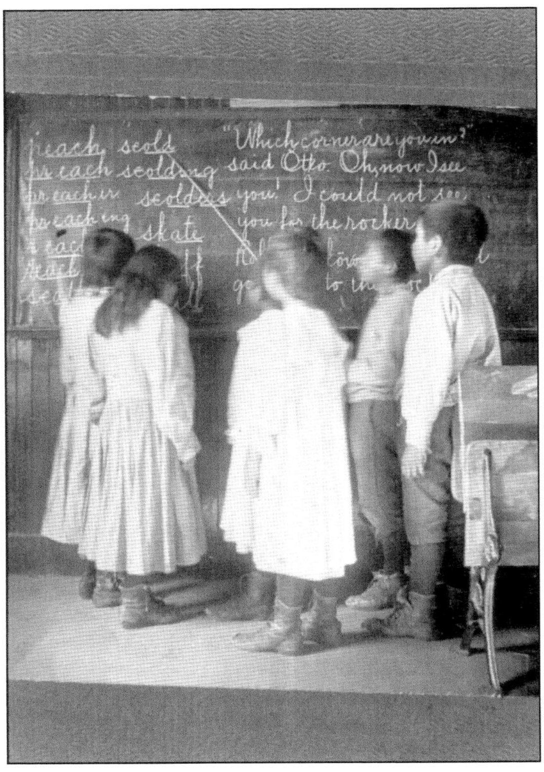

Miss Dodge teaches her students at Oahe Mission. Most of the 30 to 35 pupils were from the Cheyenne River, Standing Rock, and Rosebud Reservations. (South Dakota State Historical Society Archives.)

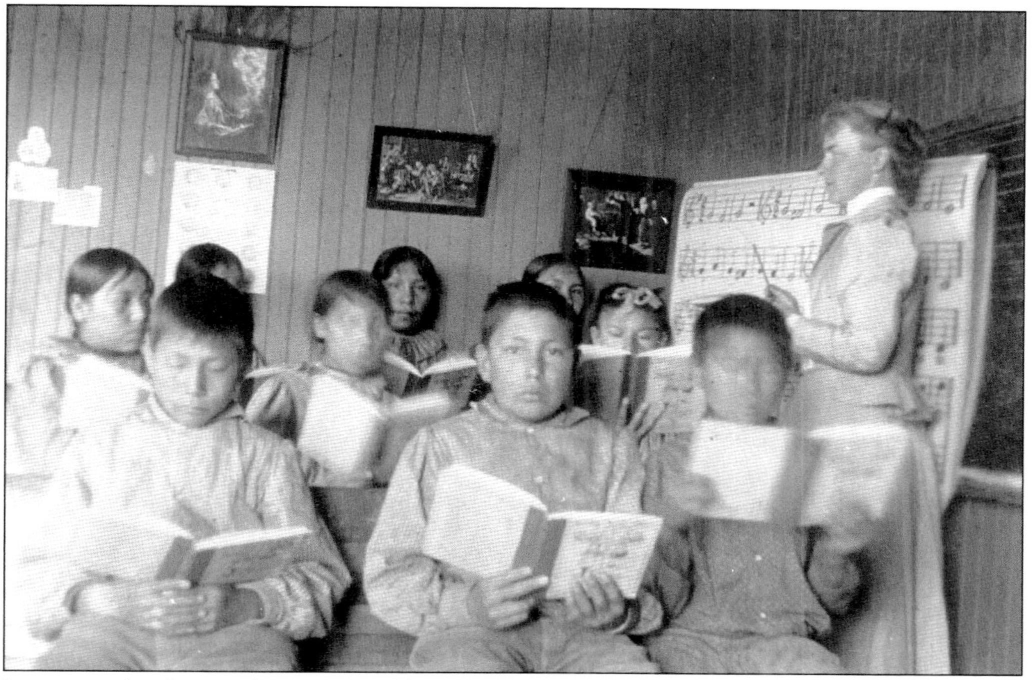

Louisa teaches her students music. Thomas Riggs married Louisa Irvine at the Oahe Mission in 1885. She became principal in 1886 and served the school until its closure in 1914. (South Dakota State Historical Society Archives.)

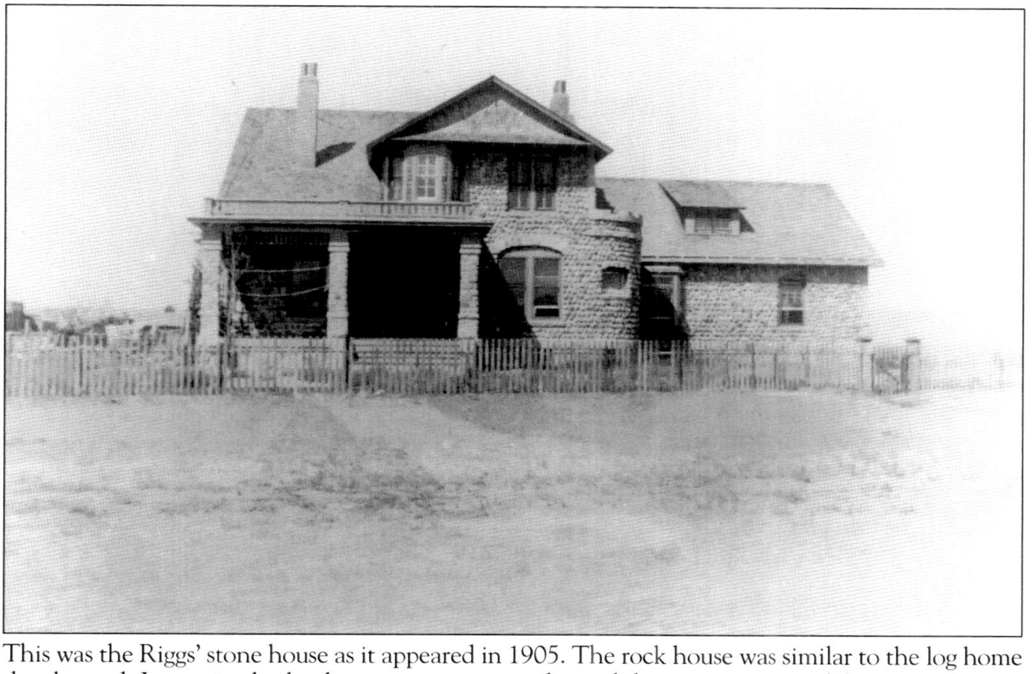

This was the Riggs' stone house as it appeared in 1905. The rock house was similar to the log home that burned. Just as in the log house, one room in the rock home was reserved for women to use while they were working at the mission. (South Dakota State Historical Society Archives.)

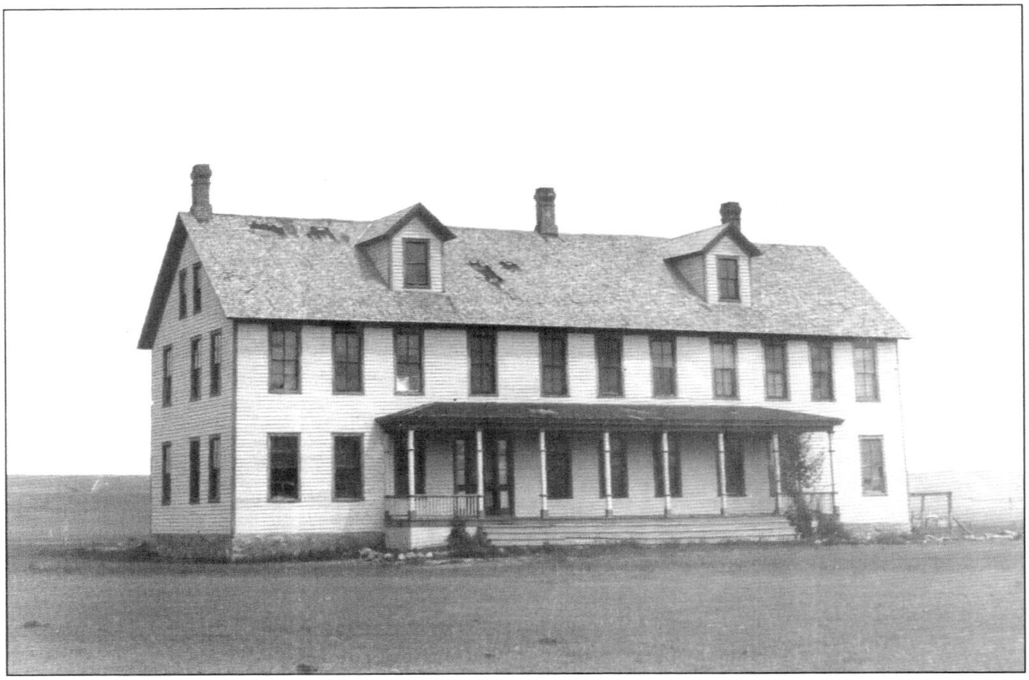

The Oahe Industrial School began as a day school for girls. Later it developed into a boarding school for both boys and girls. (South Dakota State Historical Society Archives.)

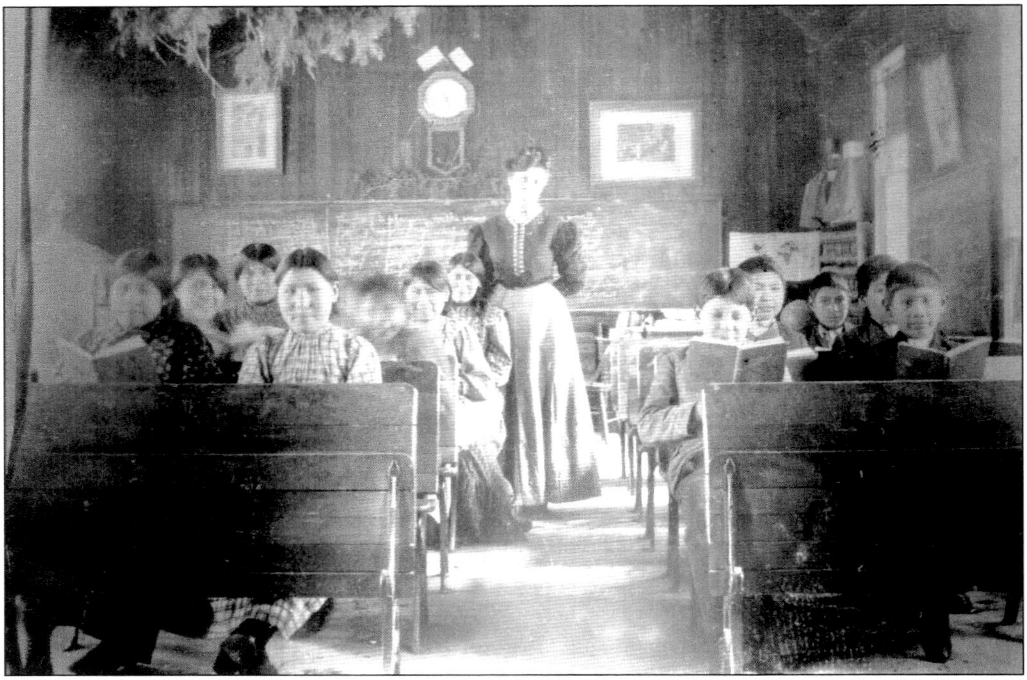

A 1907 class at Oahe Mission is in session. (South Dakota State Historical Society Archives.)

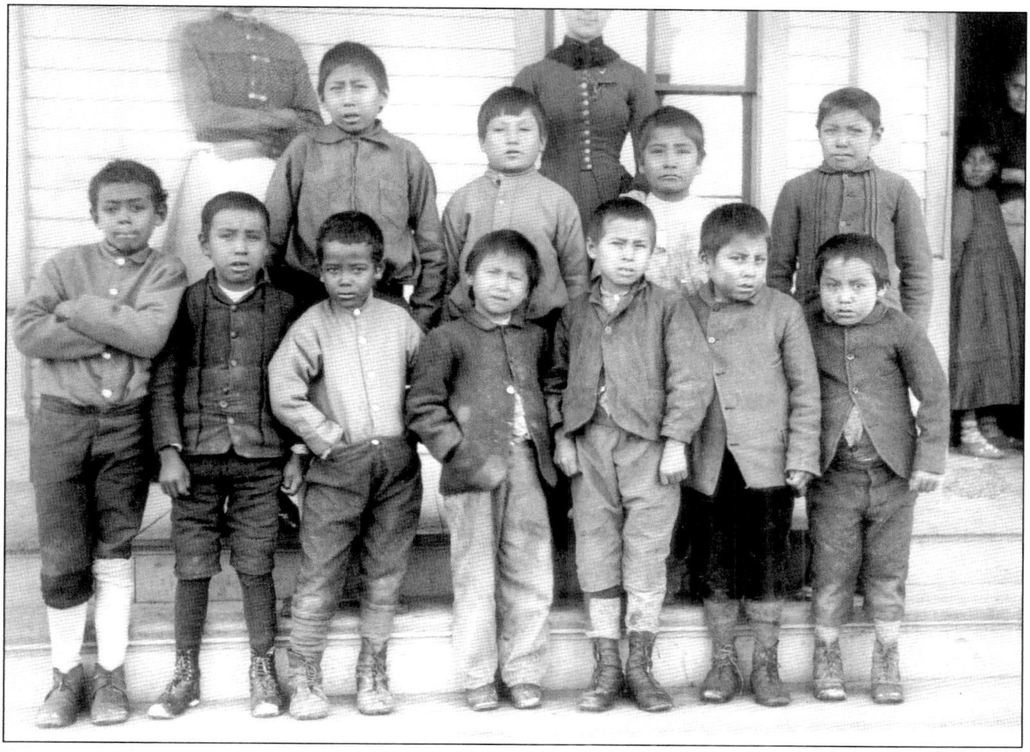

Boys pose for a picture at the Oahe mission in this undated photo. (South Dakota State Historical Society Archives.)

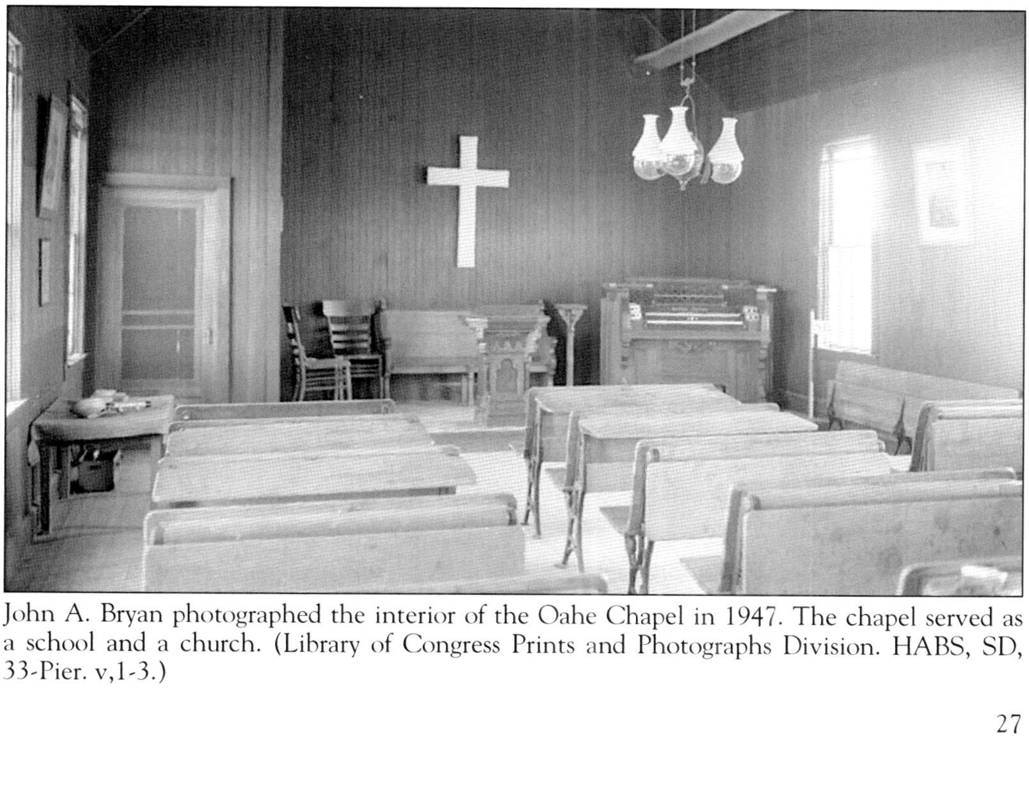

John A. Bryan photographed the interior of the Oahe Chapel in 1947. The chapel served as a school and a church. (Library of Congress Prints and Photographs Division. HABS, SD, 33-Pier. v,1-3.)

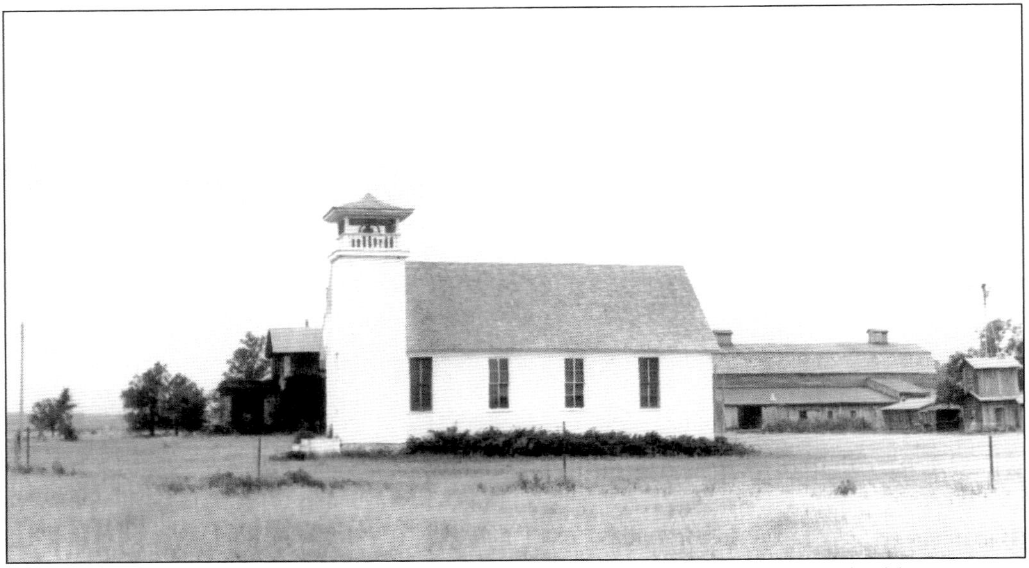

Stephen R. Riggs wrote in his book, *Mary and I, Forty Years with the Sioux*, "The building is going up—August, 1877—a neat and substantial frame, the material of which was brought up from Yankton by boat. It is forty by twenty feet, and will have a bell tower in one corner." Nina Riggs's hometown of Bangor, Maine, helped to fund the building of the church. (South Dakota State Historical Society Archives.)

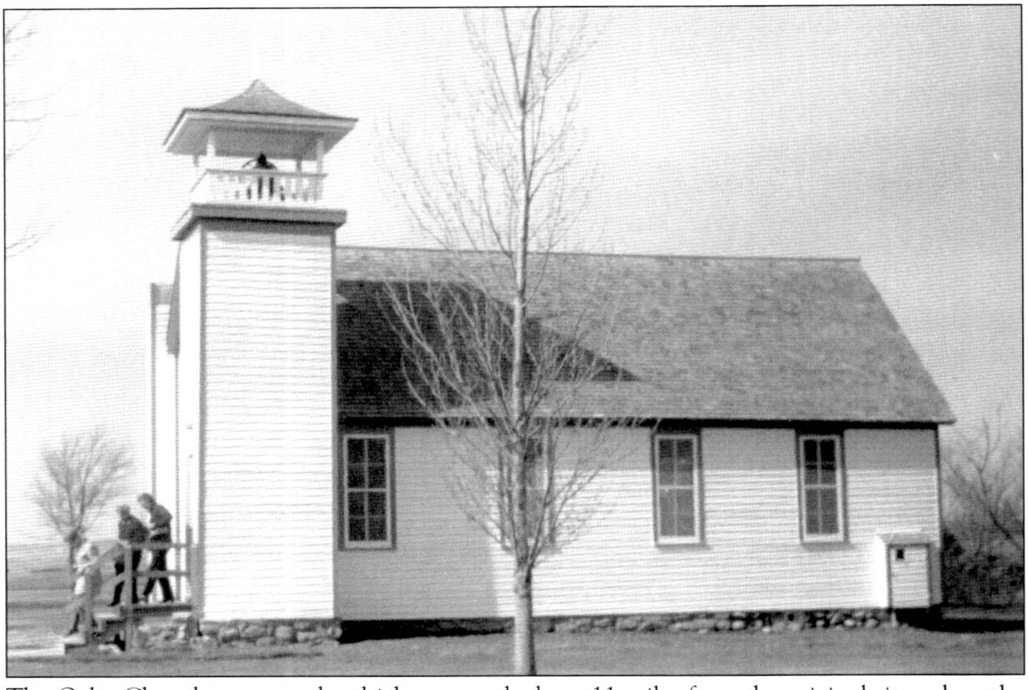

The Oahe Chapel was moved to higher ground, about 11 miles from the original site, when the Oahe dam flooded the lowlands. The building has not been changed since it served as a school and church. Some of Louisa Irvine Riggs' original blackboard writing has been preserved in the chapel.

Pictured are Mary Collins, seated in the center, Elizabeth Winyan, standing, and Elida Scott, sitting to the right. Mary C. Collins, a member of the First Congregational Church in Keokuk, Iowa, journeyed to Dakota Territory in 1875 to become a missionary. She accompanied Reverend Thomas Riggs and Nina Riggs to Oahe Mission near Pierre, South Dakota. While there, she labored as a teacher and social worker, and learned the native language. (South Dakota State Historical Society Archives.)

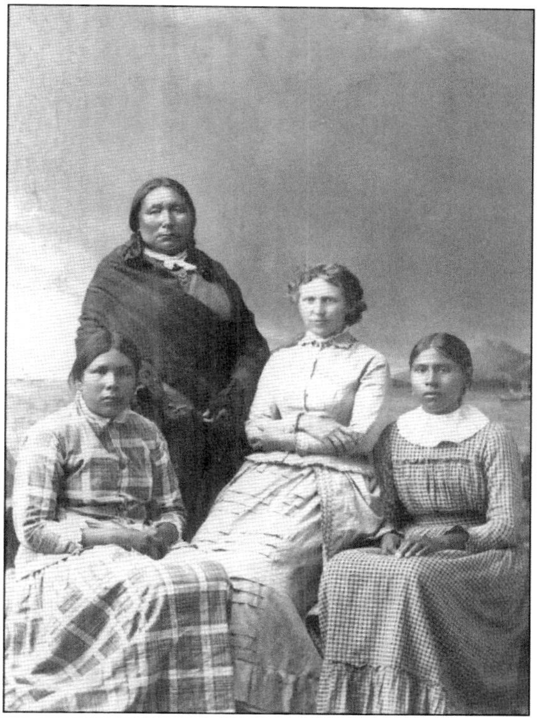

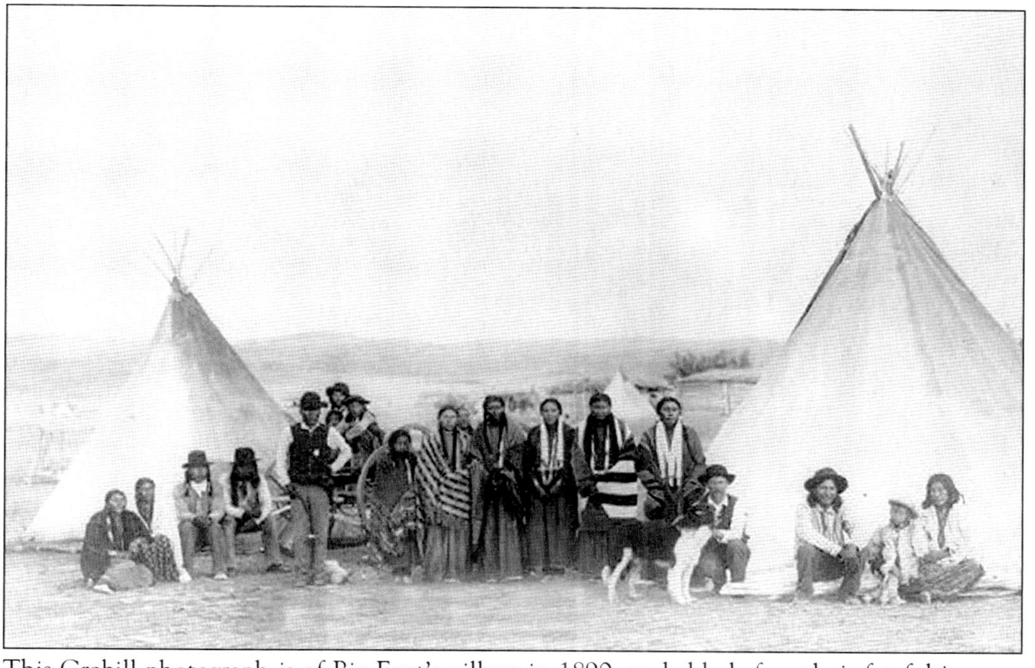

This Grabill photograph is of Big Foot's village in 1890, probably before their fateful journey to the Pine Ridge Agency. The Minneconjou, under Big Foot's leadership, were fleeing from the military. Their journey ended tragically at Wounded Knee. (Library of Congress Prints and Photographs Division; John C. Grabill Collection. LC-DIG-ppmsc-02526.)

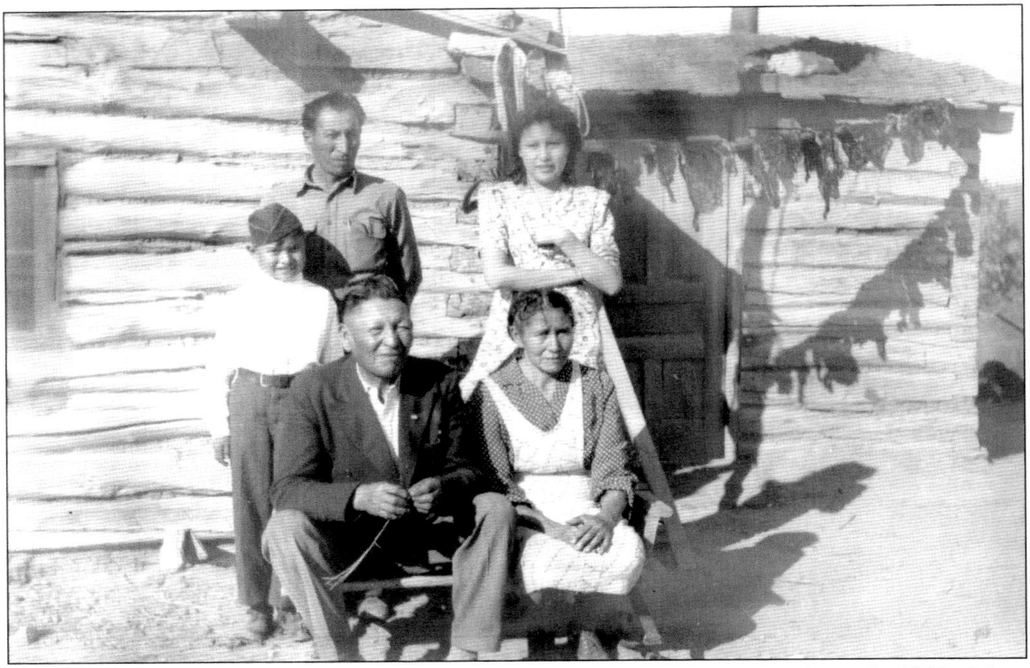

This photograph depicts a typical home on the Cheyenne Reservation in the early 1900s. Meat appears to be drying on a line near the log house. (St. Joseph's Indian School, Chamberlain.)

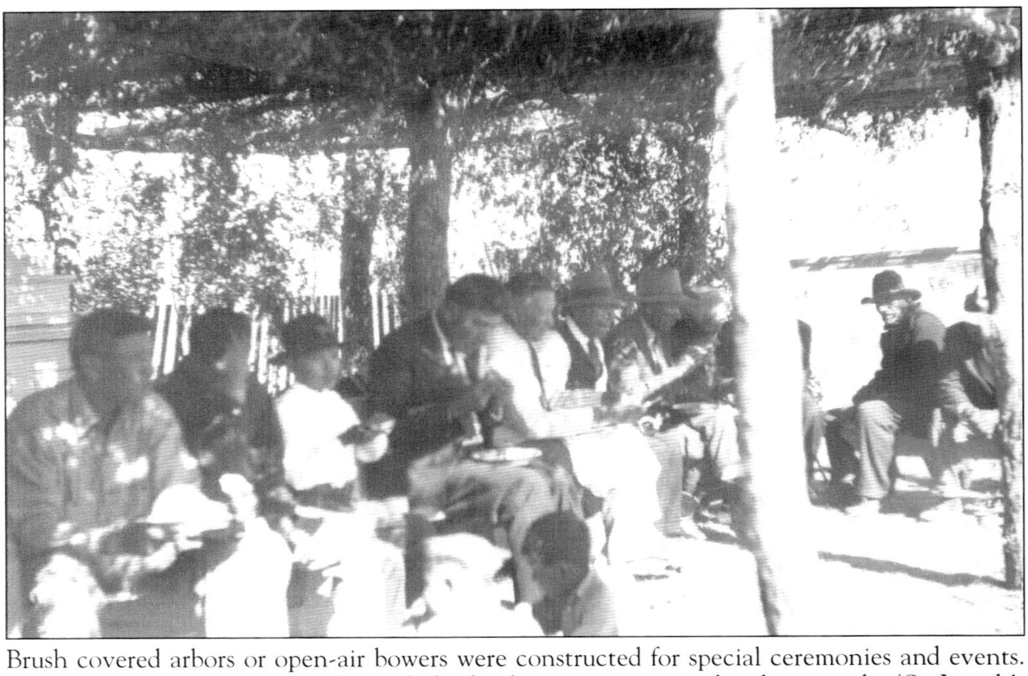

Brush covered arbors or open-air bowers were constructed for special ceremonies and events. Often, they were built in a circle, symbolic for the power contained within a circle. (St. Joseph's Indian School, Chamberlain.)

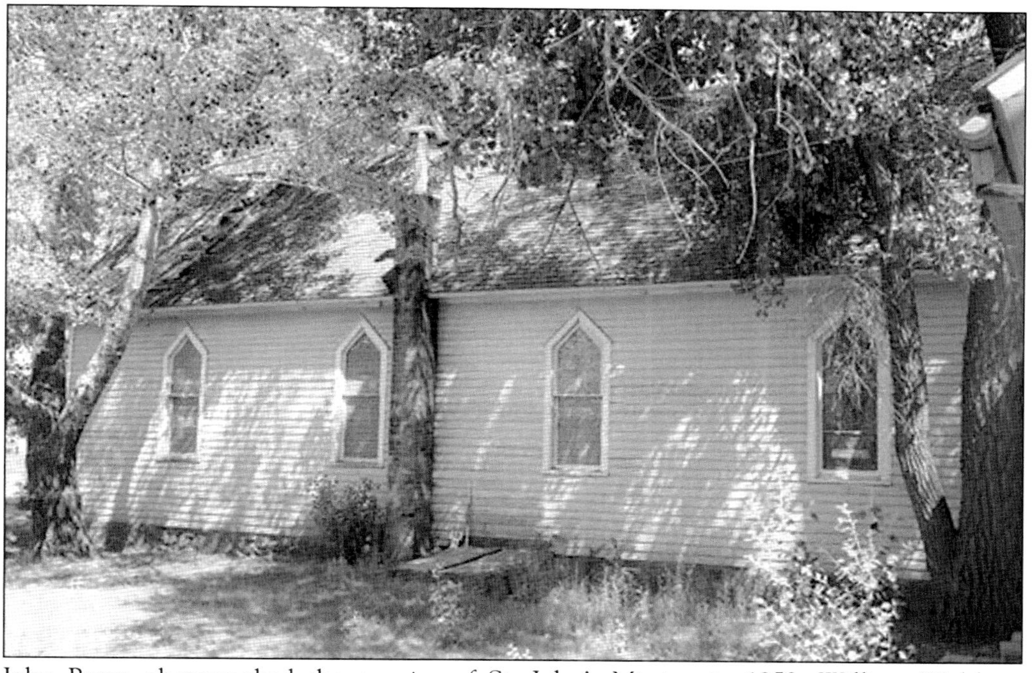

John Bryan photographed the remains of St. John's Mission in 1952. William Welsh, a wealthy Philadelphia lawyer, funded the building of St. John's Episcopal Mission in 1885. The mission was built near the site of Fort Bennett, but was later moved to another location in 1892. Reverend S.D. Frazier served the mission for many years. (Library of Congress Prints and Photographs Division. HABS, SD 21.)

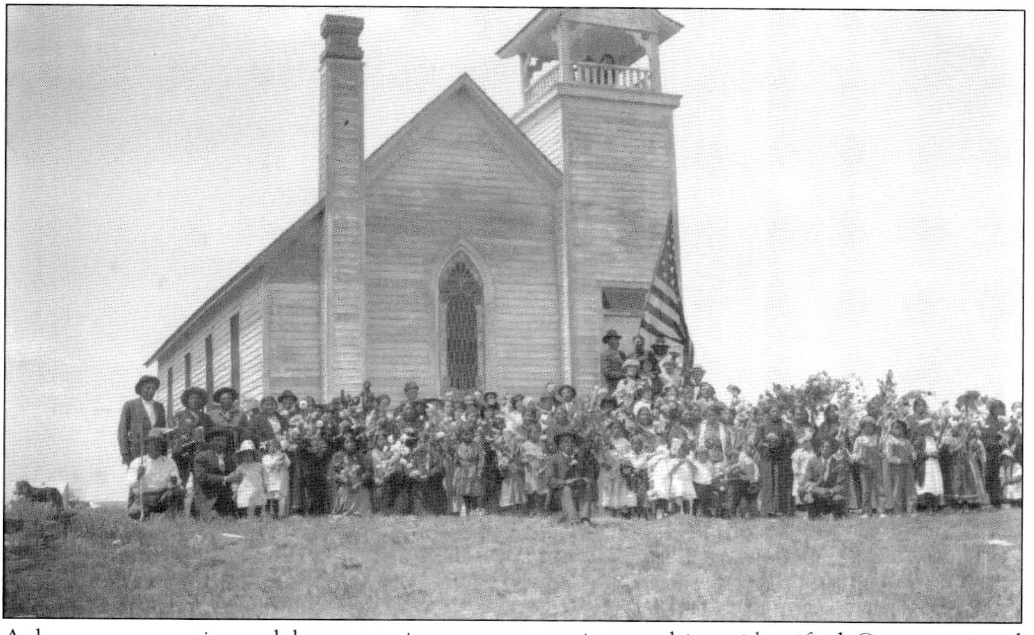

A large congregation celebrates an important occasion at this unidentified Congregational Church on the Cheyenne River Reservation. (Timber Lake and Area Historical Society.)

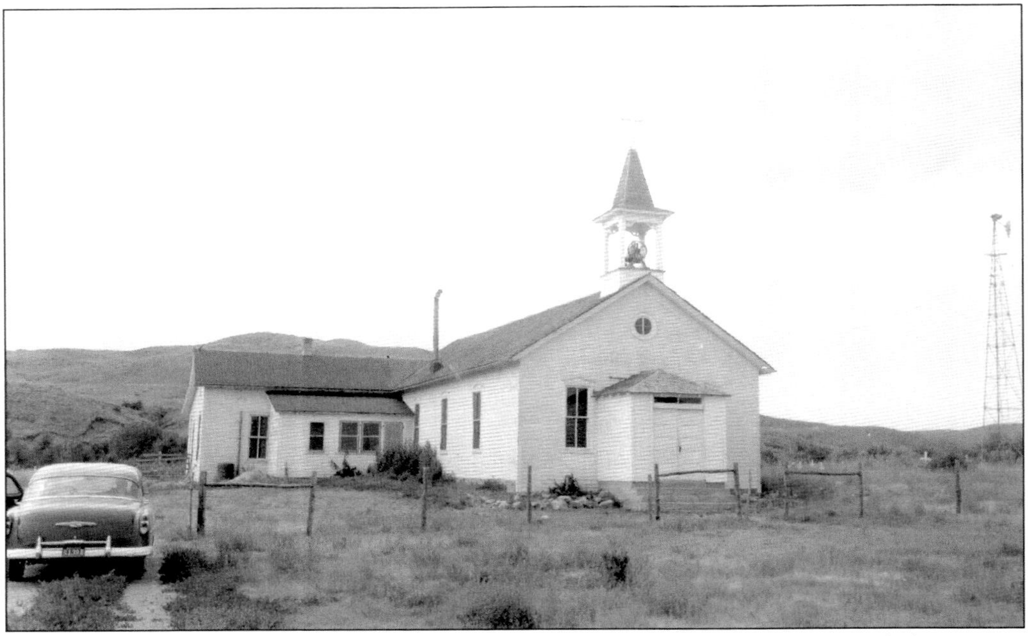

The Cheyenne Indian Agency served St. Joseph Catholic Church at Cherry Creek from 1901-1919 until it was assigned to All Saints Parish, Eagle Butte. This photo is *c.* 1950. (St. Joseph's Indian School, Chamberlain.)

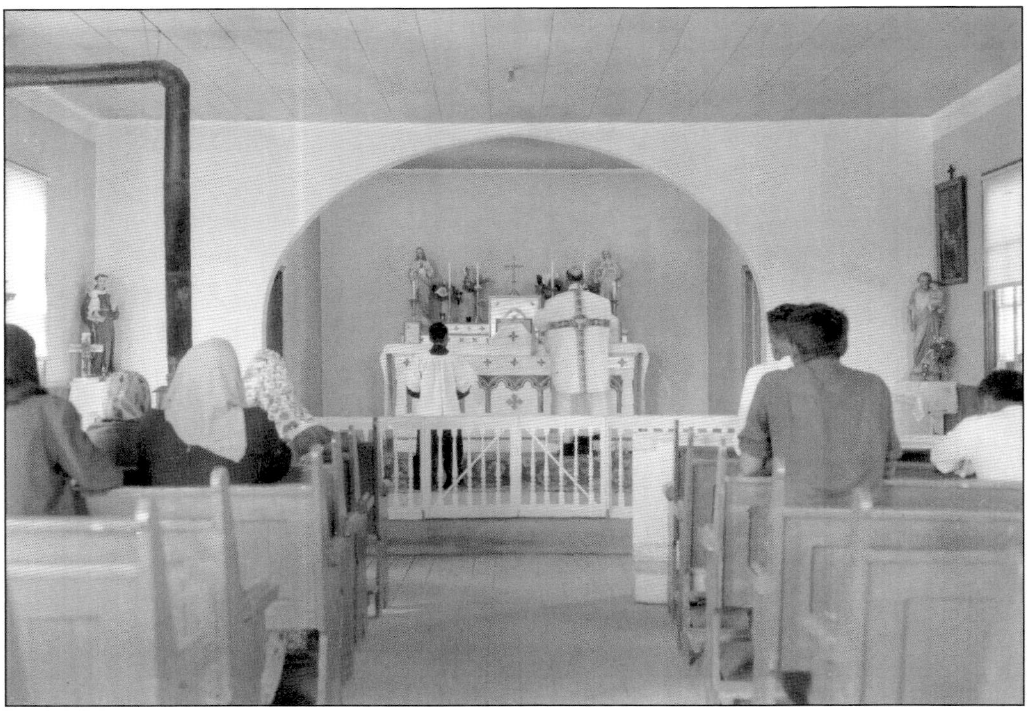

Members of the Cherry Creek Church worship during the 1950s. (St. Joseph's Indian School, Chamberlain.)

St. Mary's Catholic Church at LaPlant was established in 1889. The Congregationalists built a church nearby in the same year, and the Episcopalians established a church northeast of LaPlant in 1873. Theodore Riggs, Thomas Riggs' young son, remembers making a trip to the Congregational sub-station church near LaPlant when he was driving a team and wagon loaded with paint and supplies. The team got away from him, but to his relief he managed to get them under control. (St. Joseph's Indian School, Chamberlain.)

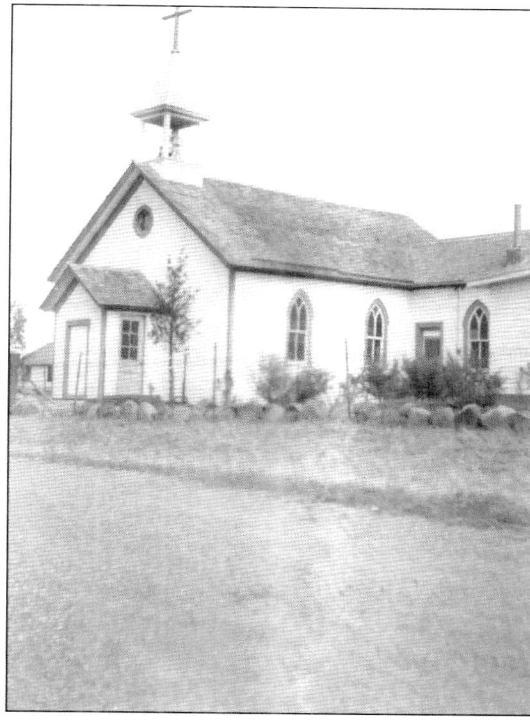

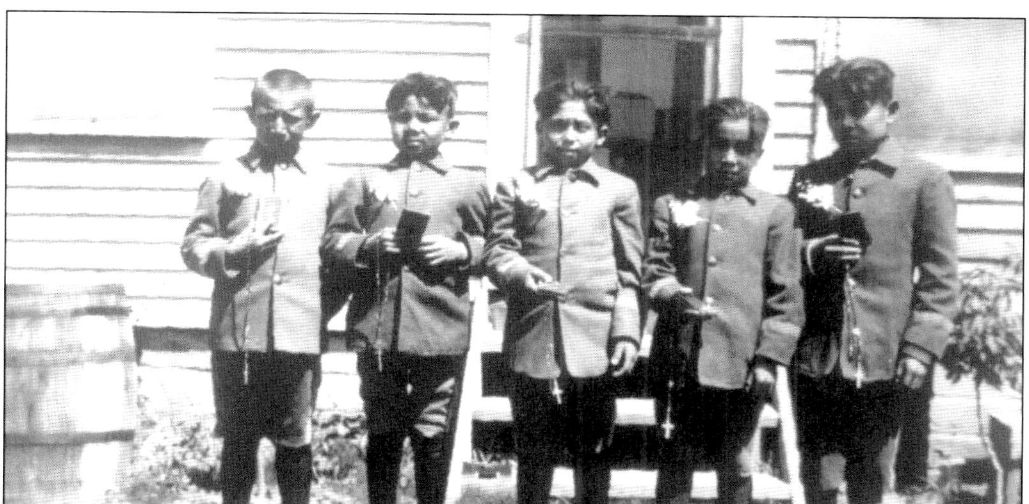

A first Holy Communion class of boys stands in front of an unidentified church on the reservation. (St. Joseph's Indian School, Chamberlain.)

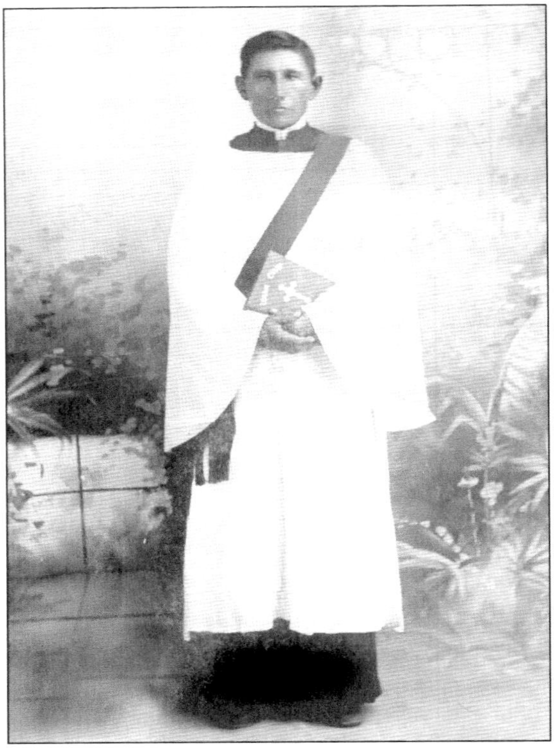

Eugene Standing Bull, pictured, was one of many Episcopal clergy who ministered on the Cheyenne Reservation. In 1873, Hobart Hare sent Reverend Swift to the Cheyenne, followed by Rev. Ffennell, Rev. Handford, Rev. Ashley, Rev. Good Teacher, Reverend Frazier, and Rev. Deloria. Many others have since served. (Timber Lake and Area Historical Society.)

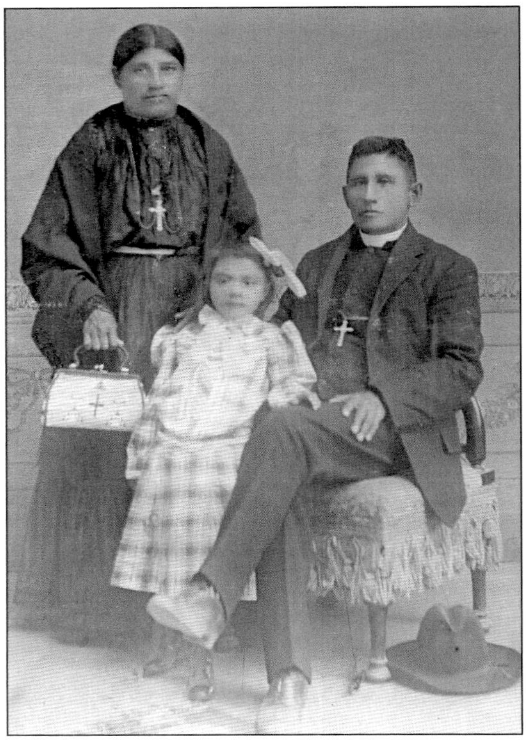

Eugene Standing Bull was born in 1857 and died in 1920. He ministered at the Emmanuel Church. He is shown in the photograph with his wife and an unidentified child. (Timber Lake and Area Historical Society.)

Three

Standing Rock

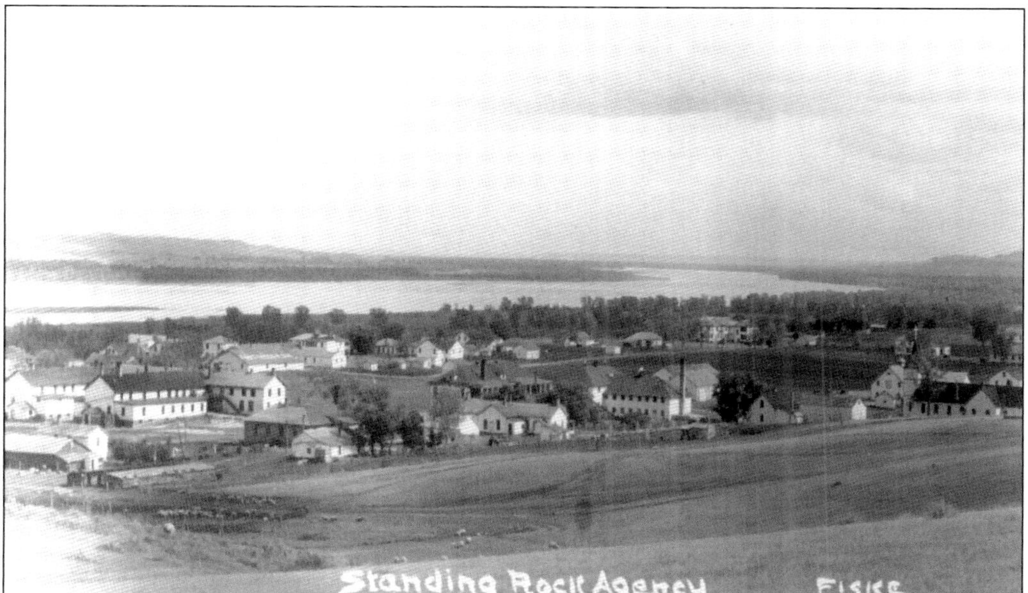

The Standing Rock Agency was established at Fort Yates, now in North Dakota. Under Grant's Peace Plan, the Roman Catholics were given permission to set up missions on Standing Rock. (Klein Museum, Mobridge; Frank Fiske Collection.)

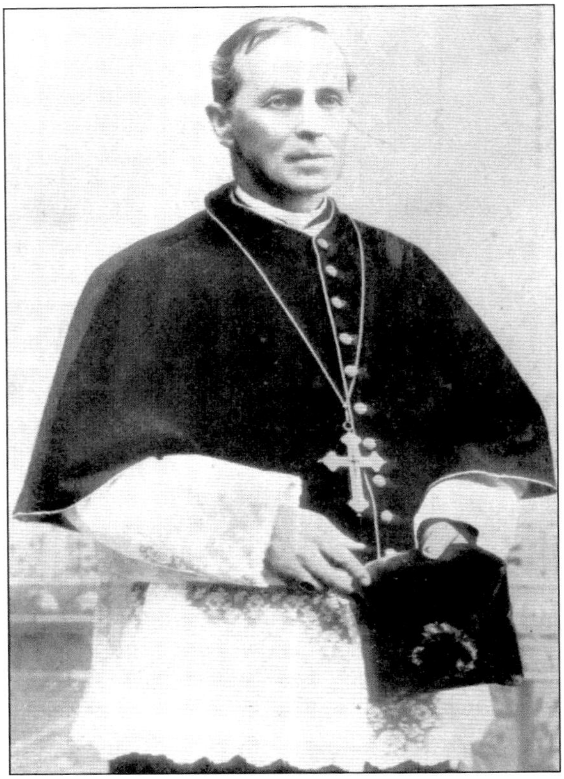

Bishop Marty worked tirelessly among the Sioux, beginning in 1876, establishing Catholic missions on the reservations. Bishop Marty first worked on the Standing Rock, but when Grant's Peace Policy plan was lifted, Marty appealed to the Jesuits and Franciscan Sisters to help establish missions on the Rosebud and Pine Ridge Reservations. Marty Mission on the Yankton Sioux Agency was named for him. (South Dakota State Historical Society Archives.)

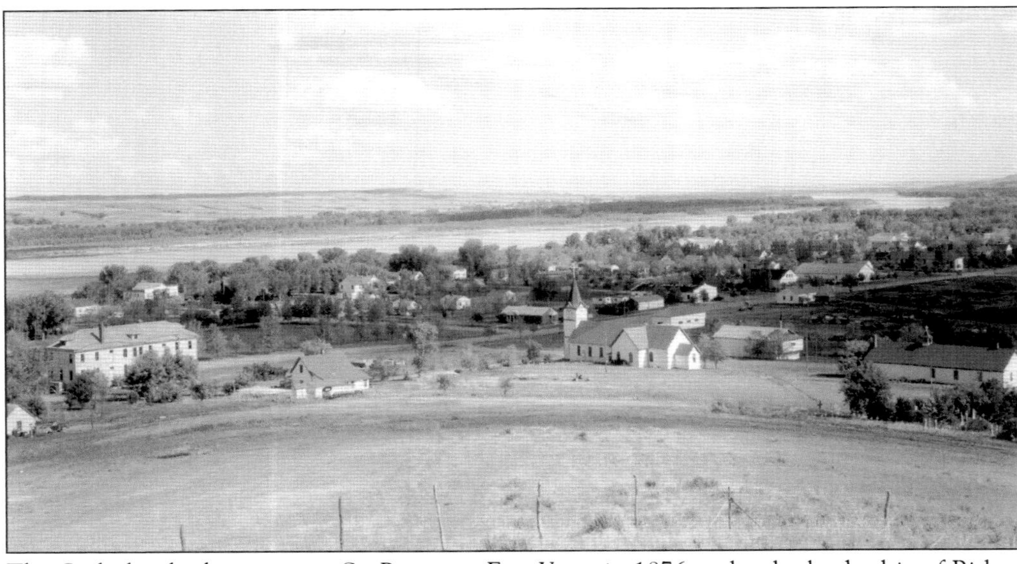

The Catholics built a mission, St. Peters, at Fort Yates in 1876 under the leadership of Bishop Marty, Foffa, and Brother Giles Laugel. In 1878, they established St. Benedict at Kennel. Other missions and sub-stations on the Standing Rock included St. Elizabeth at Cannonball, St. Aloysius at Bullhead, St. James at Shields, St. Bede at Wakpala, and St. Edward at Mad Bear Camp. (South Dakota State Historical Society Archives.)

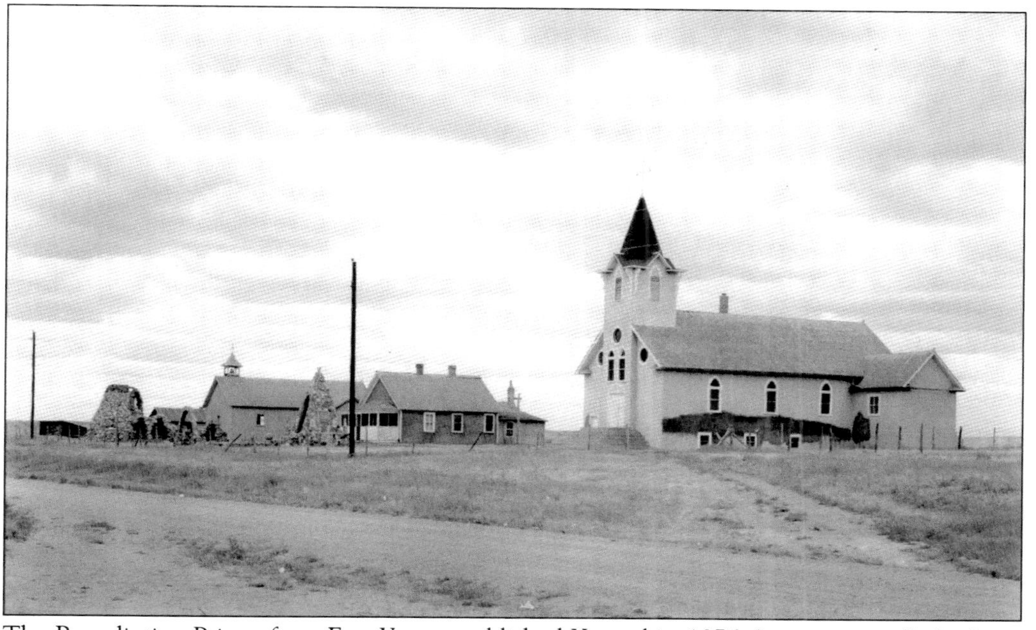

The Benedictine Priests from Fort Yates established Kennel in 1876. It was originally built on the site of Old Fort Manual Lisa and operated primarily as an agricultural school. Because the Oahe Project would flood the mission, it was moved in 1961. (South Dakota State Historical Society Archives.)

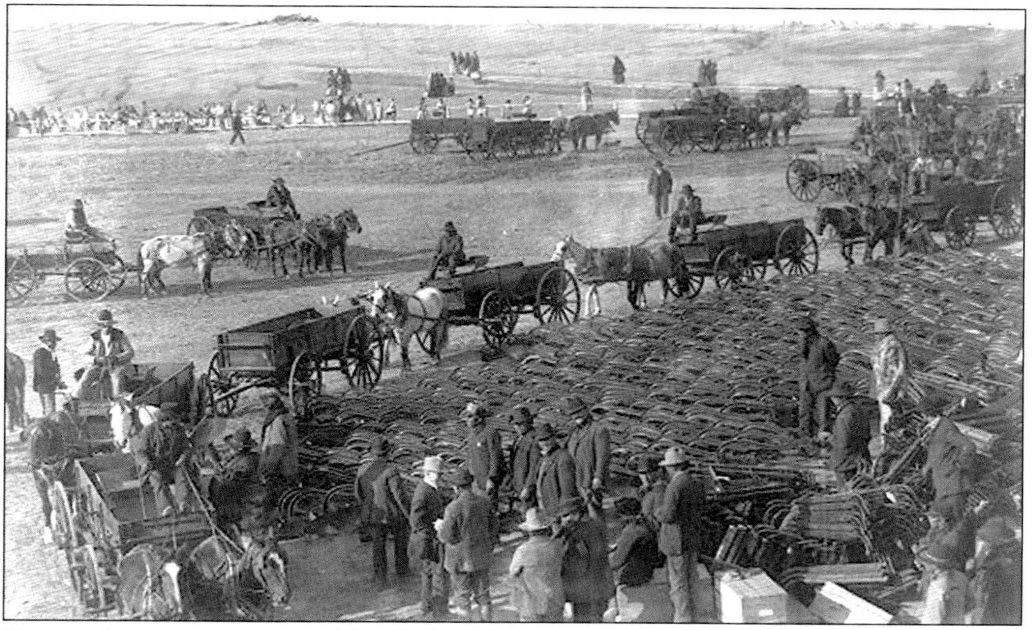

Sioux gather in wagons around hundreds of new plows. The government encouraged them to become farmers. Schools such as the one in Kennel provided instruction in agriculture. However, the push for the Sioux to become agriculturalists never worked on a large scale. (Library of Congress Prints and Photographs Division; Frank B. Fiske Collection. LC-USZ62-93150.)

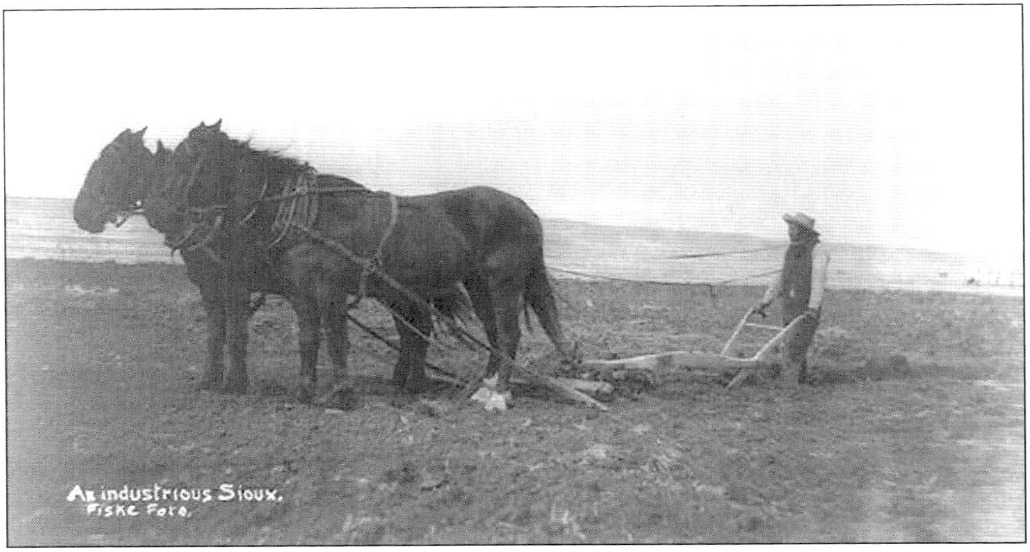

This Lakota man plows a field. Many Sioux abandoned the idea of becoming farmers, feeling it was degrading work for men to do. Often the land set aside for them to cultivate was not conducive to agriculture. (Library of Congress Prints and Photographs Division; Frank B. Fiske Collection. LC-USZ62-93149.)

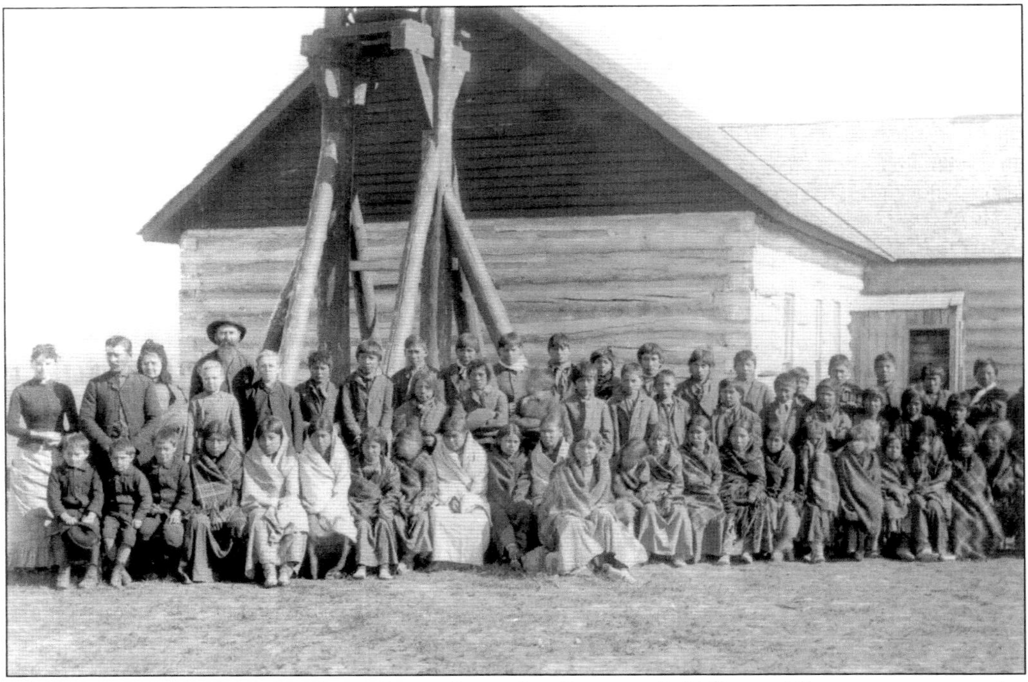

This government day school was located on the Cannon Ball River. The government also instituted government schools on the reservation. This photograph is c. 1890. (South Dakota State Historical Society Archives.)

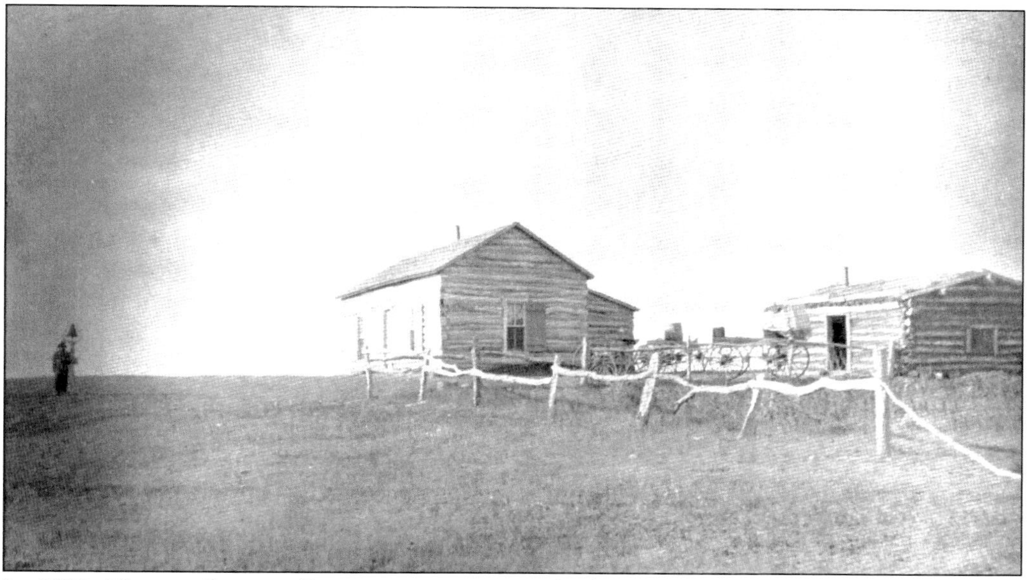

In 1882, Thomas Riggs, a Protestant missionary, built an out station at Running Antelope Village, later known as Little Eagle. A native teacher's house was built along side of the mission school. A church bell can be seen on a post to the far left. Reverend Reed conducted the marriage ceremony for Ethel Collins, Mary Collin's niece, and Elias Jacobsen here on August 5, 1892. (South Dakota State Historical Society Archives.)

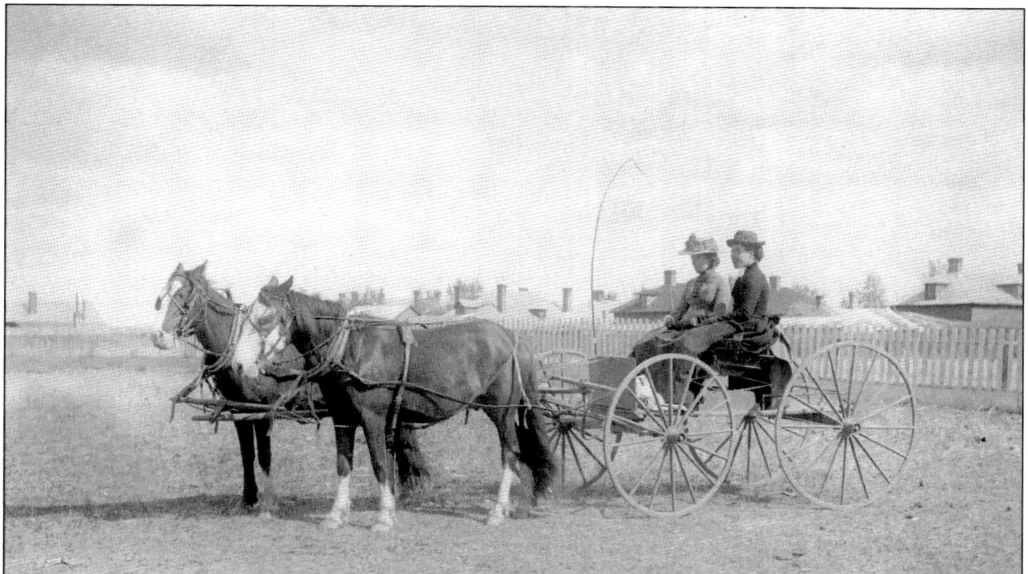

In 1885, Mary Collins left the Oahe Mission, Cheyenne River, for Standing Rock and remained at Little Eagle from 1885-1910. Her large mission field required her to travel long distances with her buckboard and her horses, Bessie and Gumbo. Seated on the buckboard are Mary Collins and Josephine Barnaby at Standing Rock Agency. Josephine, an Omaha Indian girl, graduated from Hampton Institute and was a great help to Mary Collins. (South Dakota State Historical Society Archives; Mary Collins Collection.)

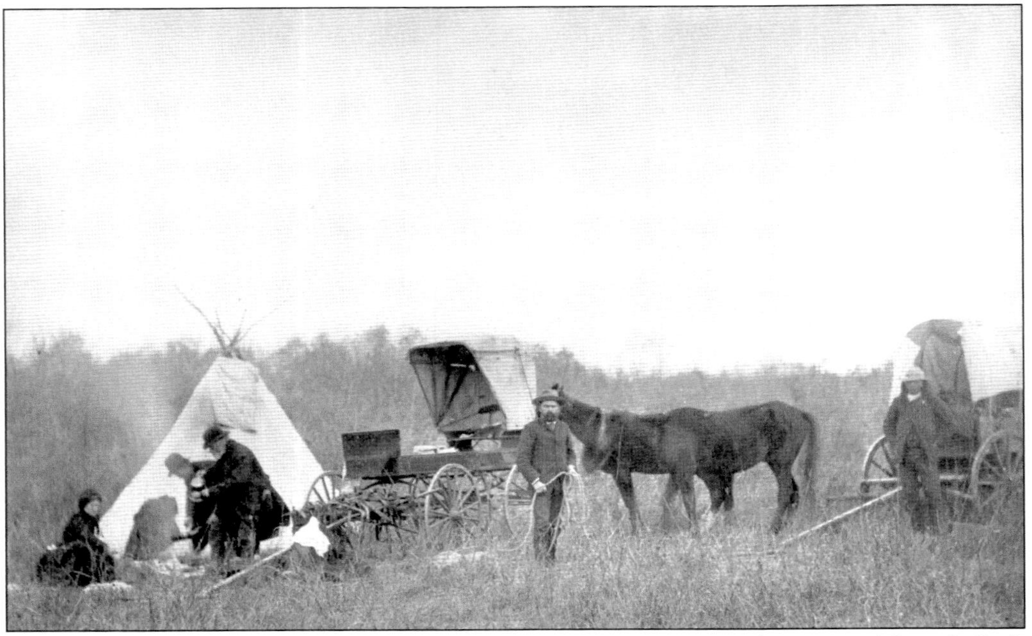

Thomas Riggs is pictured in the center of this missionary camp. Wakutemani, Mary Collin's exceptional Bible student and valuable assistant, is pictured in front of the wagon. Wakutemani became an ordained minister. (South Dakota State Historical Society Archives.)

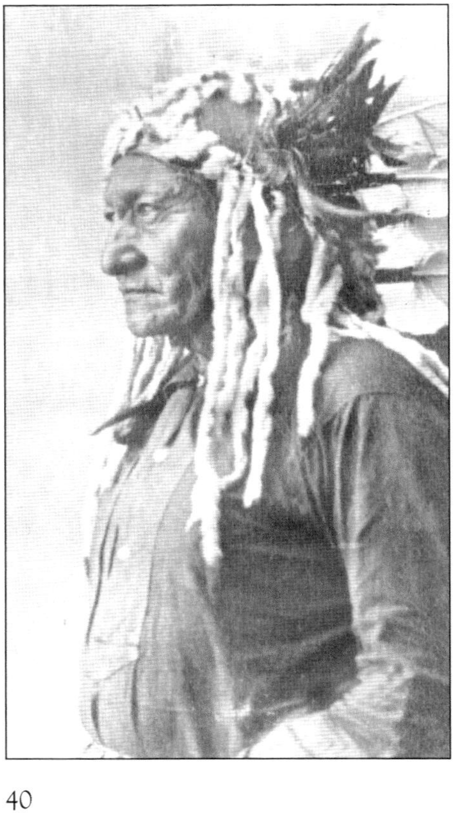

David F. Barry took this portrait of Sitting Bull in Bismark, North Dakota, in 1885. While at Little Eagle, Mary Collins became acquainted with Sitting Bull. Although they often disagreed on the assimilation issue, Sitting Bull considered her a relative since she spoke the Lakota language. He and other members of his tribe referred to her as Winona. (Klein Museum, Mobridge.)

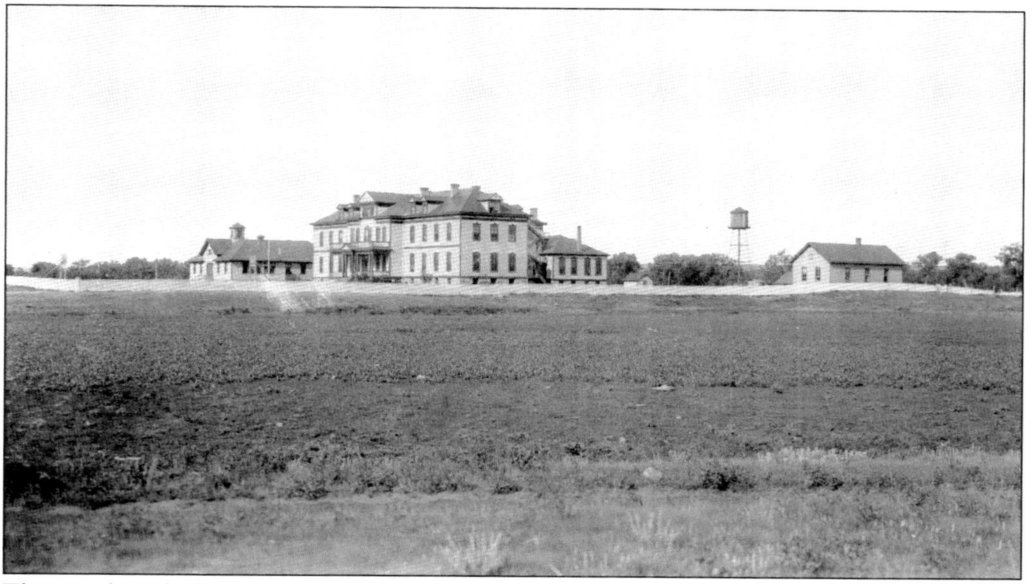

This unidentified school and church was built in Little Eagle. (South Dakota Historical Society Archives.)

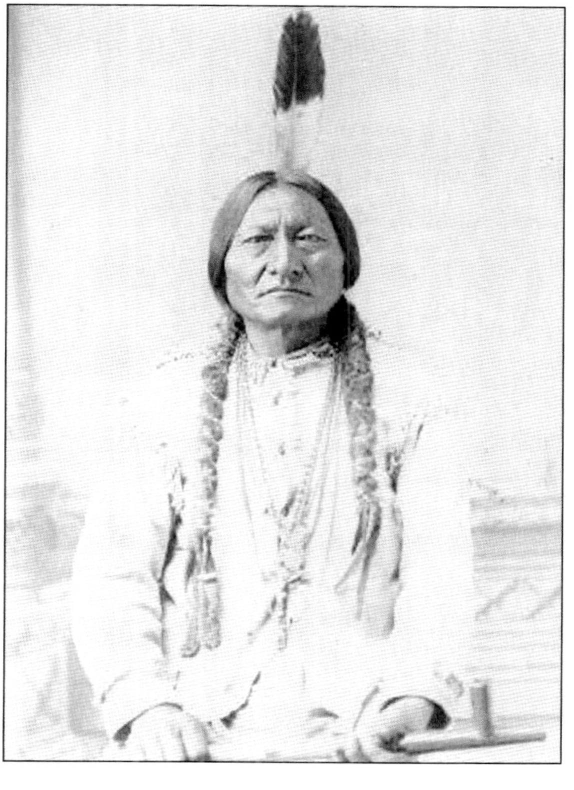

Sitting Bull, one of the most noted of Lakota leaders, adamantly opposed assimilation into white culture and fiercely fought to preserve the Sioux way of life. He refused to sign the Ft. Laramie Treaty and continued to distrust the U.S. government. Sitting Bull supported the Ghost Dance Movement. He was killed when the Indian police tried to arrest him. This photo is *c.* 1885. (Library of Congress Prints and Photographs Division; D.F. Barry Collection. LC-USZ62-111147.)

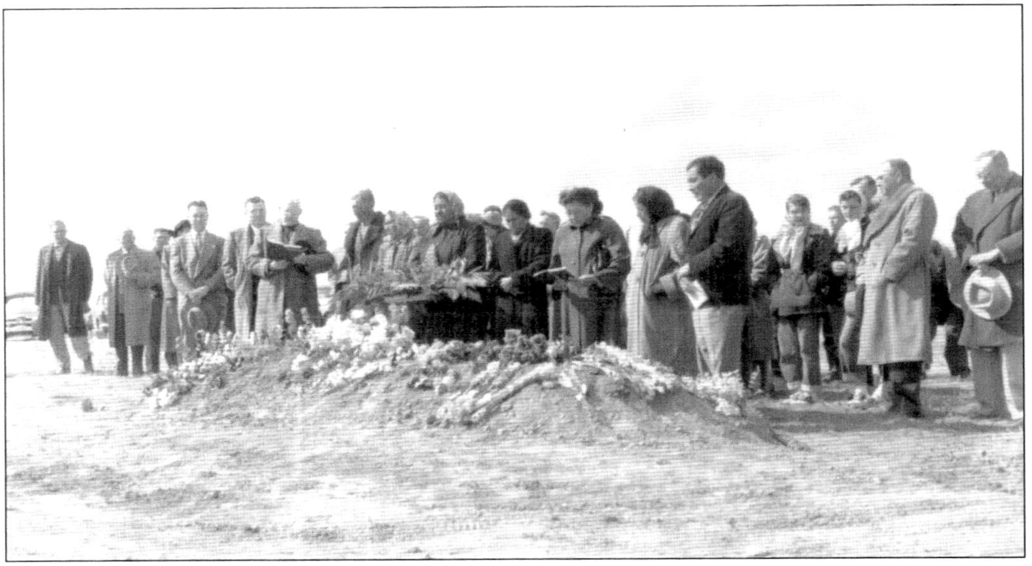

After Sitting Bull was killed, the military took his body to Ft. Yates and buried it there. Eventually the agency was abandoned, and the graves were moved to other locations. Sitting Bull's body was left in peace in a simple grave. With permission of his granddaughters, Mobridge businessmen decided to bring the famous leader home and inter him on a high bluff overlooking Mobridge and the Missouri River in 1953. (Klein Museum, Mobridge.)

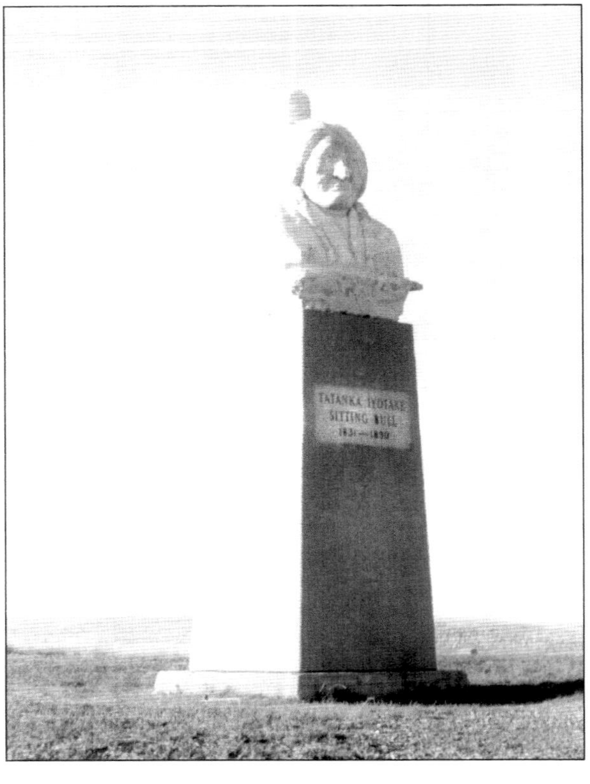

Sitting Bull's coffin was placed in a steel vault and covered with concrete, sealing the remains of the Hunkpapa leader. Korzak Ziolkowski, of Crazy Horse Monument fame, chiseled the bust of Sitting Bull, which now marks his final resting place.

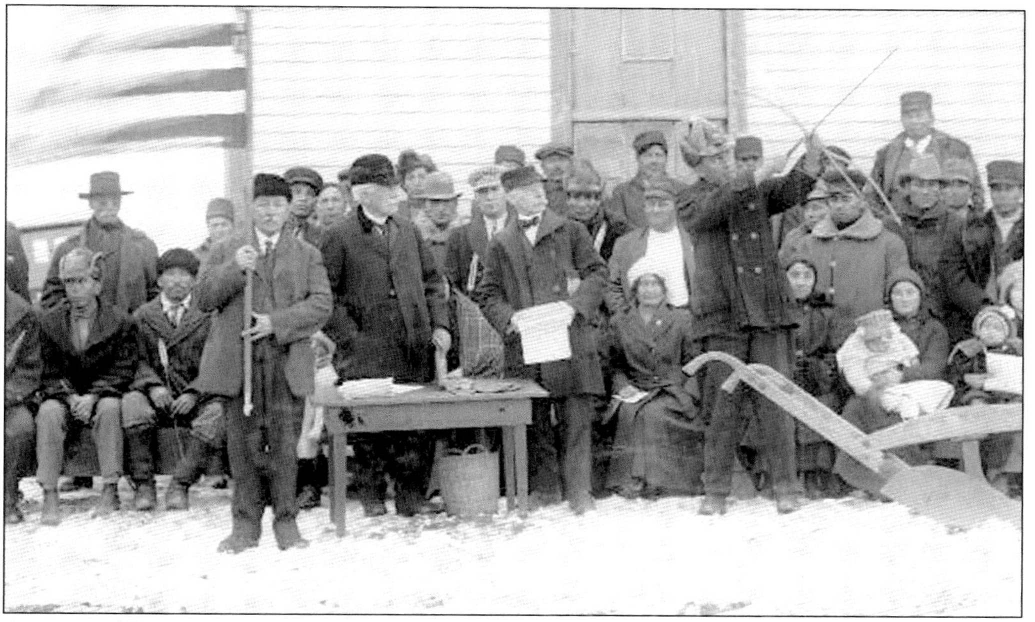

A group of Sioux at a ceremony, presumed to be the Standing Rock Reservation, shoots a last arrow skyward to symbolize a new peace agreement and a new way of life. (Library of Congress Prints and Photographs Division: Frank Fiske Collection. LC-USZ62-102685.)

Episcopal Bishop Hobart Hare arrived at the Yankton Agency in 1873 where he established his mission base. The reservations on which he hoped to maintain missions were hundreds of miles from Yankton Agency. He divided the territory to be served into smaller units each headed by a presbyter who was responsible for the catechists and ministers at each sub-station. Hare successfully established an efficient mission system. (South Dakota State Historical Society Archives.)

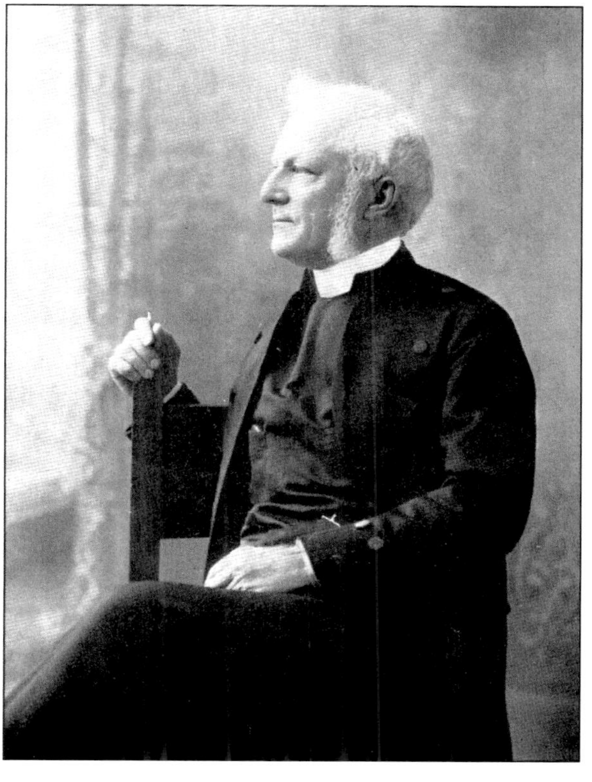

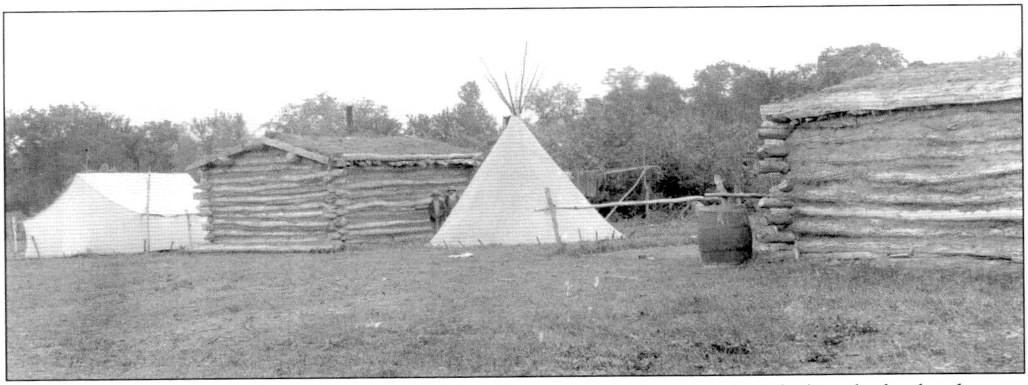

Wakpala in 1908 reveals several types of dwellings the native people inhabited: the log house, the tepee, and the government issued tent. The tepee was often preferred in summer as it was often cooler than the log house and could be moved. (Klein Museum, Mobridge.)

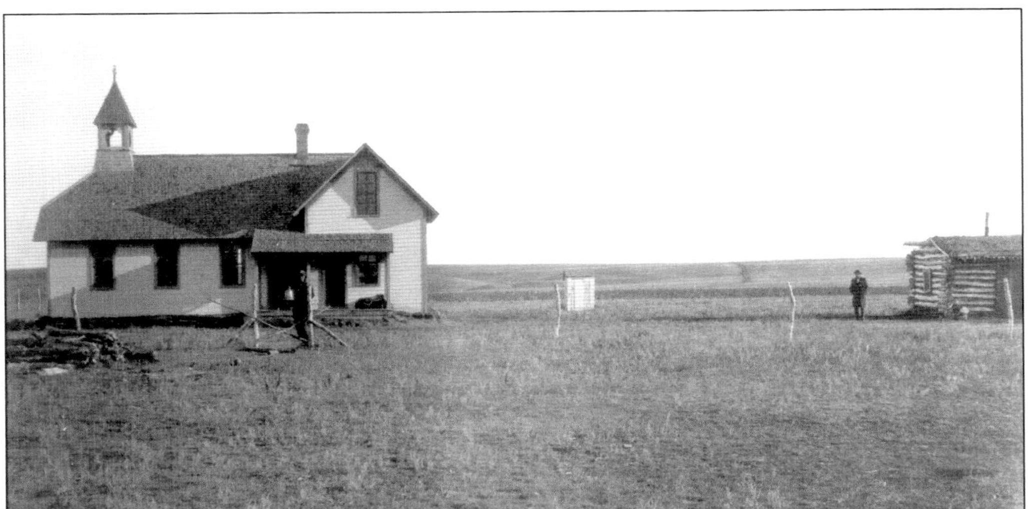

The Hunkpapa Chief Gall asked Bishop Hare for a school. The Episcopalians built St. Elizabeth's Mission in 1890. Mary S. Francis oversaw the school along with Miss Pricilla Bridge. In 1897, a fire destroyed St. Elizabeth's. The school was rebuilt with insurance money and funds obtained by the Lakota. (South Dakota State Historical Society Archives.)

Pictured, from left to right, are Rev. William Holmes, Rev. Philip Deloria, and Rev. Sherman Coolidge. In 1870, Philip Deloria was baptized in the Episcopal Church. He went to the white man's schools and later became a deacon in 1883. Bishop Hare sent Deloria to the Standing Rock Reservation. He remained at St. Elizabeth's Mission until 1925. (South Dakota State Historical Society Archives.)

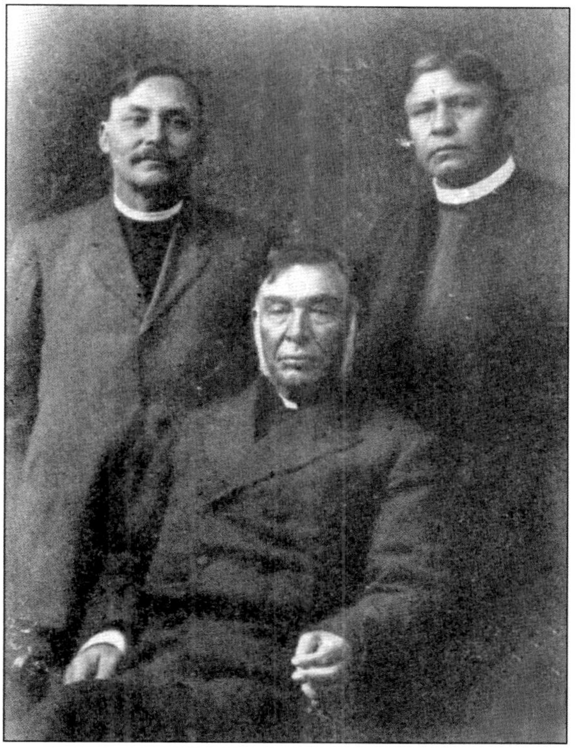

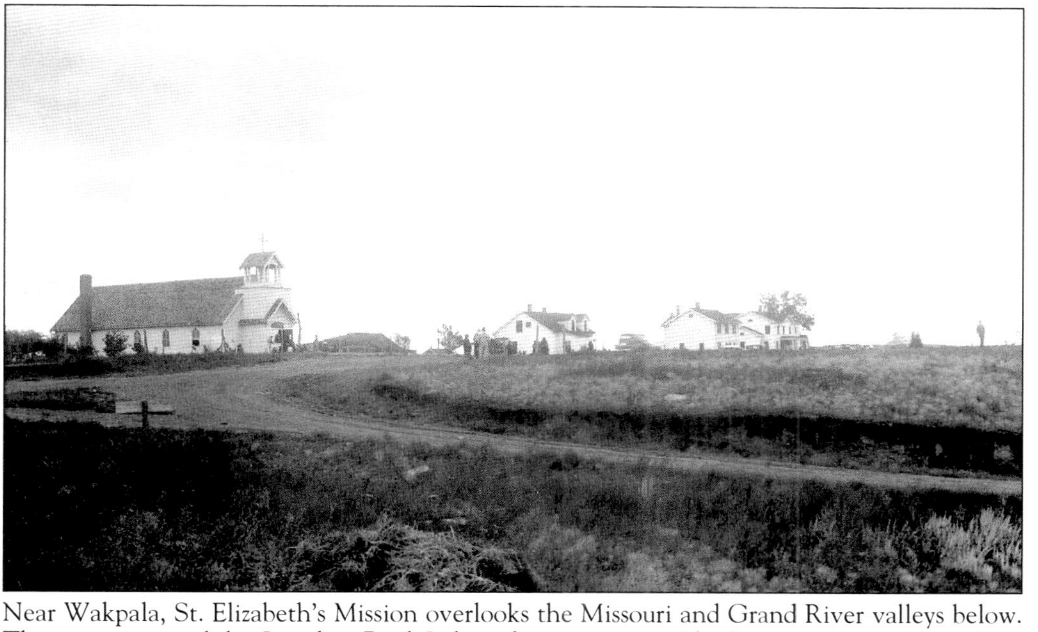

Near Wakpala, St. Elizabeth's Mission overlooks the Missouri and Grand River valleys below. The mission served the Standing Rock Lakota for many years. The Depression years forced the school to close. It then became a boarding school for students who attended public school in Wakpala. The boarding school closed also in 1967. The buildings remained vacant until 1973. (Klein Museum, Mobridge.)

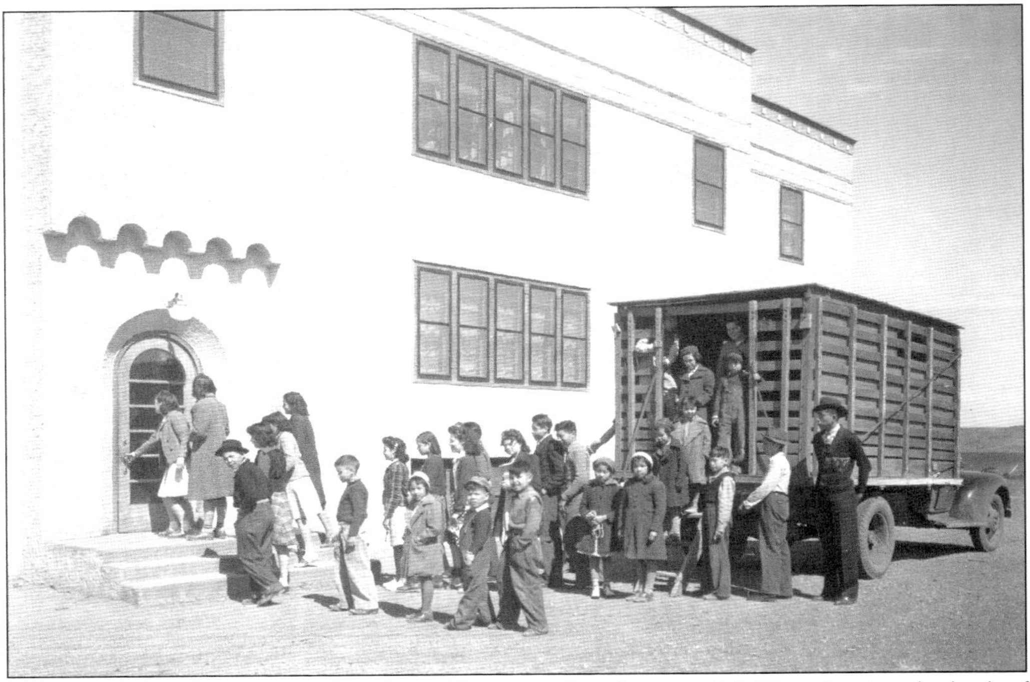

Taken by Mobridge photographer Oscar Huettner, this photo is of children leaving the back of a truck used as a bus at St. Elizabeth Mission during 1939–1941. (Klein Museum, Mobridge.)

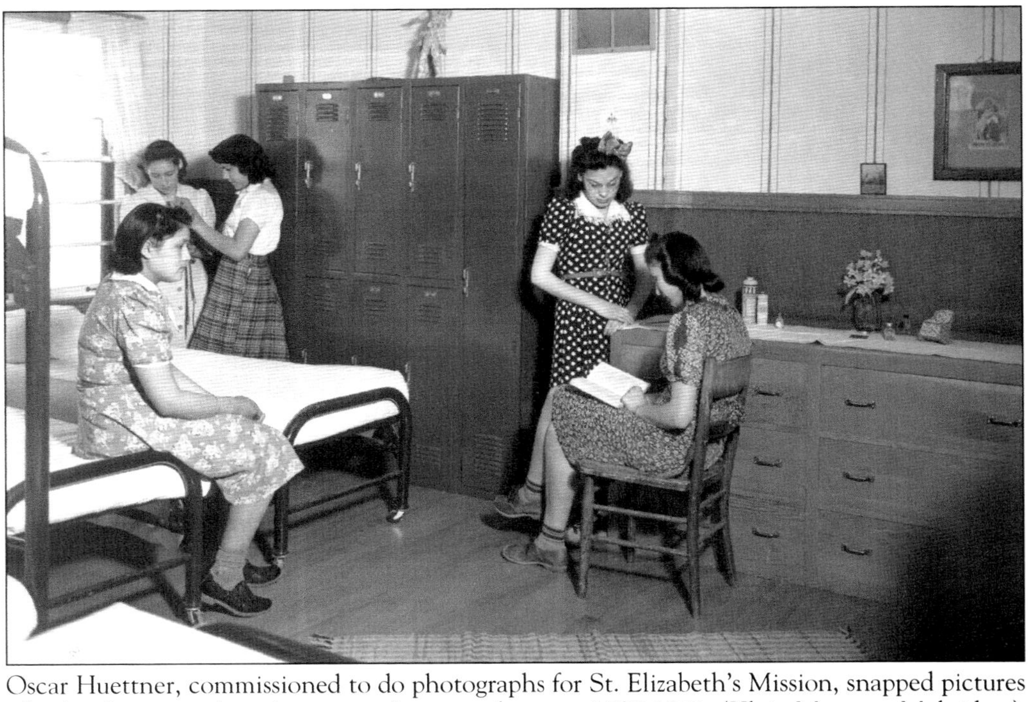

Oscar Huettner, commissioned to do photographs for St. Elizabeth's Mission, snapped pictures of girls relaxing in their dorm room between the years 1939-1941. (Klein Museum, Mobridge.)

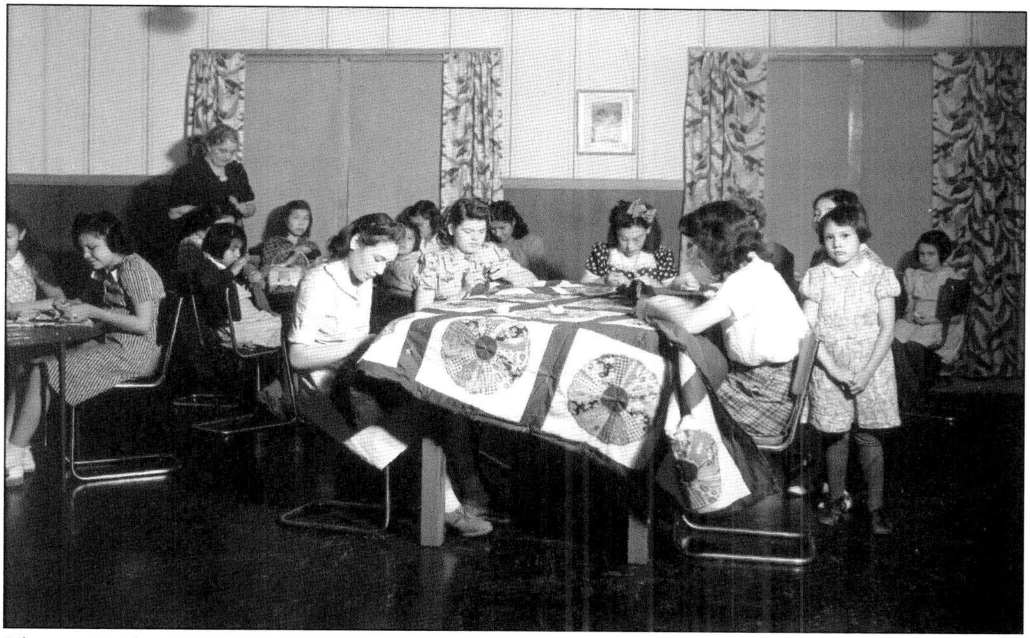

This is another commissioned photo of Heuttner's of girls sewing on a quilt at St. Elizabeth's. The native women gradually incorporated their own traditional designs into quilts. A good example is the well-known star quilt. (Klein Museum, Mobridge.)

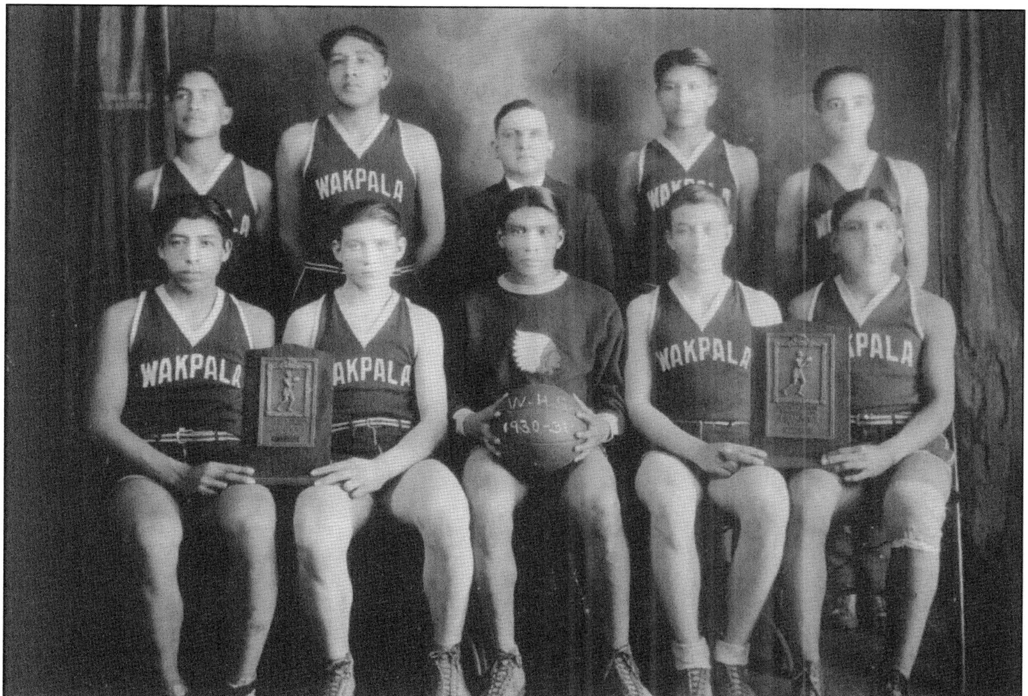

A Heuttner photograph captures a proud moment of the Wakpala boy's basketball team. (Klein Museum, Mobridge.)

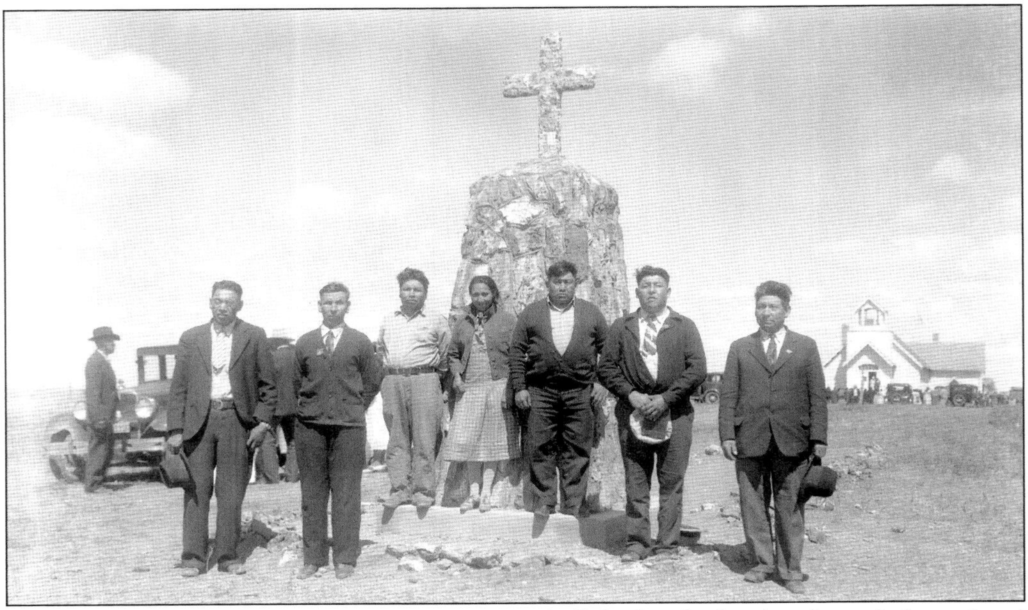

A group of people stands beside a monument, embellished with chunks of petrified wood and decorative stone, at St. Elizabeth's Mission. The marker commemorates the Episcopal Church's 50 years of service on the Standing Rock Reservation. St. Elizabeth's Church appears in the background. (Klein Museum. Mobridge.)

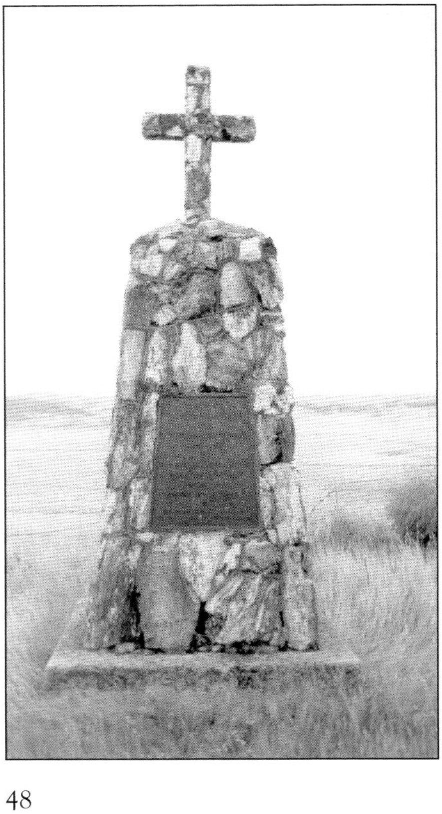

The inscription on the monument reads, "Erected to commemorate the fiftieth anniversary 1885–1935 of the establishment of the Episcopal Church among the Standing Rock Dakotas by William Hobart Hare, D.D., First Bishop of South Dakota." Bishop Hare designed a special Niobrara Cross for his Native American friends who became Christians. He gave one to each that was confirmed. The Greek letters surrounded by tepees on the oval seal translate into this motto, "That they may have life."

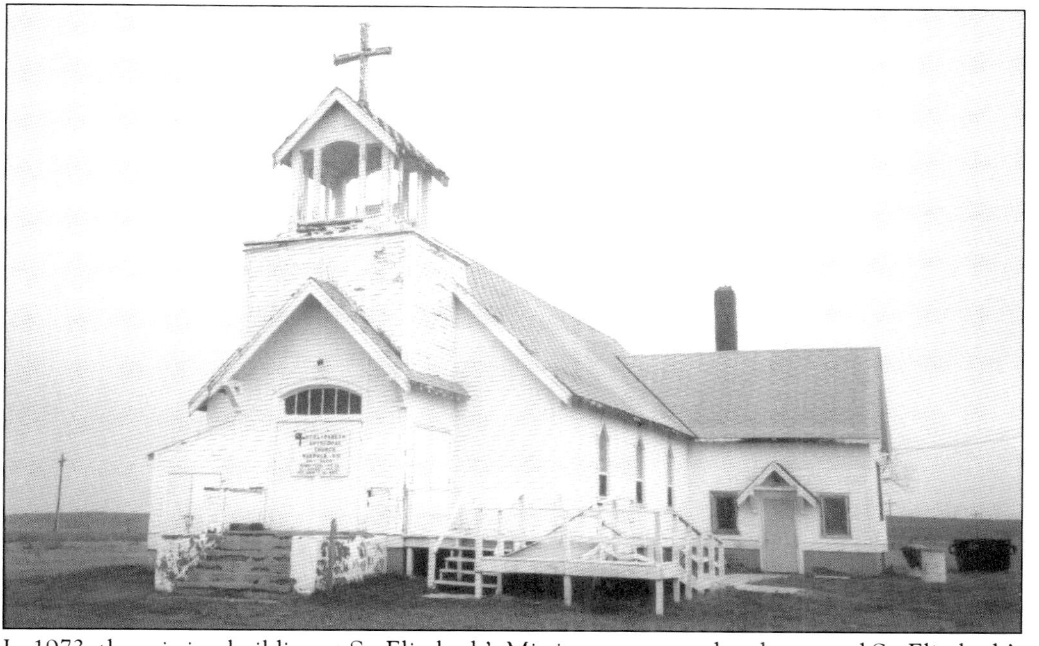

In 1973, the mission building at St. Elizabeth's Mission was opened and renamed St. Elizabeth's Training Center. Here, young men could train to become catechists and helpers. The center closed the following years and once again the buildings were vacant. The church, pictured above, has been in use throughout the years.

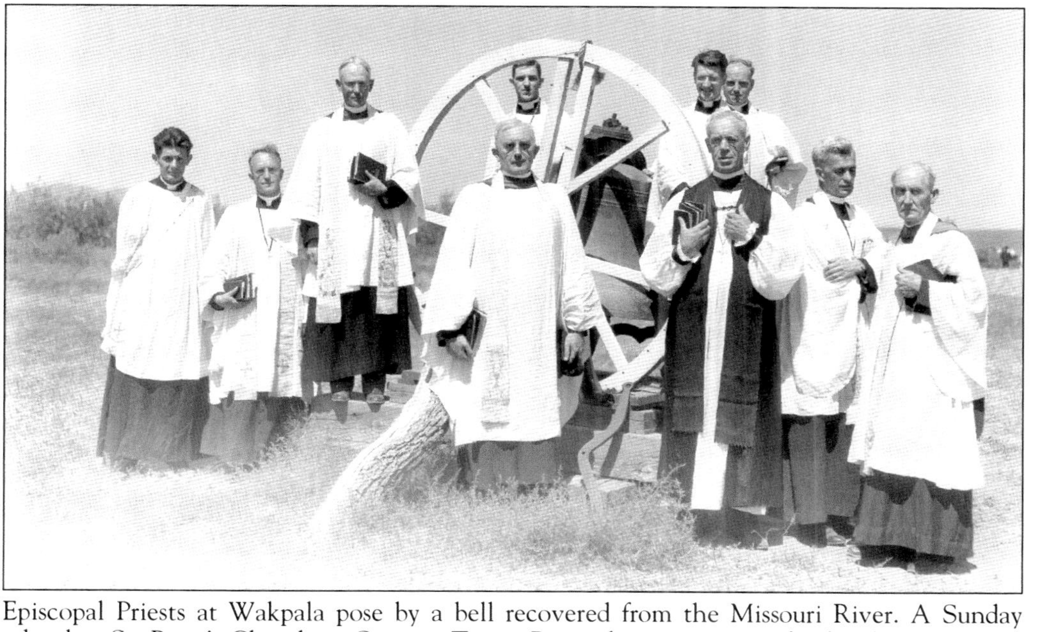

Episcopal Priests at Wakpala pose by a bell recovered from the Missouri River. A Sunday school at St. Peter's Church in German Town, Pennsylvania, sent a gift of a church bell for St. Elizabeth by riverboat. In transit, the bell was lost overboard near Chamberlain. Years later, during a time of low water, the bell was found resting on a sandbar. An inscription on the bell identified it as belonging to St. Elizabeth's. (Klein Museum, Mobridge.)

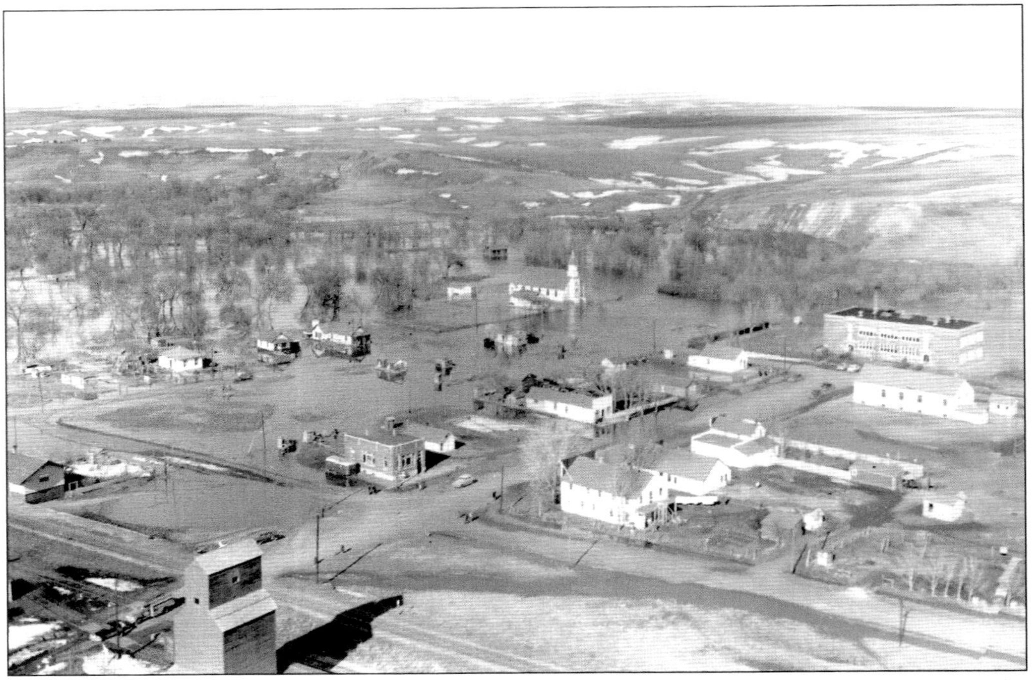

The water from a flooding Oak Creek surrounds the Catholic church of St. Bede, Wakpala. Wakpala is the Lakota word for Oak Creek. Father Bede Marty presided over the first mass in 1889. The native people donated cattle to help fund the new church, built in 1927. (Klein Museum, Mobridge.)

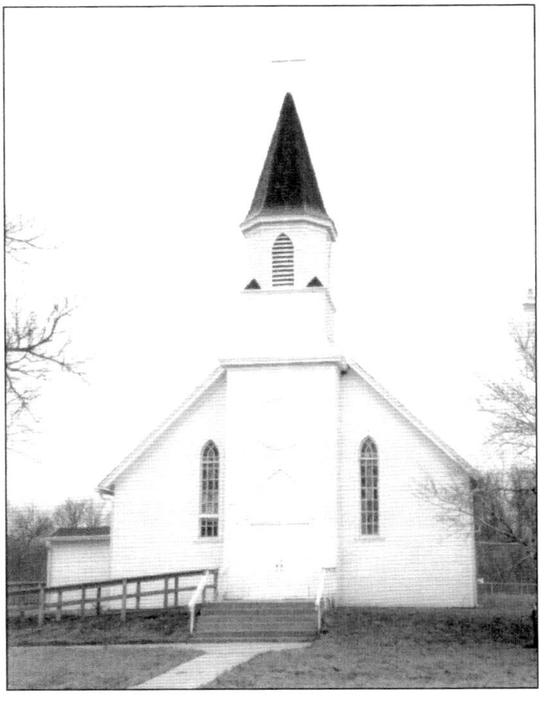

St. Bede is still in use today in Wakpala. The church was renovated in 1999 and blessed by Bishop Cupich.

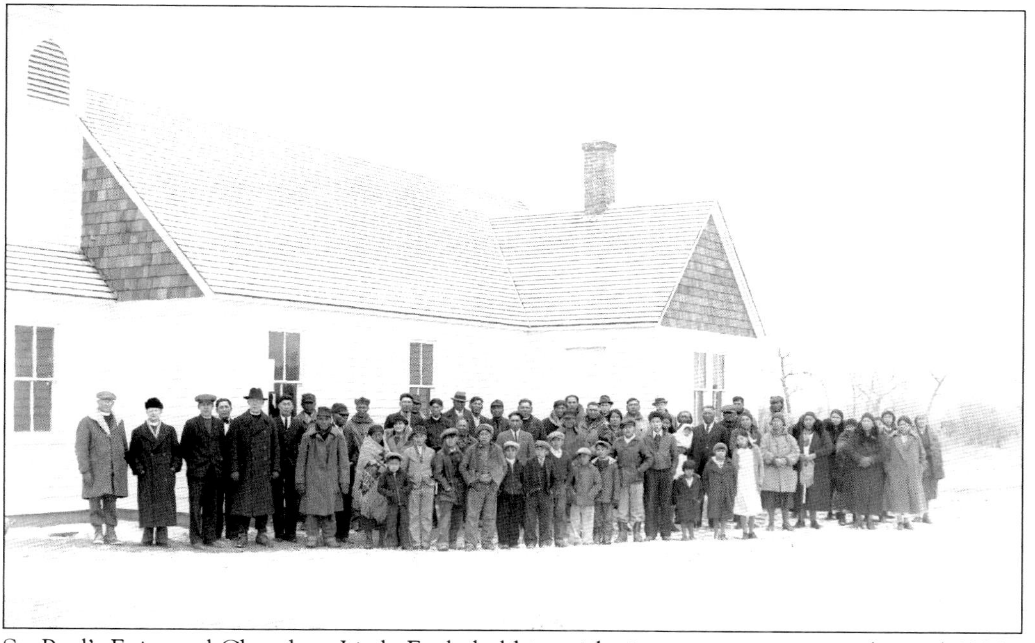

St. Paul's Episcopal Church at Little Eagle held its mid-winter convocation in the mid 1930s. In 1935, Rev. C.C. Rouilland and Catechist Paul Long Bull served the parishioners. (Klein Museum, Mobridge.)

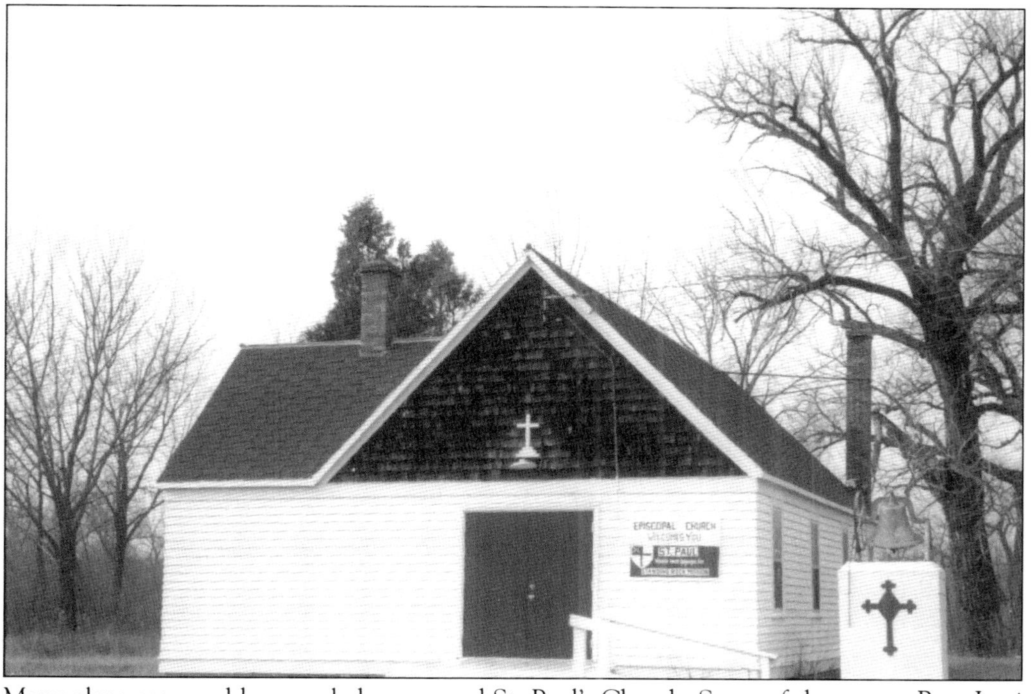

Many clergymen and lay people have served St. Paul's Church. Some of them were Rev. Levi M. Rouilland, Johnson Brown Eagle, Vernon Ashley, Wilbur Bearsheart, Victor Brown Eagle, and Levi Brown Eagle.

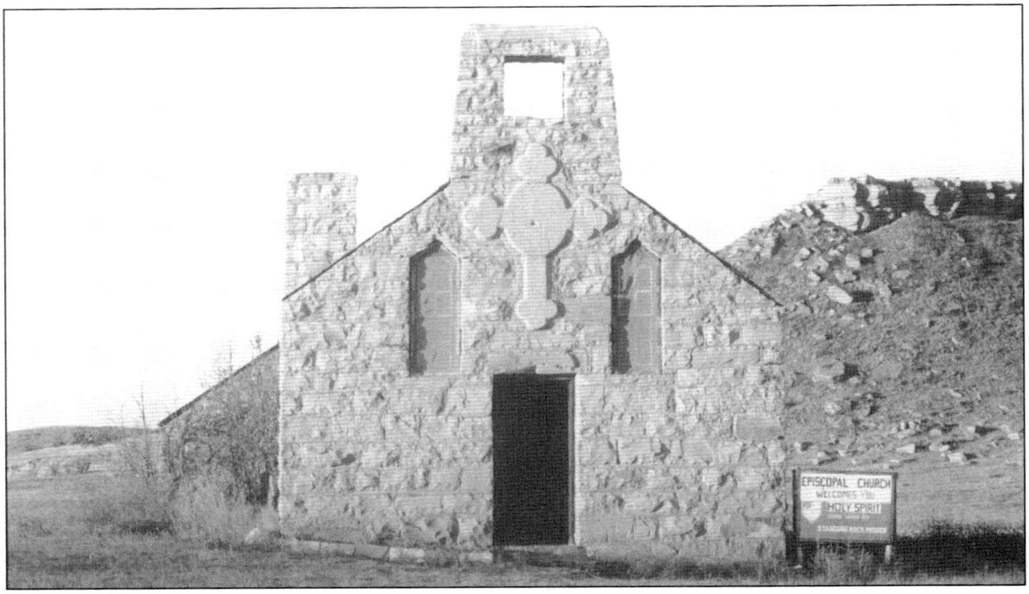

In a remote area of the Standing Rock Reservation, the Chapel of Holy Spirit, built from native stone from the bluffs above, blends into the landscape. The church was designed in 1922 by architect Alfred Morton Githens of New York, and built by Frank Waggoner of Keldon, South Dakota. Church members donated their time and money to build the church. (Timber Lake and Area Historical Society.)

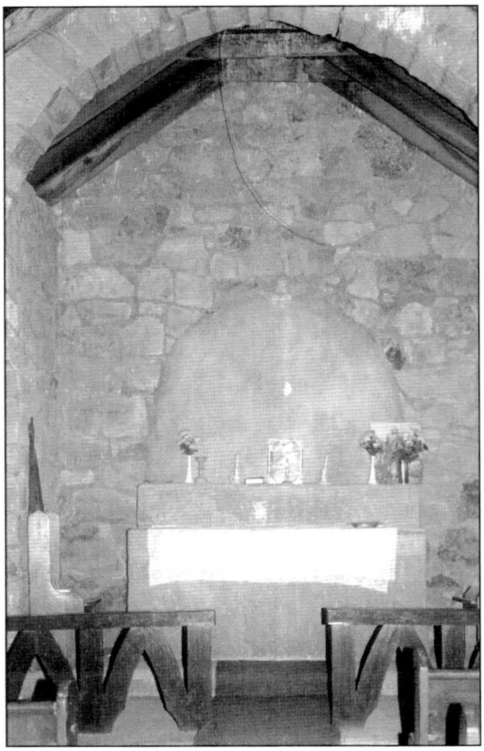

The native sandstone taken by nearby bluffs is clearly visible in this view of the altar area. The Timber Lake and Area Historical Society restored the old stone church between 2002–2004. (Timber Lake and Area Historical Society.)

Four

Rosebud

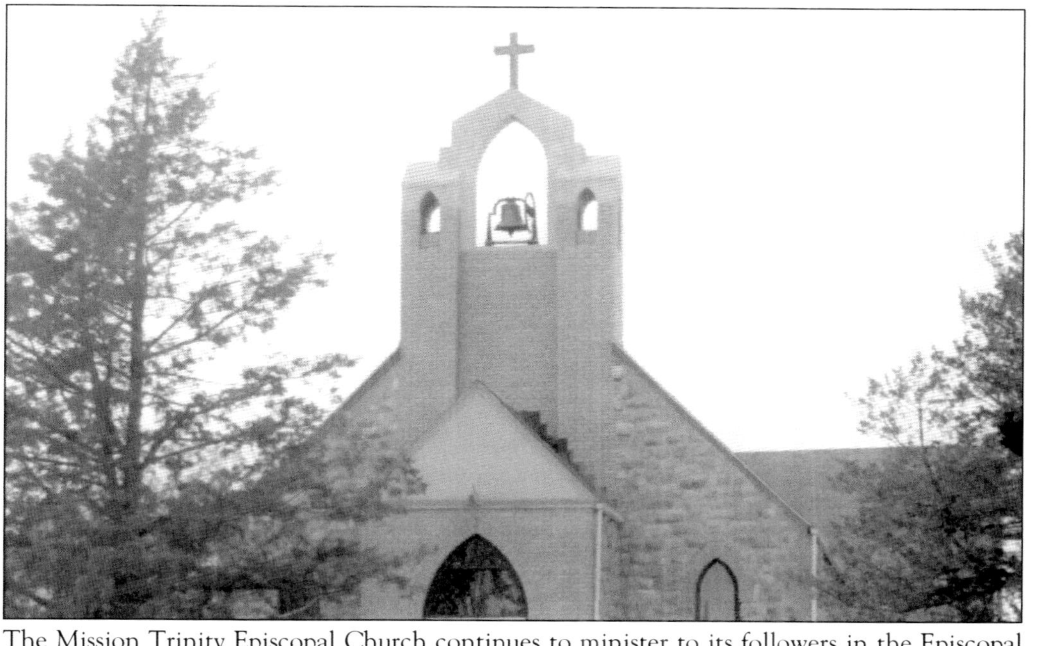

The Mission Trinity Episcopal Church continues to minister to its followers in the Episcopal tradition that began on the Rosebud when President Grant assigned the Rosebud to them. In 1875, Rev. Cleveland established a mission on the Spotted Tail Agency. The government moved the agency several times, making it difficult for a permanent mission until St. Mary's was founded near Rosebud in 1885.

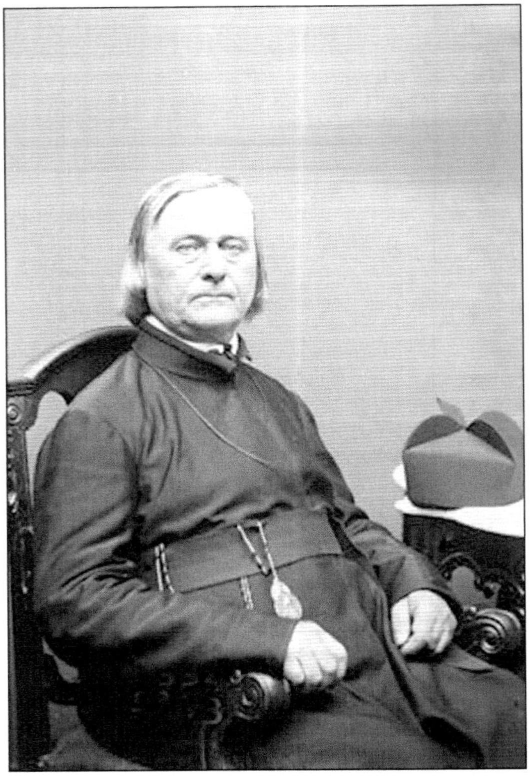

Born in Belgium, Rev. Father Pierre Jean DeSmet came to South Dakota in 1839 to mediate a dispute between the Yankton Sioux and the Potawatomi. He traveled on foot, by horseback and boat to spread the gospel to the Sioux. Whites and Native Americans alike looked forward to his trips up the Missouri River. Impressed with his imposing height, physical strength, and moral goodness, people flocked around him waiting to be baptized. (Library of Congress Prints and Photographs Division. LC-DIG-cwpbh-03561.)

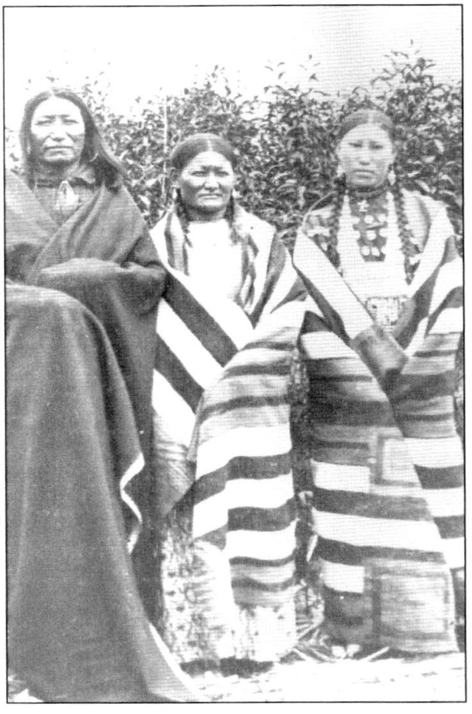

Spotted Tail, pictured with his wife and daughter, at first protested when the Brule Sioux were assigned to the Episcopal Church because of Grant's Peace Policy. The Brule remembered Father DeSmet and desired the Black Robes (Jesuits) to come and minister to his people. However, in 1870 Spotted Tail contacted William Welsh to send Episcopal missionaries. Spotted Tail never converted to the white man's religion. (South Dakota State Historical Society Archives and O.H. Over Museum; Morrow Collection.)

Hollow Horn Bear, like all Sioux chiefs, initially fought against the white invasion of their land. Later, he accepted the inevitable and favored peace. He became involved in treaty negotiations as one of the main spokesman. He also became a Catholic and is buried near St. Francis. (Library of Congress Prints and Photographs Division. LC-USZ62-102873.)

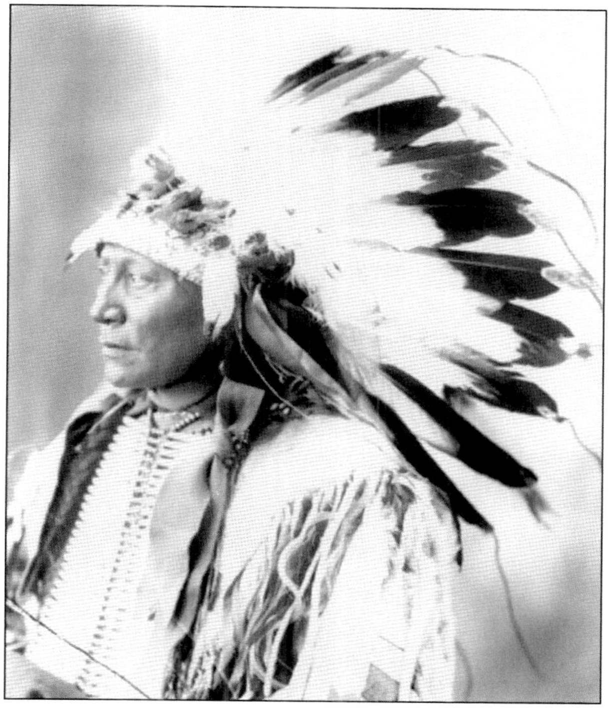

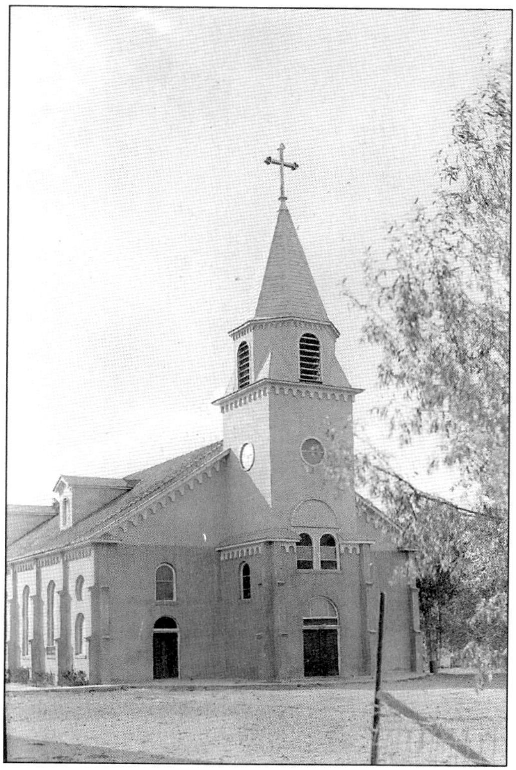

At the request of Spotted Tail, the Jesuits, Father Jutz and Brother Nunlist, established St. Francis Mission in 1885. Father Digmann arrived one year later with additional teaching staff. The native children found adjusting to life at St Francis' Boarding school difficult at first, but by 1900, 500 Indian students were enrolled, making St. Francis, a government contract school, one of the largest boarding schools in the nation. (St. Francis Mission.)

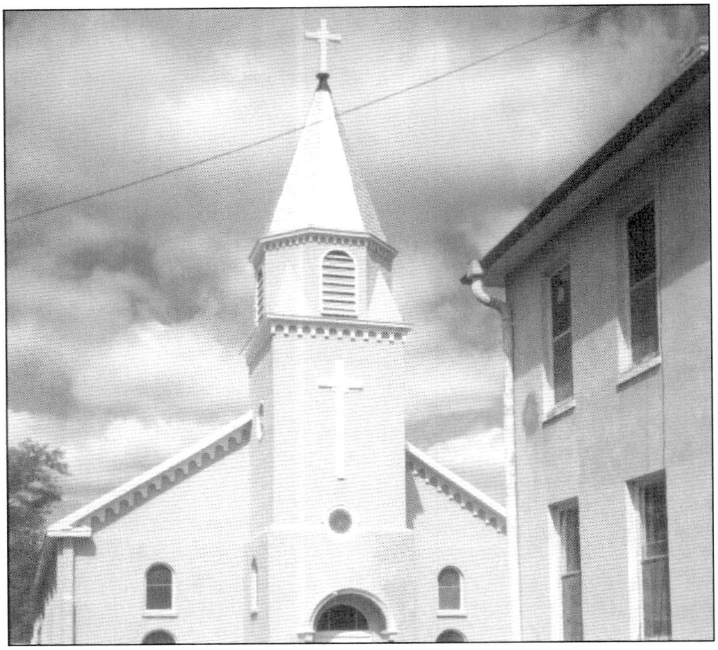

A new St. Charles replaced the original wooden church, which burned to the ground in January of 1915. The pouring of concrete for the new church began in 1917. The concrete, carried by buckets, was used for the foundation and the eighteen-inch thick walls. When St. Charles Church was completed on June 10, 1922, Father Digmann offered a Solemn High Mass for the occasion. Bishop J.J. Lawler of Lead, South Dakota, dedicated the Romanesque-style church on Octocber 24, 1922.

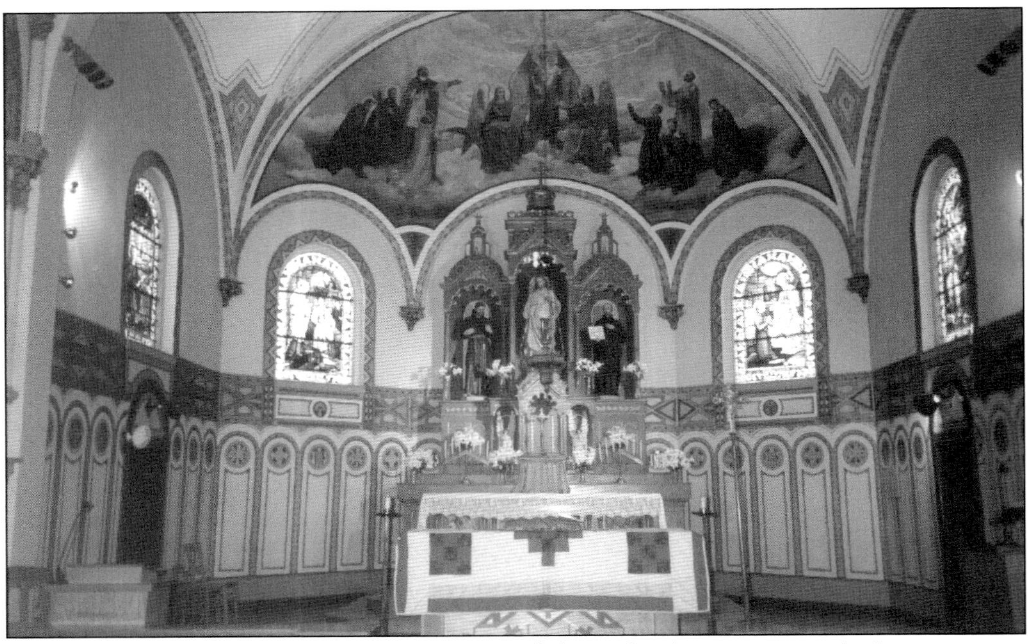

Joseph Lights, a former student, painted the mural above the altar portraying the Jesuit martyrs, St. Isaac Joques, St. John De Brebeuf, and Companions. Eight of the ten stained glass windows came from Germany, and were donated by Lakota students as memorials.

The statues on the main altar are of St. Francis of Assisi, Sacred Heart of Jesus, and St. Ignatius of Loyola. Brother Andrew Hartman, S.J., and others made the three main altars and communion rails. Brother Joseph Schwarzler, S.J., and Clarence Packard designed the small altar.

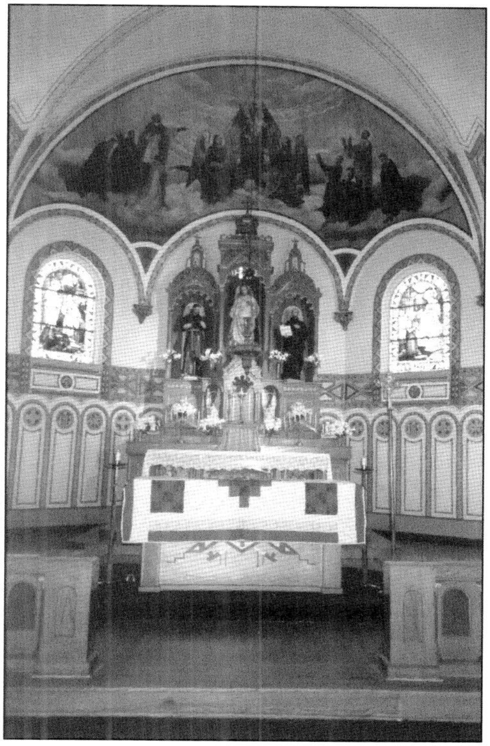

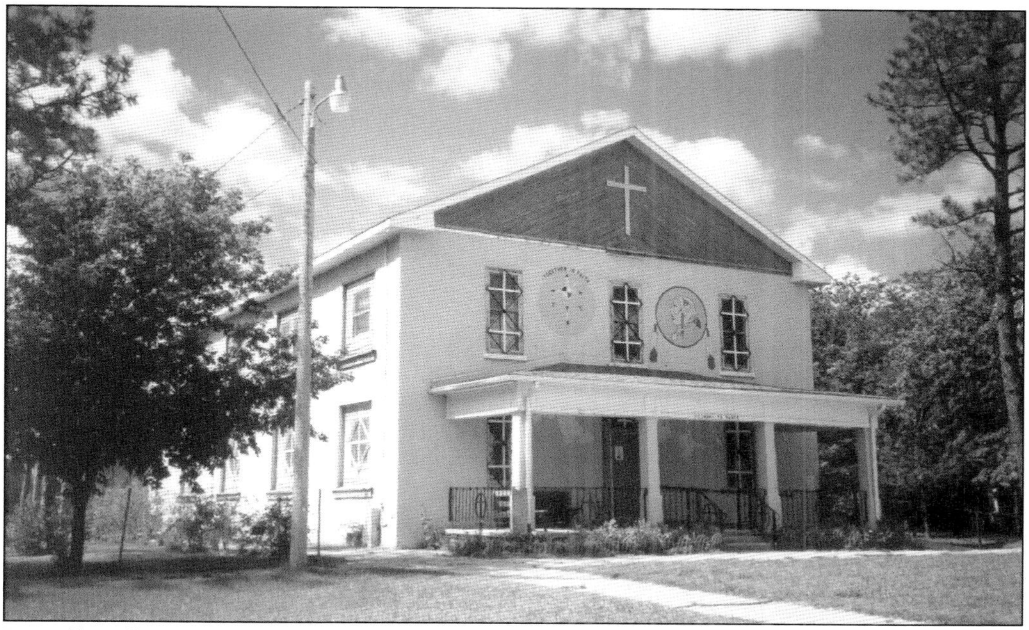

Drexell Hall, where the Sisters resided, was named for Katharine Drexel. Drexel supported various missions throughout the country and abroad, including the Rosebud and Pine Ridge Reservation. She pronounced her vows in 1891 as the first Sister of the Blessed Sacrament. Pope John Paul II canonized her in 2000.

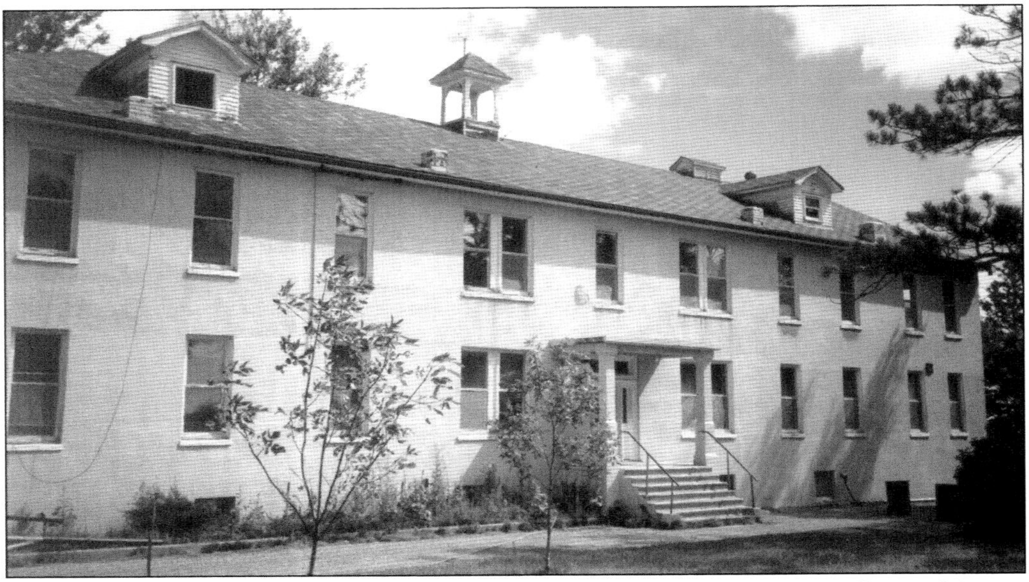

Hartman Hall was named for Brother Andrew Hartman, S.J., who came to St. Francis Mission in 1905 and remained until his death in 1949. He was a master carpenter who trained his Lakota workmen in the building of Drexel Hall at St. Francis, Red Cloud Hall for Holy Rosary, as well as mission buildings on the Wind River Reservation. Over 20 mission chapels on both the Pine Ridge and Rosebud were evidence of his handiwork.

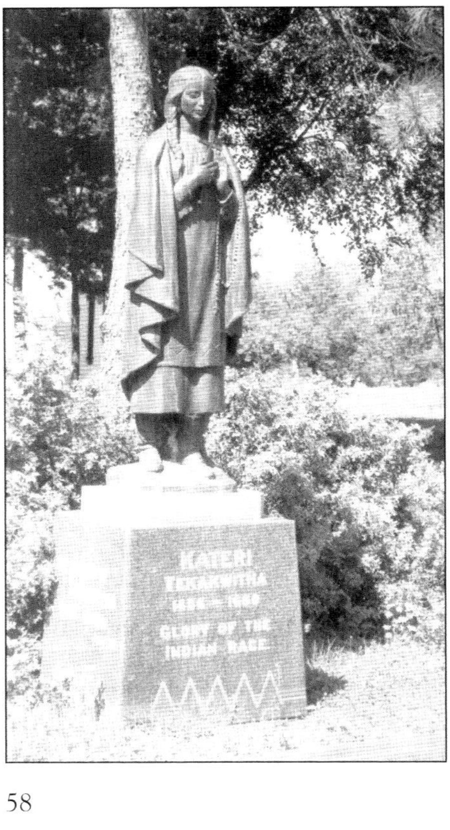

The statue of Kateri occupies a place of honor at St. Francis. Born in 1656 in New York State to a Mohawk father and an Algonquin mother, Kateri Tekakwitha was the first Native American nominated for Sainthood. Taught by the Jesuits, Kateri was baptized in the Catholic faith on Easter 1676. She dedicated her life to God and died at the age of 24.

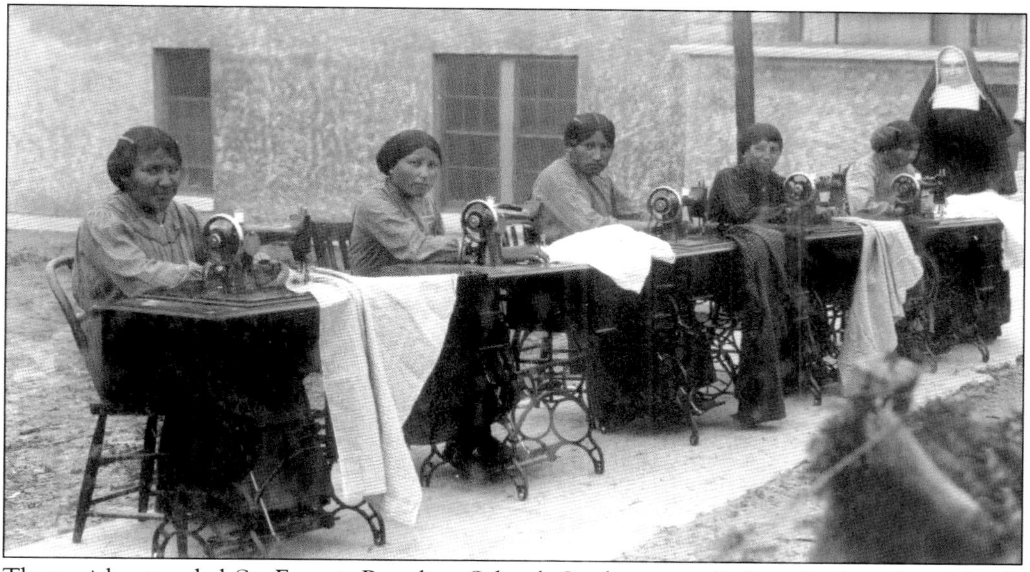

These girls attended St. Francis Boarding School. Students enrolled in the boarding schools received intense instruction seven days a week. In addition to the academic curriculum, pupils were taught various trades. The girls learned domestic skills such as sewing, cooking, cleaning, and laundering. The schools taught boys shoemaking, farming, carpentry, gardening, and blacksmithing. Every student above the fifth grade performed three hours of manual labor a day. (St. Francis Mission.)

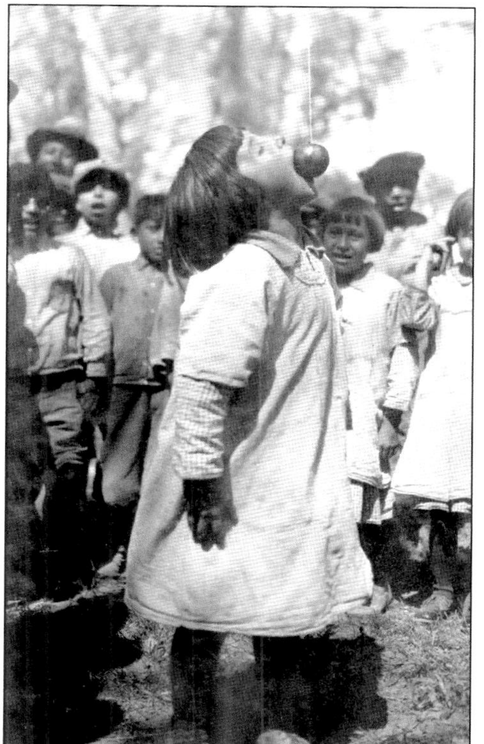

The boarding school students adhered to a rigid curriculum but time was made for parties and fun. (St. Francis Mission.)

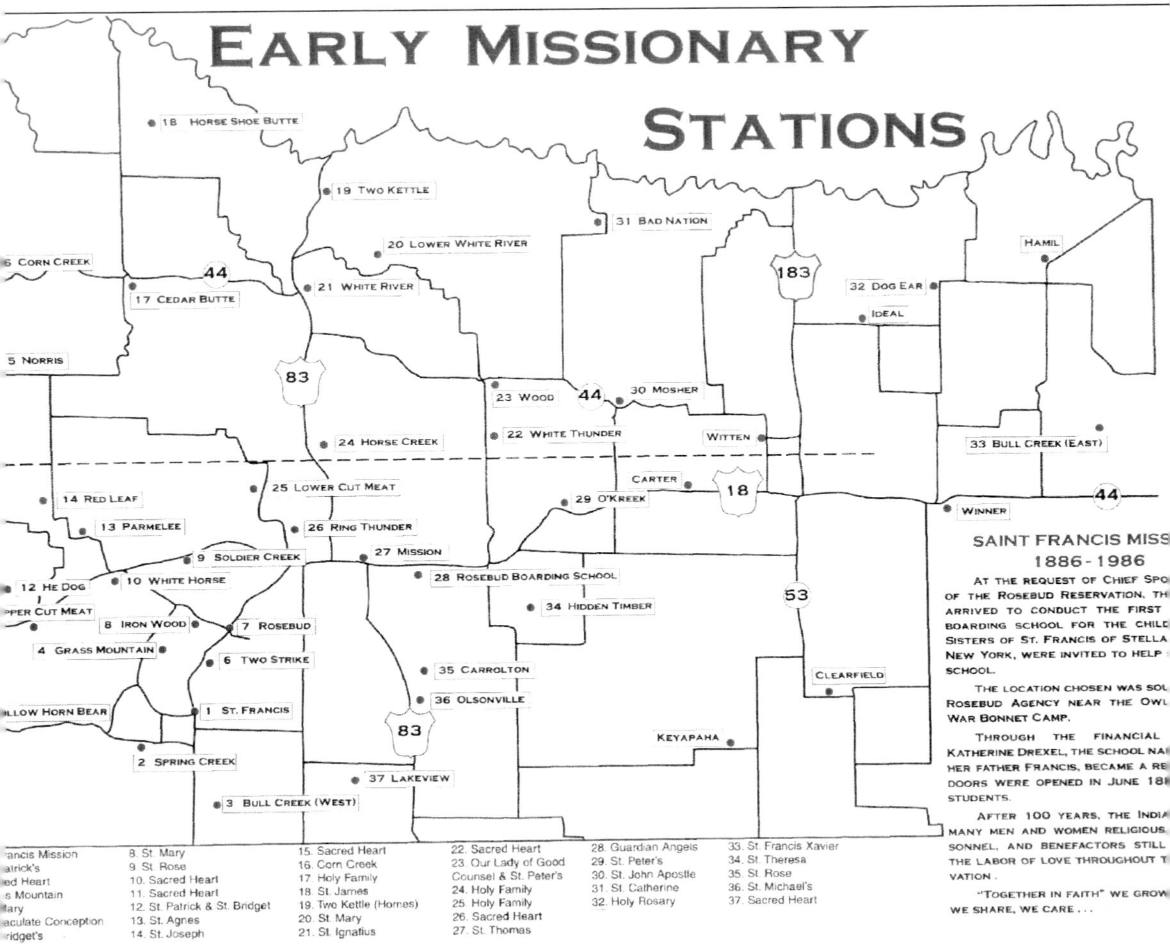

This map shows the extensive missionary stations on the Rosebud. (St. Francis Mission.)

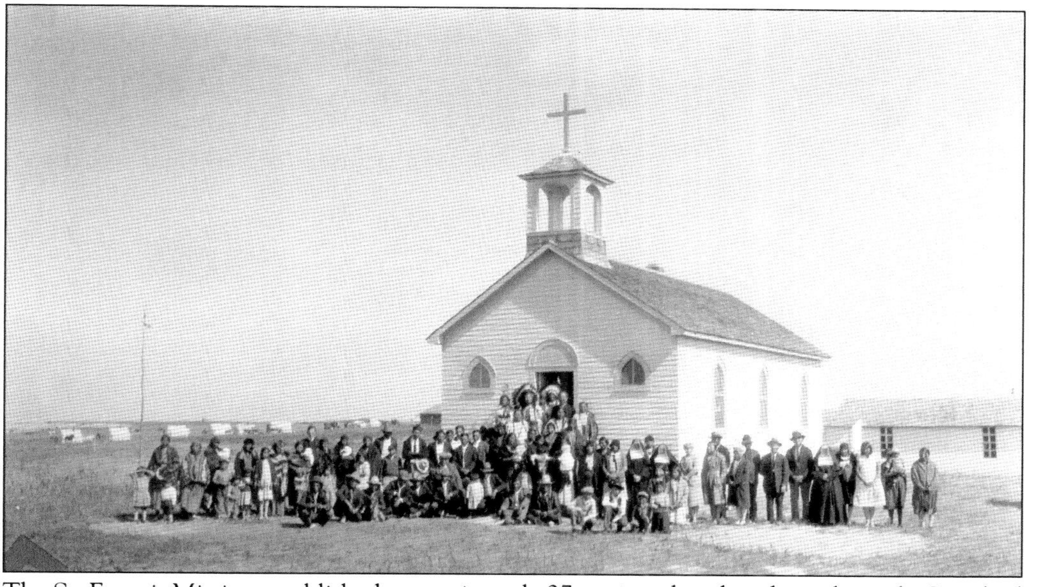

The St. Francis Mission established approximately 37 station churches throughout the Rosebud Reservation. The Sacred Heart Church, built in 1911 near Ring Thunder, was one of them. Father Groethe originally made the circuit visiting each church. His successor, Father Buechel, made the rounds in his Model T. (St. Francis Mission.)

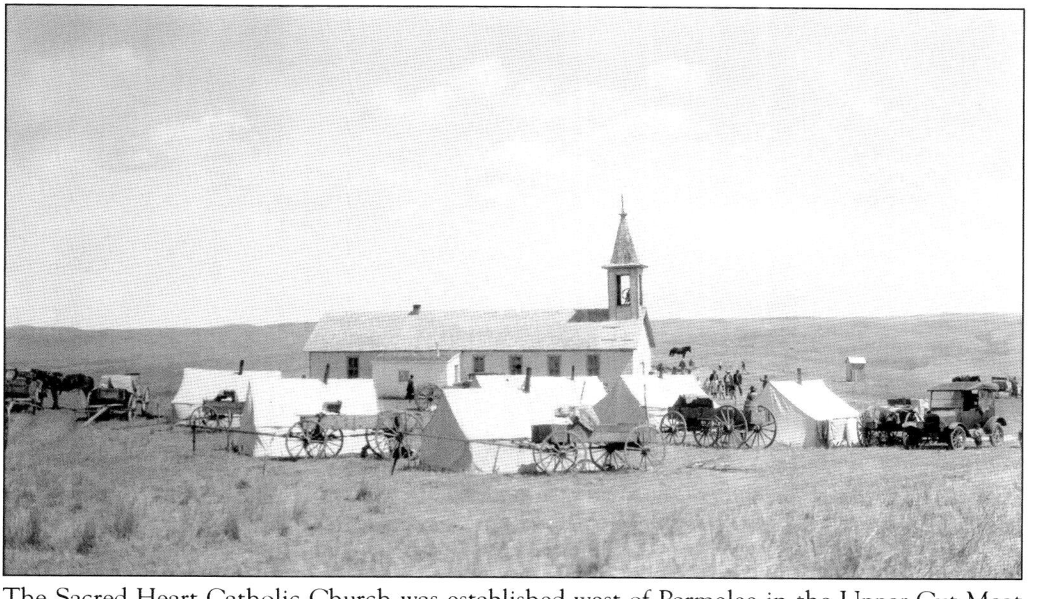

The Sacred Heart Catholic Church was established west of Parmelee in the Upper Cut Meat area. The Cut Meat name came from the three slaughter stations, located at Cut Meat and at Lower and Upper Cut Meat. The government issued beef on the hoof. The Lakota would kill the cattle and butcher them here. (St. Francis Mission.)

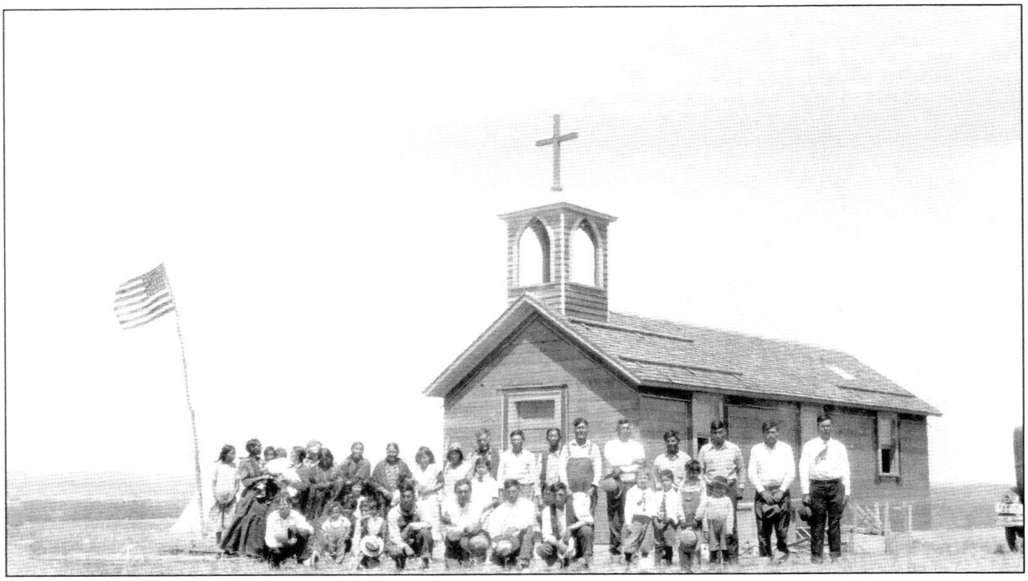

St. James Church, south of Belvidere, was located near Horse Shoe Butte. All that remains of the church is the foundation. (St. Francis Mission.)

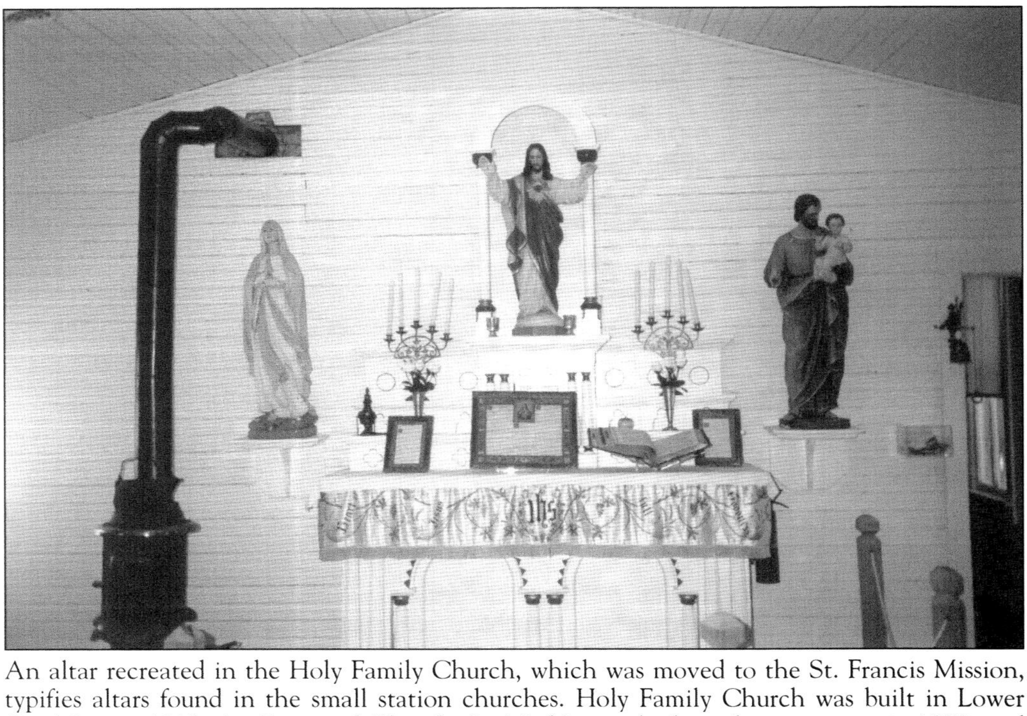

An altar recreated in the Holy Family Church, which was moved to the St. Francis Mission, typifies altars found in the small station churches. Holy Family Church was built in Lower Cut Meat in 1913. An Episcopal Church, St. Mark's, was built in this same area in 1890, and destroyed by fire in 1993.

A primitive log chapel was used before the building of this Spanish-style church in 1927. Although St. Agnes in Parmelee still stands, it is no longer used. In 1974, a new building replaced it.

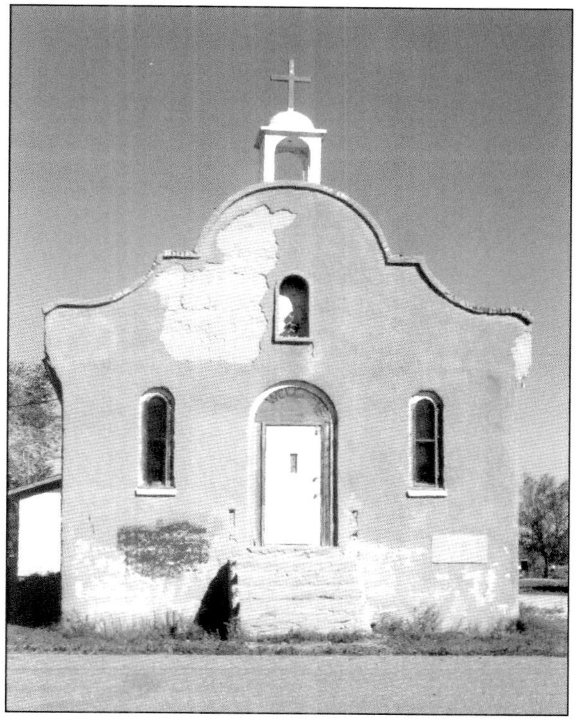

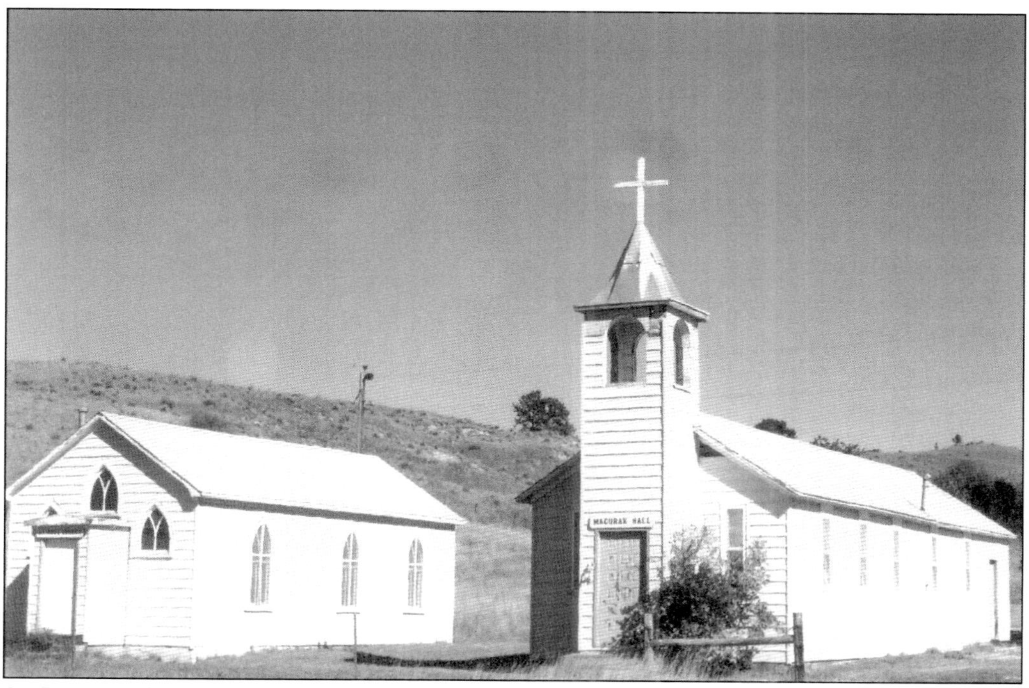

St. Rose, to the left, was first used at Mosher, and then moved to Soldier Creek in 1962. The building to the right had been used as a church in Midway and Hidden Timber and was moved to Soldier Creek in 1938. It is renamed Macurak Hall in honor of Father Macurak, S.J.

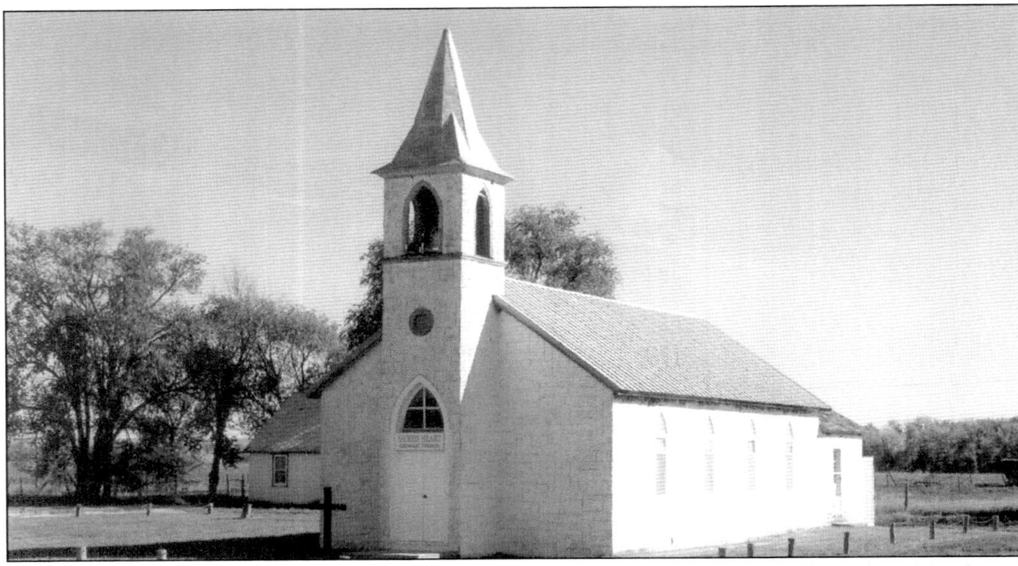

The first Sacred Heart Catholic church was moved to Norris and was used until 1955, when a larger church replaced it. The Jesuits ministered to a native and non-native congregation.

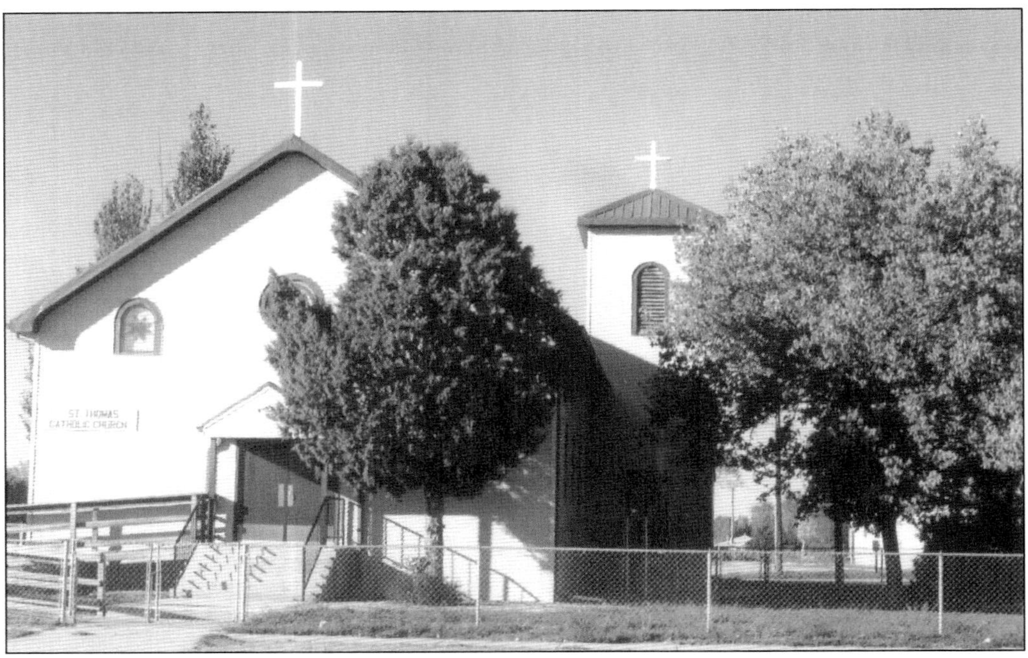

Father Digmann celebrated the first mass in a federal boarding school until he was restricted from doing so. Father Gerald Stakemeier established St. Thomas Catholic Church in Mission at the request of Bishop John Lawler in 1936. Brother Hartman, S.J., from St. Francis Mission built the rectory with help from Lakota men.

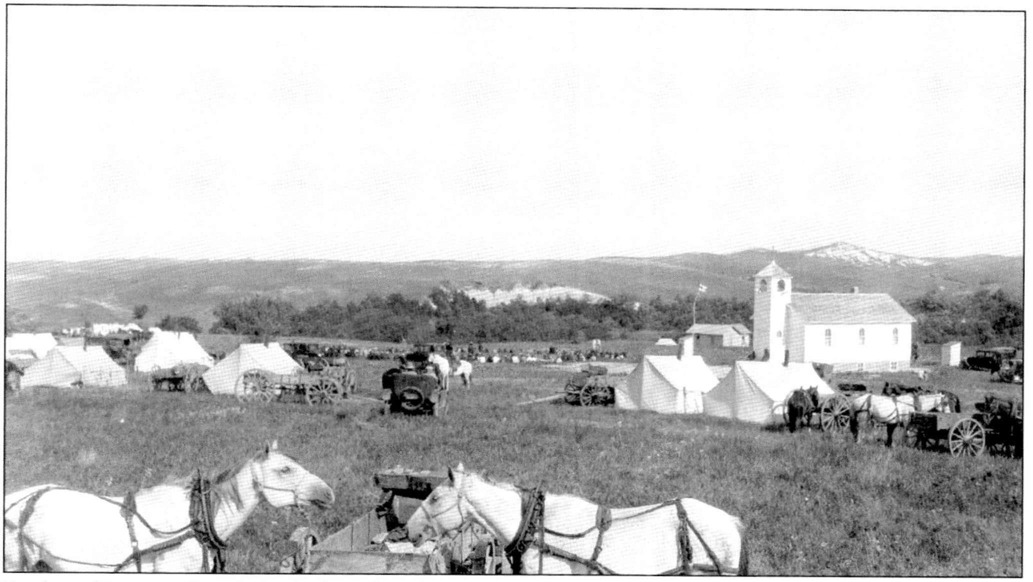

Both an Episcopal and Catholic Church, St. Patrick's and St. Bridget's, appear near He Dog in this 1930 photograph. (St. Francis Mission.)

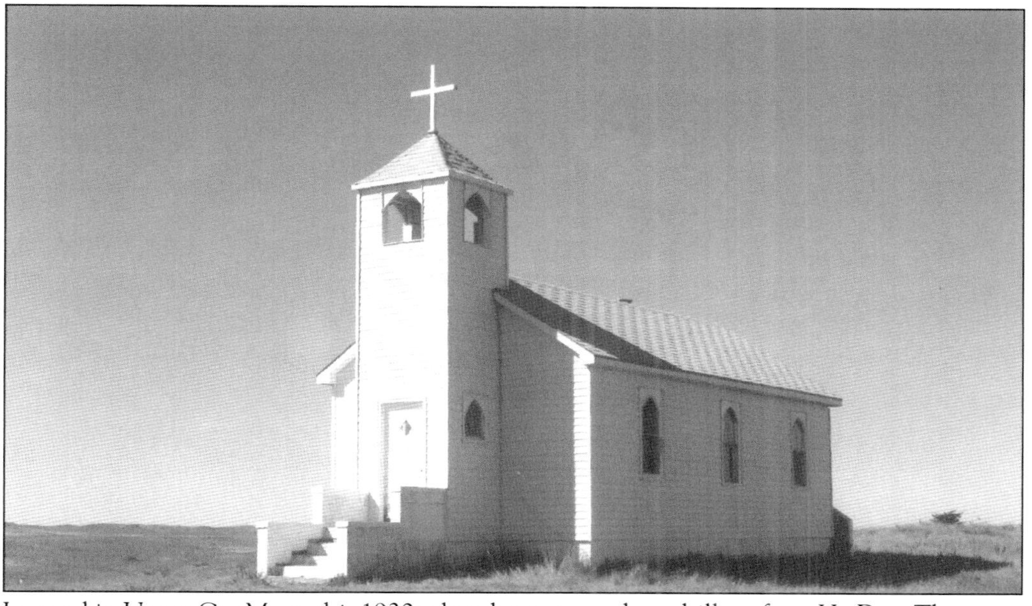

Located in Upper Cut Meat, this 1930s church was moved to a hilltop from He Dog. This same church can be seen in the previous photograph. Father Robert Demeyer, S.J., had the original 1911 church torn down.

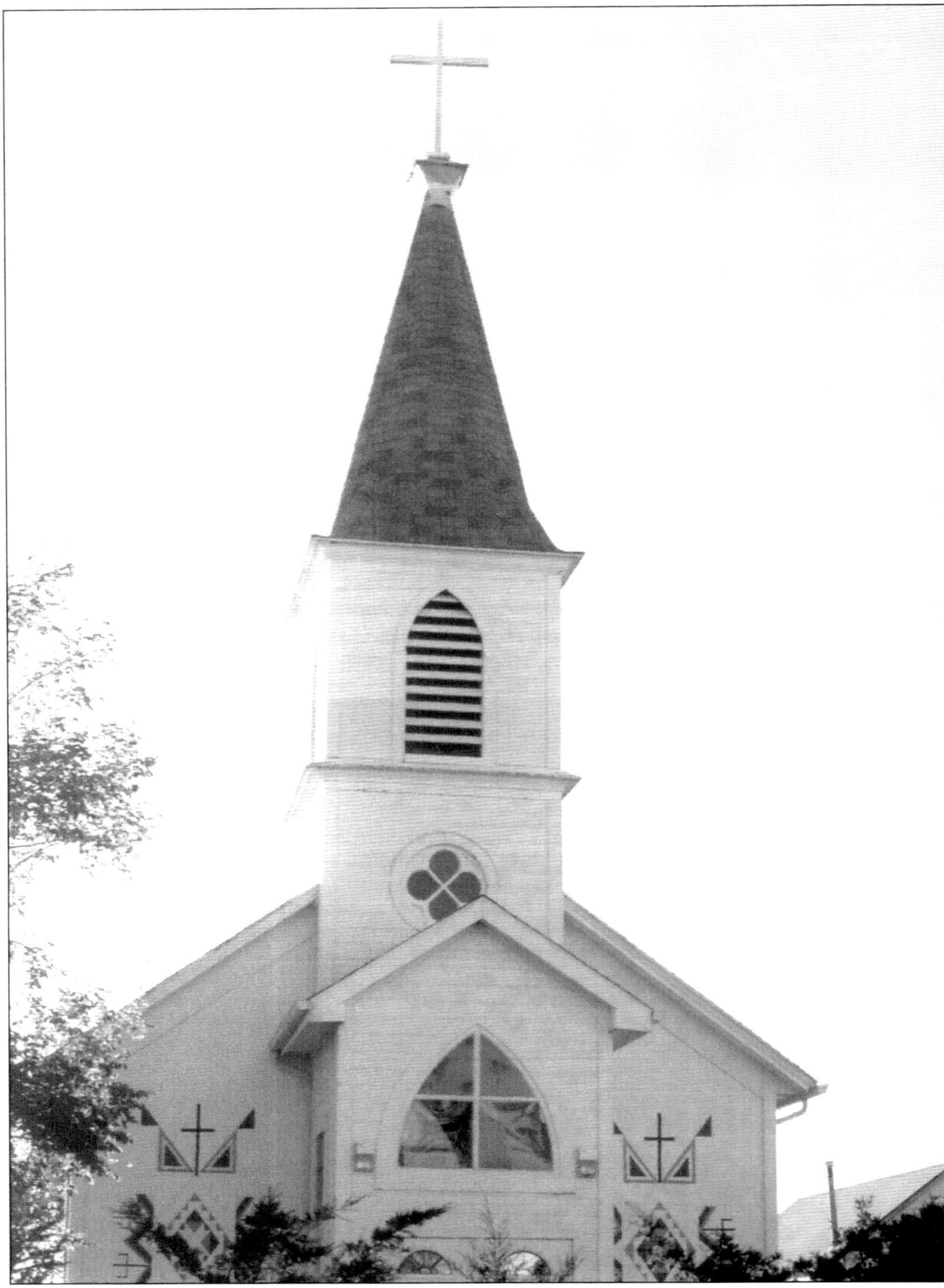

In 1892, Lakota from the Two Kettles band requested baptism. Father Digmann went to the area to accommodate their request. The government donated land and Katharine Drexel made a contribution towards the building of the church. St. Ignatius, located at White River, was moved twice and is the oldest church on tribal lands still in use.

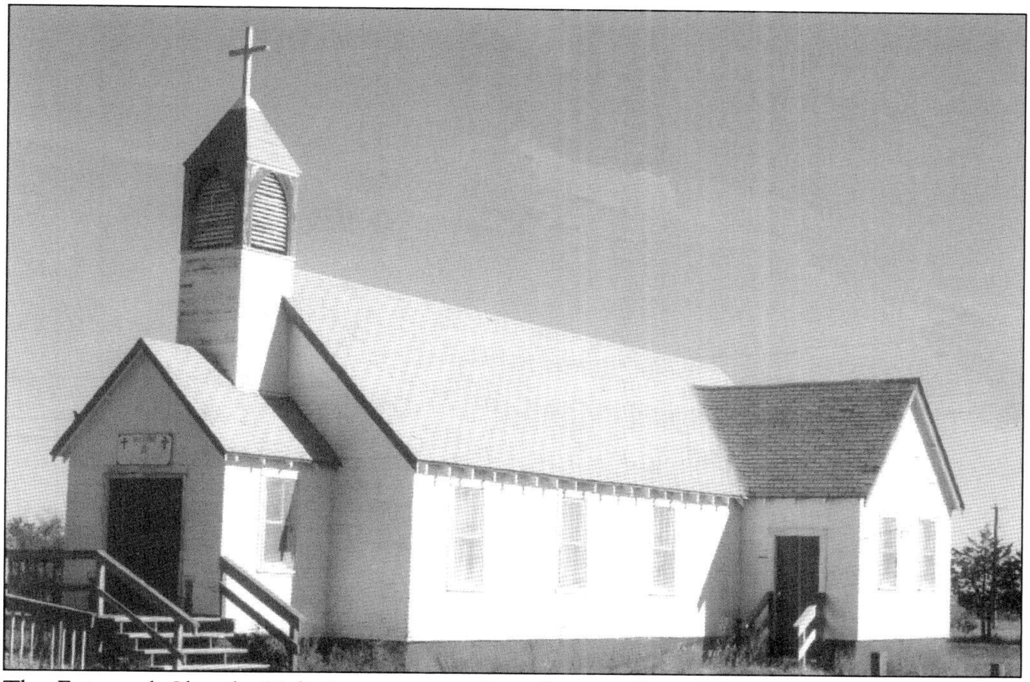

The Episcopal Church, Holy Innocents, at Parmelee is still an active church. Over the years many catechists and clergy have served the church. Stephen Murray was Senior Catechist of Holy Innocents in 1910. In 1935, Rev. S.H. King and his helper Silas Standing Bear held services. Several Niobrara Deanery Convocations were held here in 1936, 1949, 1965, and 1971.

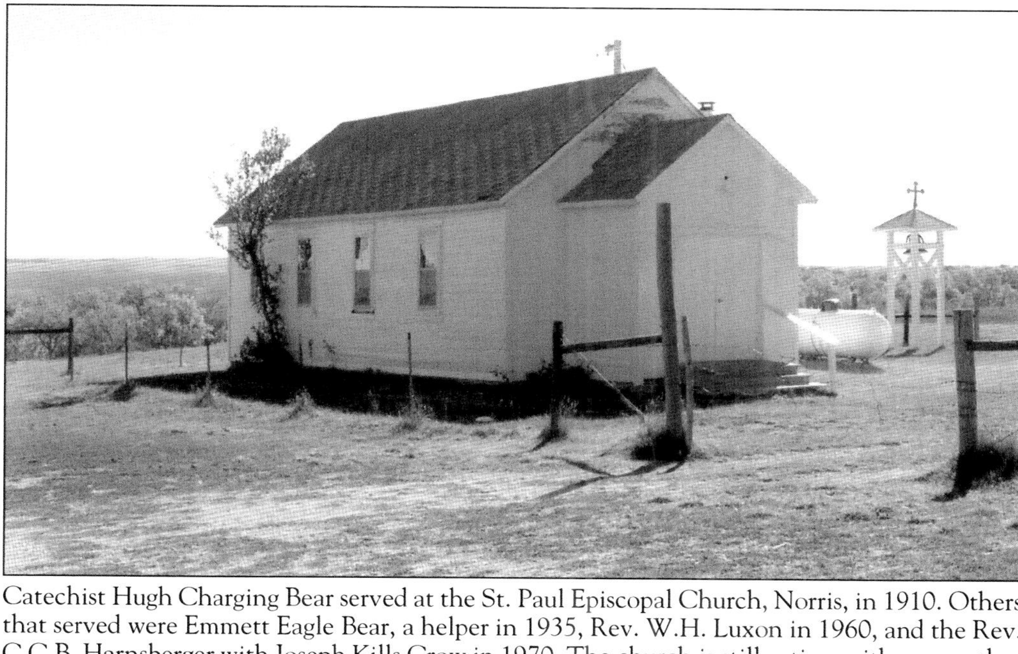

Catechist Hugh Charging Bear served at the St. Paul Episcopal Church, Norris, in 1910. Others that served were Emmett Eagle Bear, a helper in 1935, Rev. W.H. Luxon in 1960, and the Rev. C.C.B. Harnsberger with Joseph Kills Crow in 1970. The church is still active, with many other clergy who have served since.

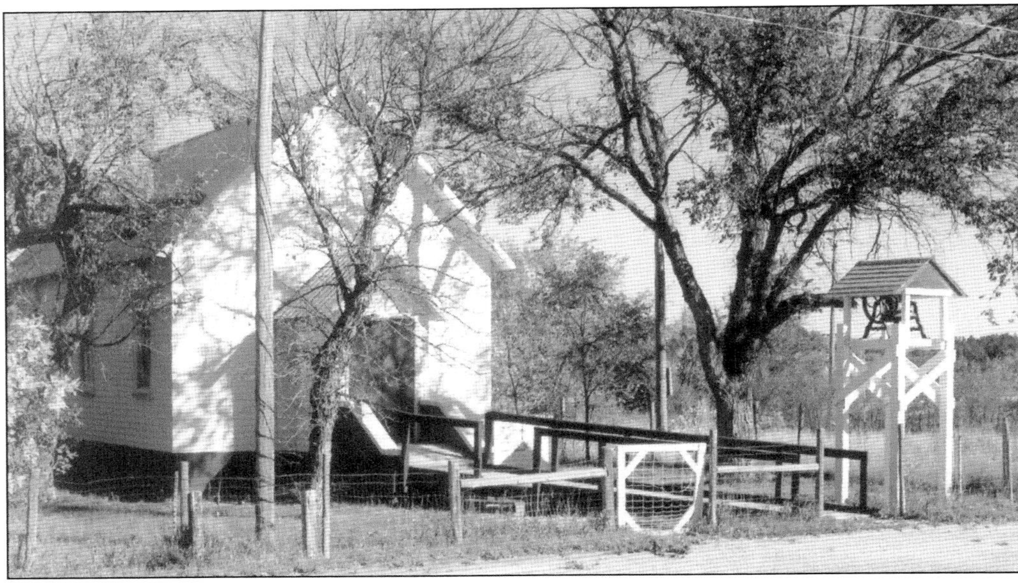

Still in use, Rosebud Episcopal Mission, Church of Jesus, was established in 1875. In 1910, Samuel Broken Rope served as catechist. Rev. John DeCory served terms beginning in 1935, Rev. Paul Barbour in 1945, Rev. W. B. Luxon in 1960, Rev. Fredrick E. Jessett and Theodore Lunderman in 1970. A host of other clergy has served since.

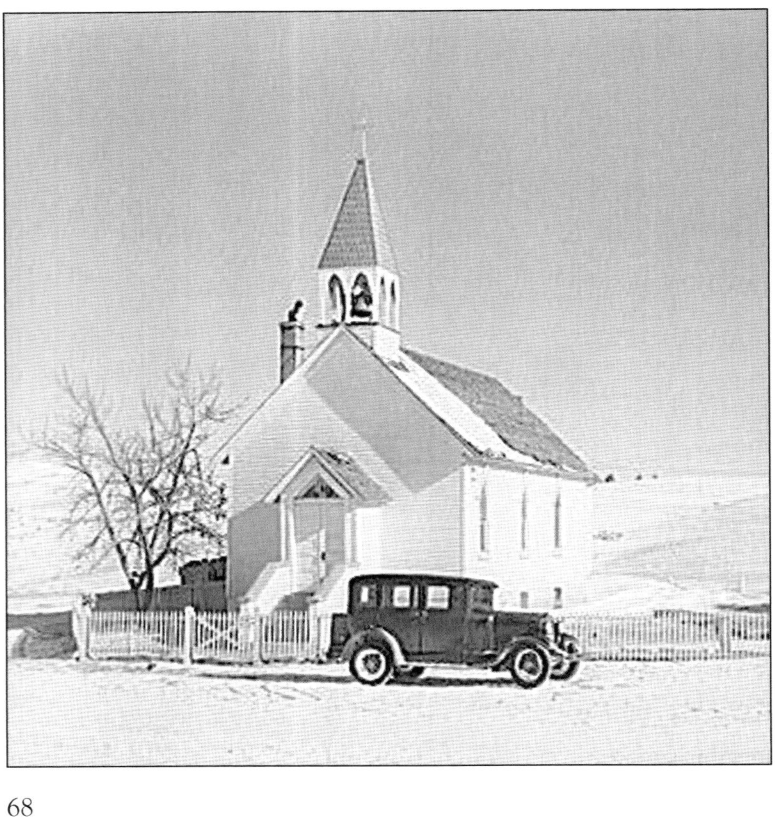

John Vachon took this winter photograph of an unidentified Catholic Church on the Rosebud in 1940. (Library of Congress Prints and Photographs Division; John Vachon. LC-USF34-061760-D.)

Four

PINE RIDGE

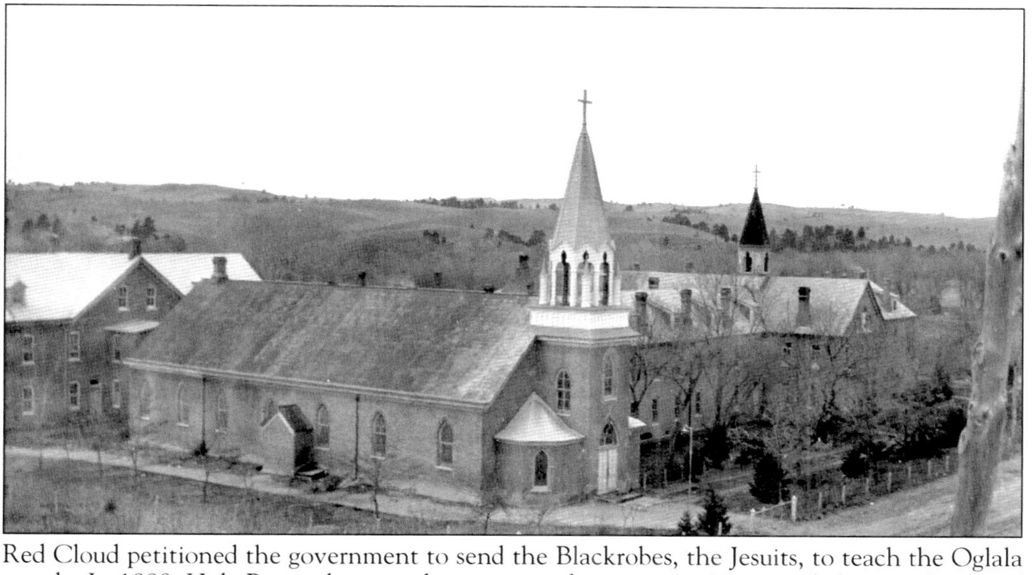

Red Cloud petitioned the government to send the Blackrobes, the Jesuits, to teach the Oglala people. In 1888, Holy Rosary became the answer to his petition. 28 stained glass windows and hand carved wood adorned the hand made brick church. Holy Rosary earned the distinction of being the first brick county church west of the Missouri. (St. Francis Mission.)

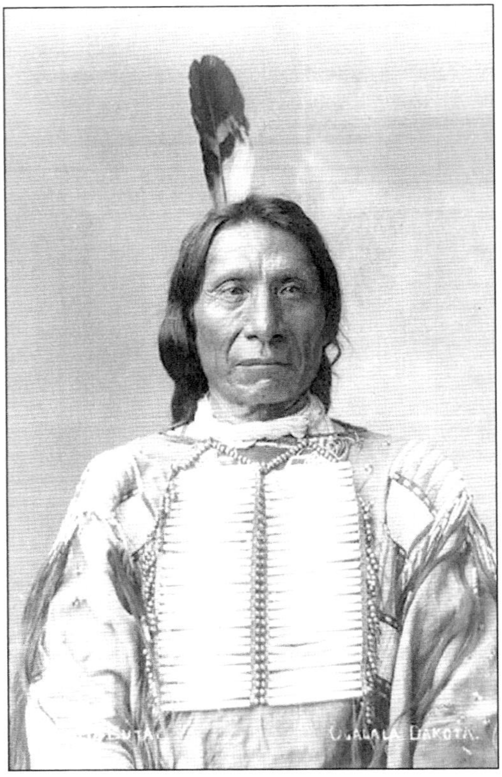

Red Cloud was one of the most prominent of agency chiefs. He waged wars to protect his people and negotiated treaties to bring peace. His oratorical abilities were recognized in Washington when he traveled there to speak in behalf of the Lakota. (Library of Congress Prints and Photographs Division. LC-USZ62-91032.)

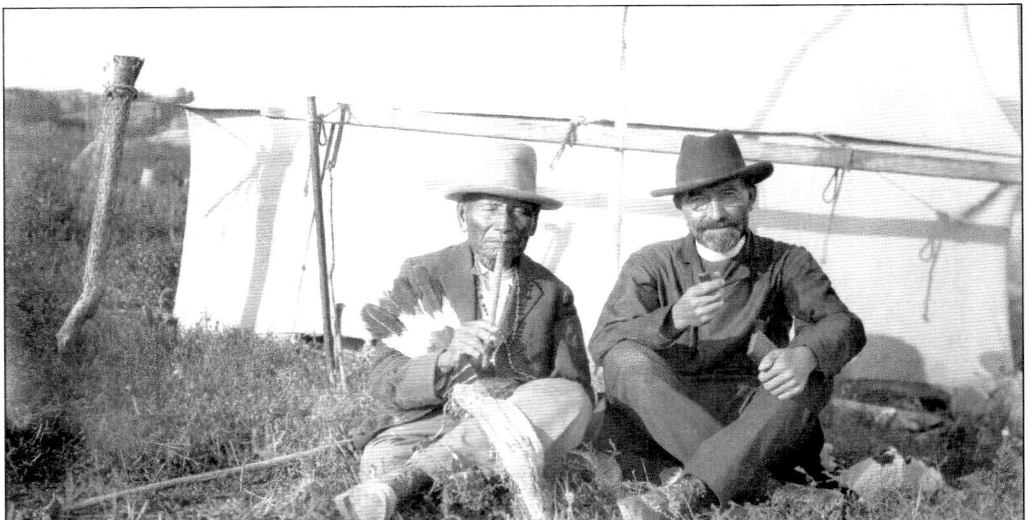

Father Eugene Buechel, S.J., pictured with Red Feather, came to the Pine Ridge and Rosebud Reservations to work with the Lakota in 1902. He studied the Lakota language and began to compile a Lakota Bible history, a prayer book, a hymnal, and a Lakota grammar. His collection of word and phrase cards was published as a Lakota dictionary in 1970. In addition to being a photographer, he collected Sioux artifacts, which are displayed in the Buechel Memorial Lakota Museum. (St. Francis Mission.)

This original Holy Rosary Mission building, constructed of handmade bricks, houses the administrative offices of Red Cloud Indian School and The Heritage Center, which features Lakota art. Since 1969, Red Cloud Indian School has hosted the Red Cloud Indian Art Show, where Native American artists from throughout the continent display their art.

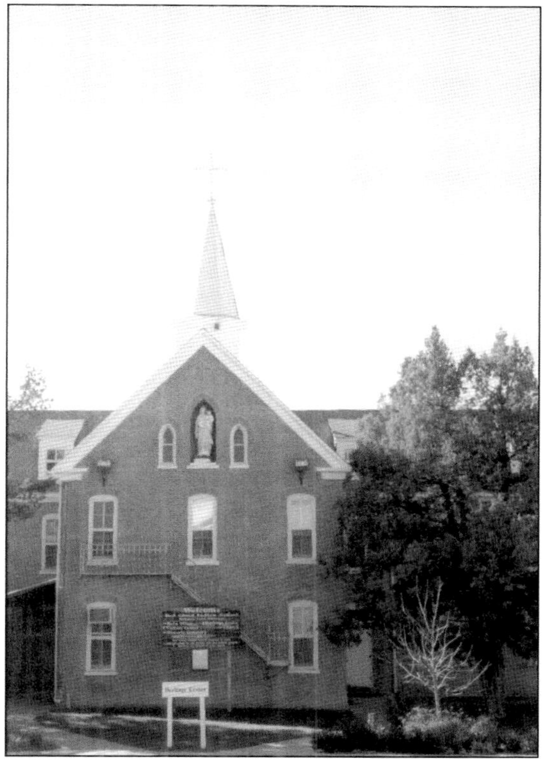

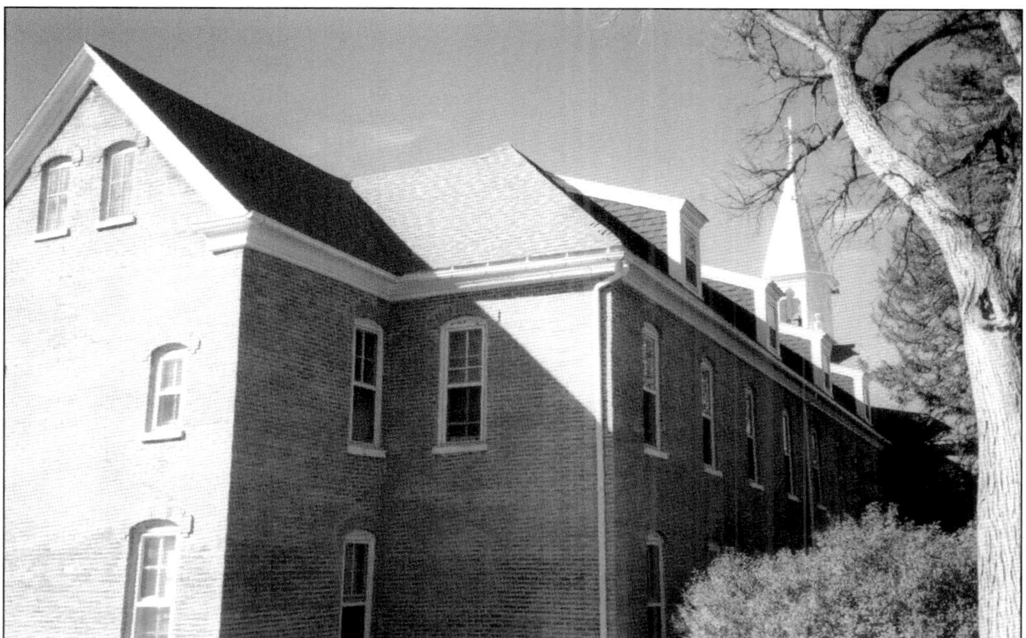

Holy Rosary Mission, now also referred to as Red Cloud Indian School, still educates children in a manner in which traditional cultural values are incorporated into Jesuit Catholic teachings.

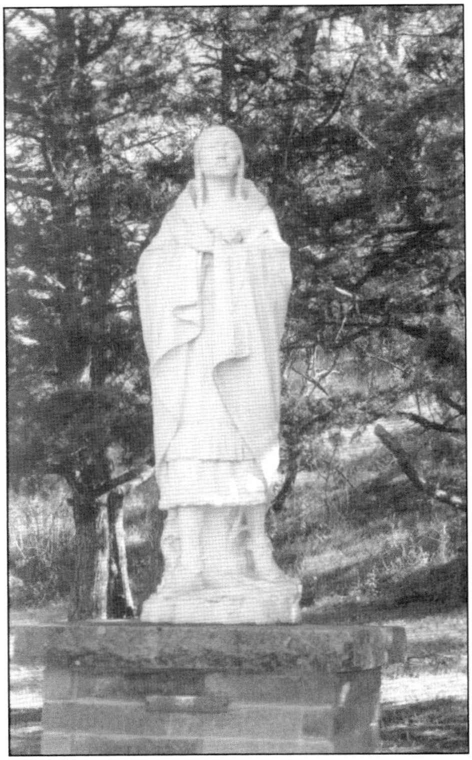

A copse of evergreens frames a statue of Saint Kateri on the Holy Rosary Mission grounds. Kateri was born in 1656 to a Christian Algonquin woman and a pagan Mohawk chief. A smallpox epidemic took her parents and baby brother, leaving her scarred and weak, with impaired vision. After she regained partial health, she dedicated her life to Christianity. At the time of her death at 24 years of age, two Jesuits and her Native American friends witnessed the miraculous disappearance of her scars.

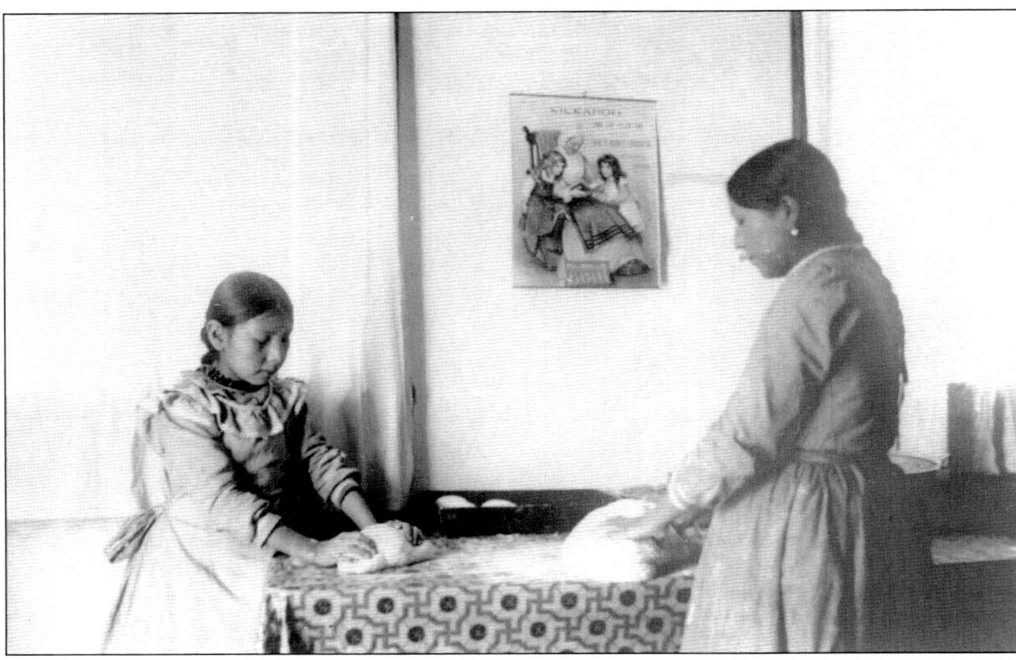

Students at the mission learn to bake bread. The teaching of domestic skills was an important part of the curriculum. (South Dakota State Historical Society Archives.)

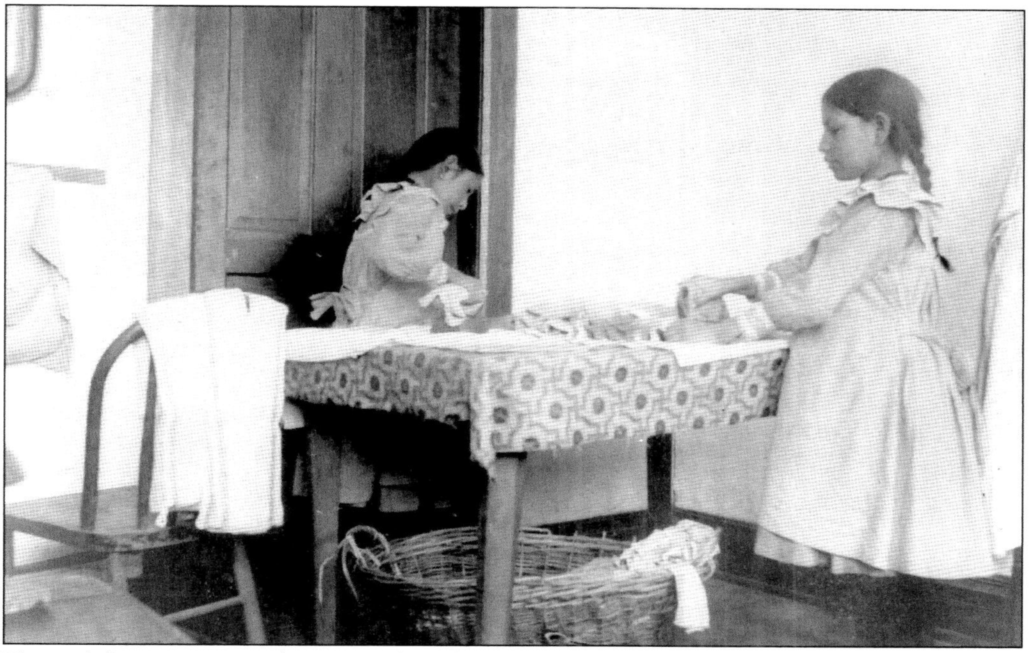

Two girls learn to iron at the mission boarding school. The boarding schools stressed cleanliness. (South Dakota State Historical Society Archives.)

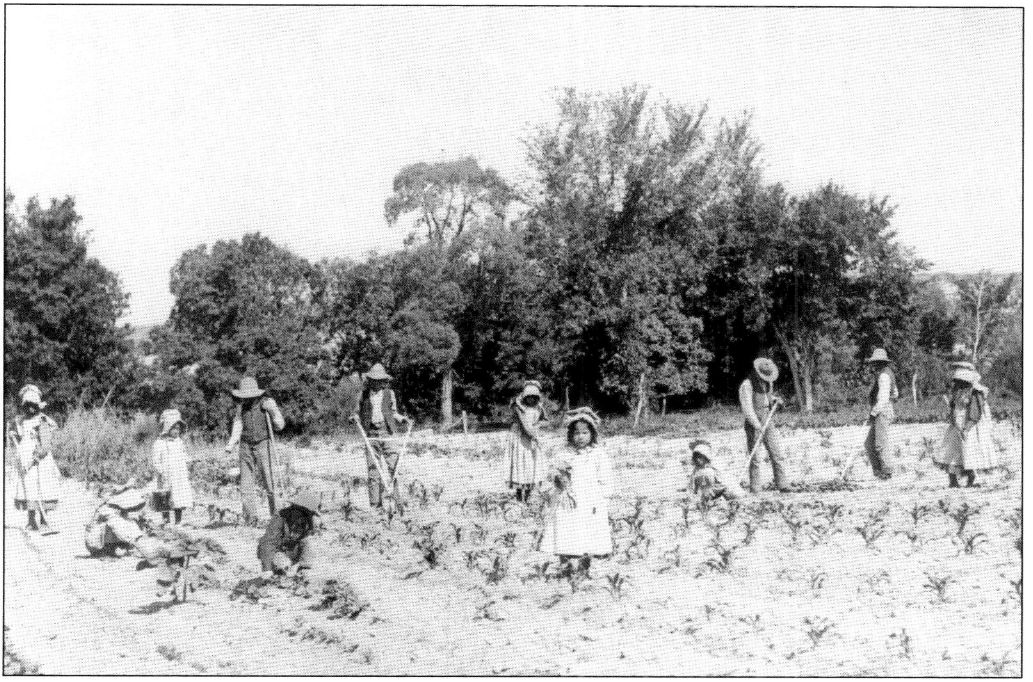

Boys and girls learn to garden in the reservation schools and provide food for the students as well. The girls learned to prepare the various vegetables harvested from the garden. (South Dakota State Historical Society Archives.)

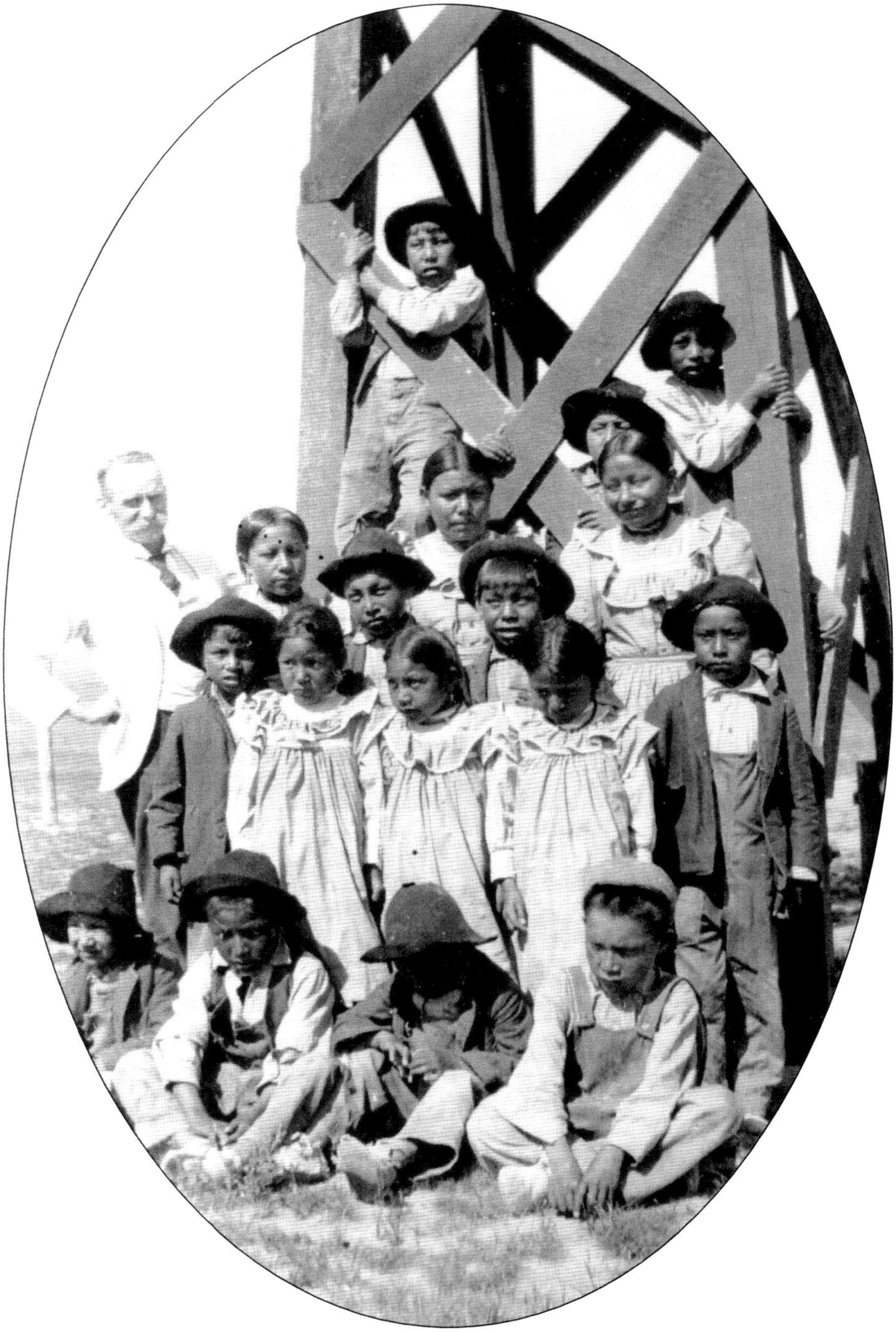

The government as well as churches provided day schools for the native students. At the end of the day the children could return to their homes, as opposed to boarding schools where the children were required to remain for long periods of time. Educators and missionaries disagreed on which type of education was most beneficial. (South Dakota State Historical Archives.)

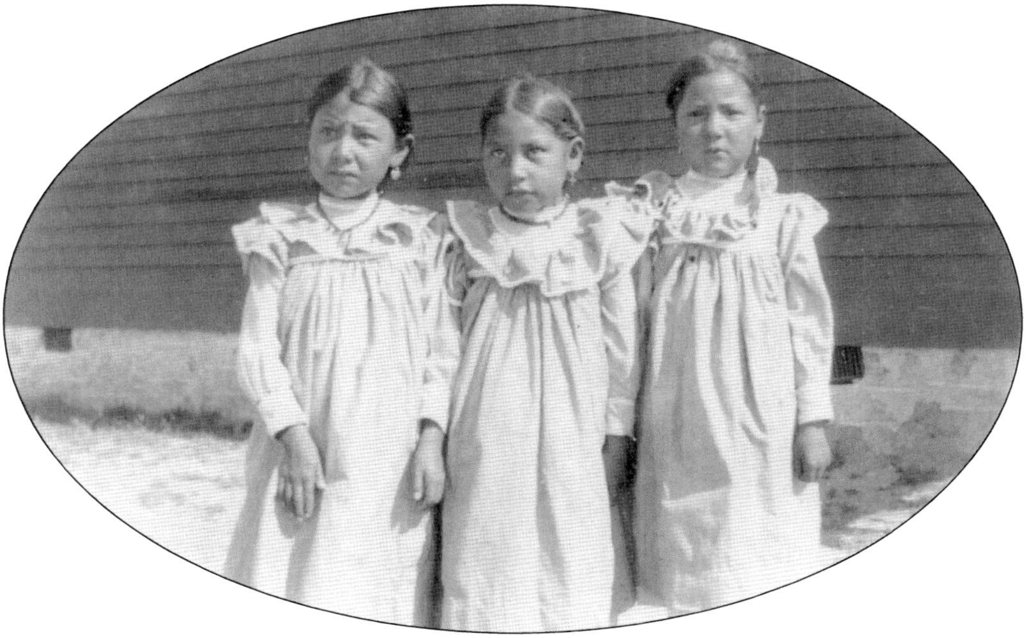

These three girls attend day school number 29. Their dresses are very similar, much like a uniform. Their hair appears not to be cut as it often was at boarding schools. (South Dakota State Historical Society Archives.)

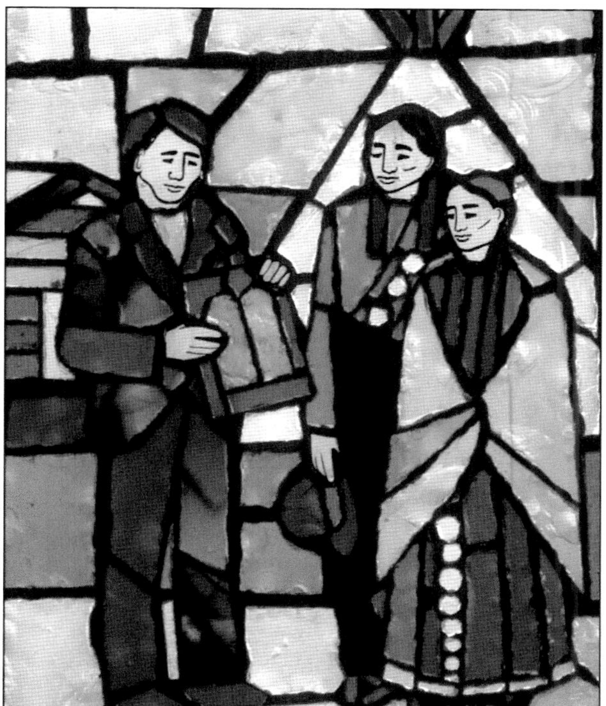

This stained glass window from Our Lady of the Sioux Chapel depicts the important role of the catechists. Native American lay leaders instructed their people in the Christian teachings as well as performed ceremonies when priests were unable to do so because of the great distances they were required to travel. (St. Joseph's Indian School, Chamberlain; David Meyer photographer.)

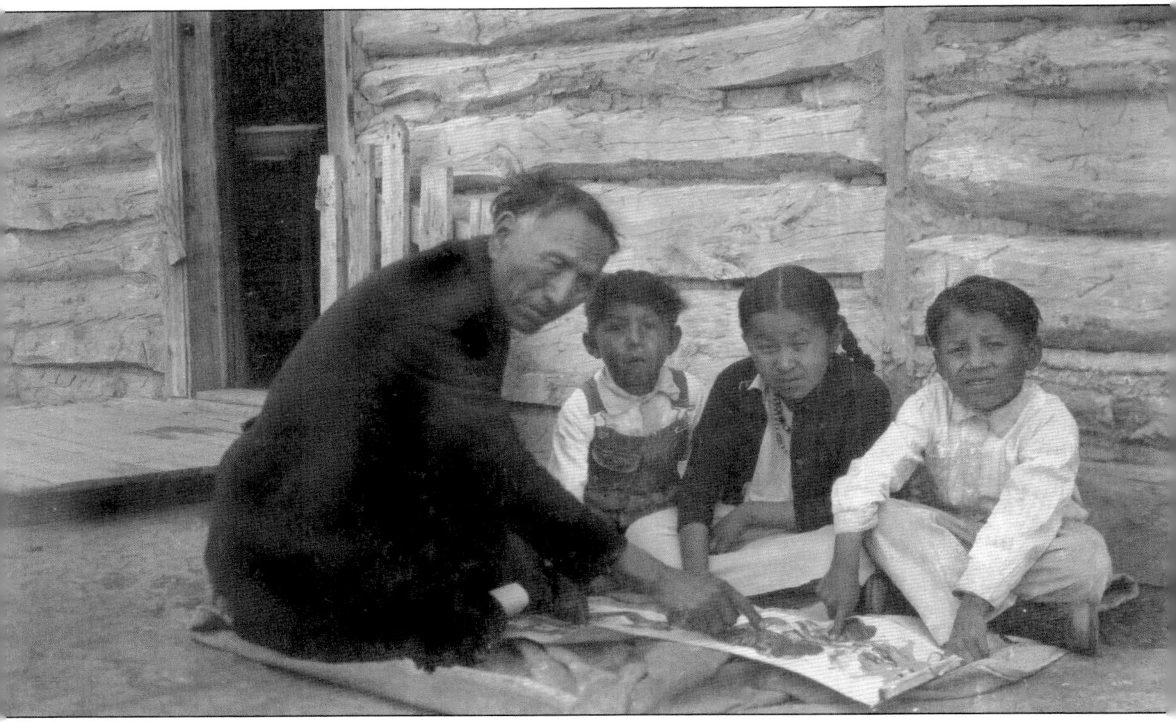

Black Elk, a Lakota Holy Man noted for his book, *Black Elk Speaks*, became a catechist and spent forty years of his life teaching the Catholic faith. In this photograph, Nicholas Black Elk teaches Broken Nose's children using the Two Roads, a picture Catechism. The Two Roads was constructed from a strip of paper one foot wide and five feet long, containing the Catechism teachings. A red road depicted the way to heaven and a black road lead to hell. Father Albert Lacombe, a French missionary to Canada's Black Feet, created the document in the 1880s, picturing a list of virtues and doctrines of the Catholic Church in addition to important events in the church's history. Protestants objected to its use because Martin Luther was pictured on the black road. (St. Francis Mission.)

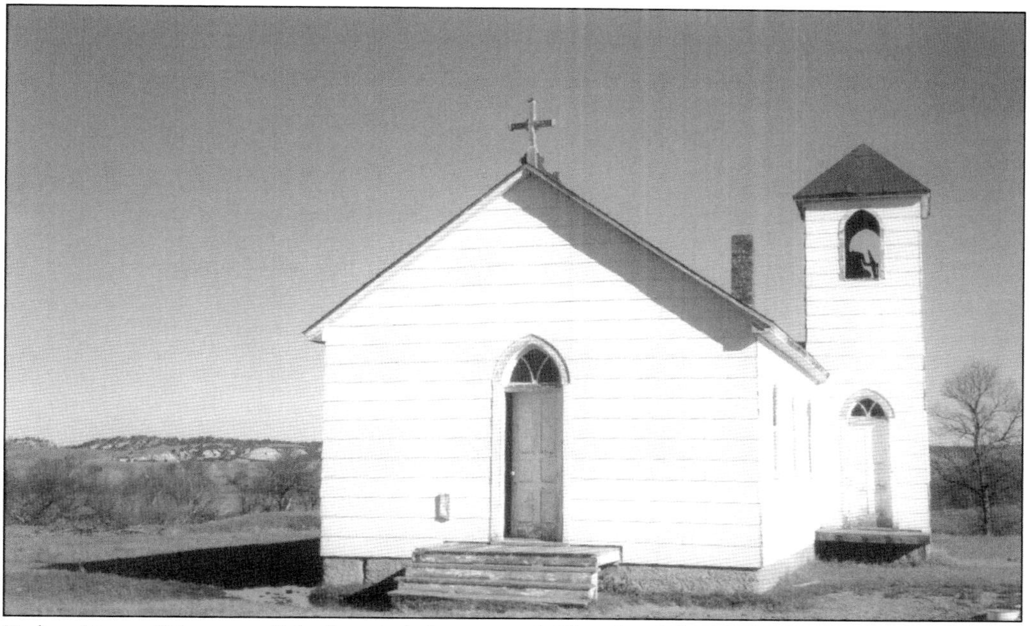

Father Henry Westropp, S.J., founded the original Church of the Holy Angels in 1905 at Slim Buttes. A larger chapel, St. Anthony's, was built, but was destroyed by a tornado in 1939. The present chapel pictured, Church of Our Lady of Lourdes, was built in 1940.

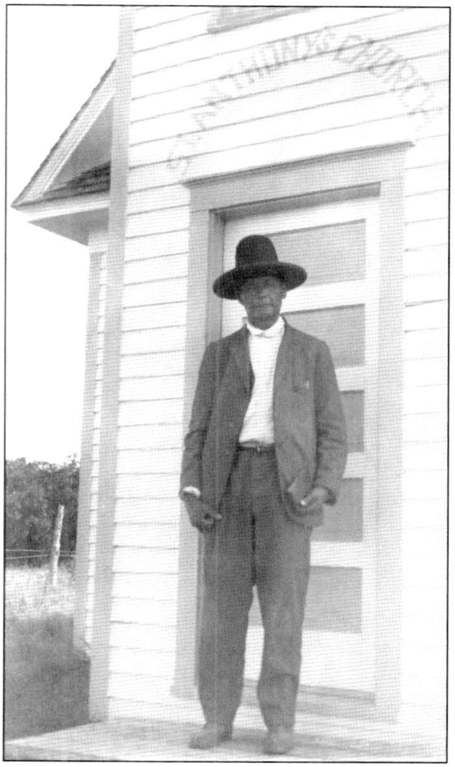

John Fool Head stands in front of St. Anthony's Church at Slim Buttes. Fool Head was a catechist along with Joseph Horn Cloud. Catechists played an important role in spreading the Christian faith to the Lakota. Often catechists, blessed with oratorical skills, shared the message with their relatives, friends, and neighbors. (St. Francis Mission.)

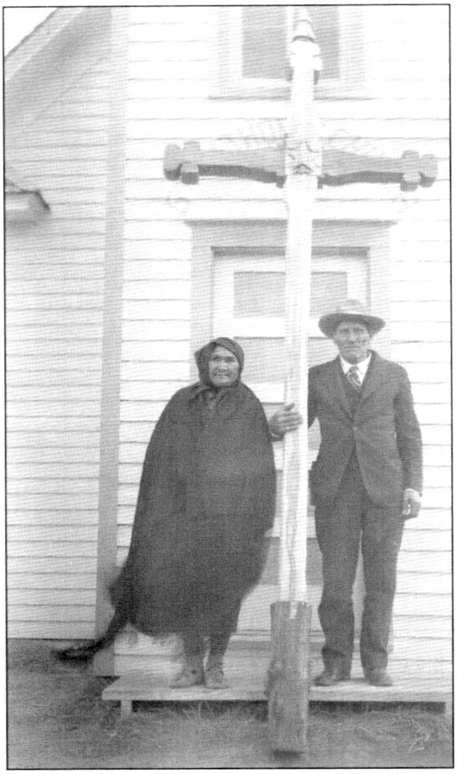

Peter Shangreau and his wife hold a cemetery cross in front of St. Anthony's Church, Slim Buttes, in this undated photo. Large crosses marked the cemeteries across the reservation. (St. Francis Mission.)

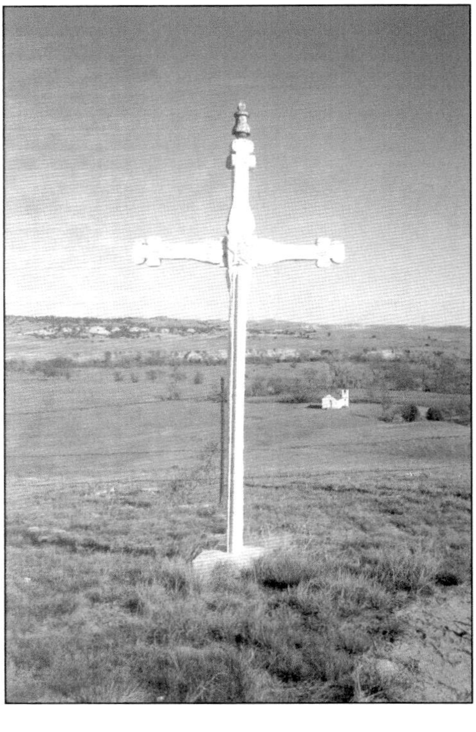

The cemetery cross the Shangreaus held in the above photo still marks the cemetery overlooking the golden clay buttes in the distance and Our Lady of Lourdes Church below. The church was still attended until recently.

Traditionally, the Lakota did not bury their dead. As pictured here, they placed the body in a tree to be closer to the Great Spirit. They believed that burying a body in the ground would offend the spirits. (South Dakota State Historical Society Archives and O.H. Over Museum; Morrow Collection.)

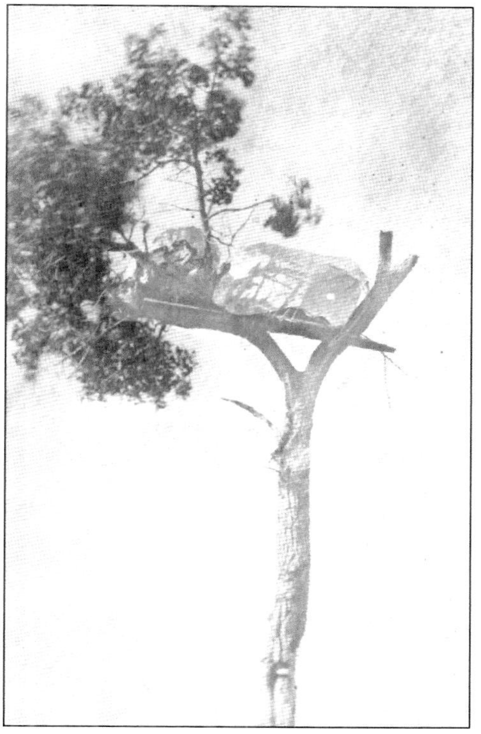

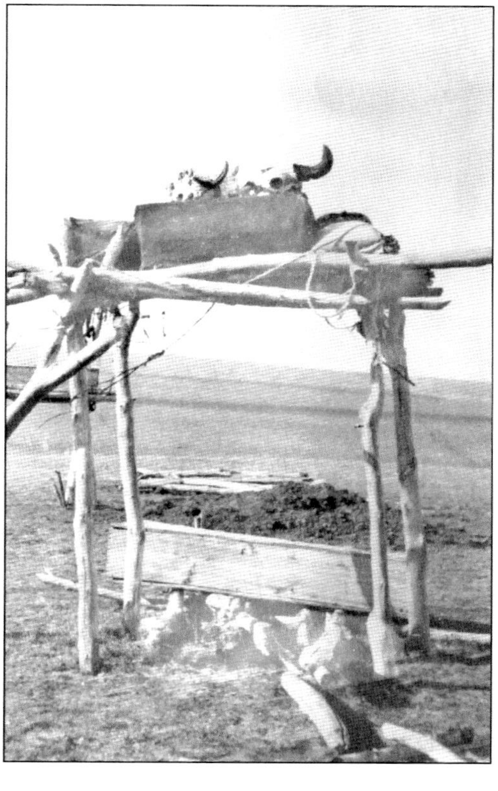

When trees were not available, a scaffold was built and the body placed on top. Sometimes bodies were placed in boxes and set upon a hill. Eventually, the churches convinced the Lakota to bury the deceased in cemeteries. (South Dakota State Historical Society Archives and O.H. Over Museum; Morrow Collection.)

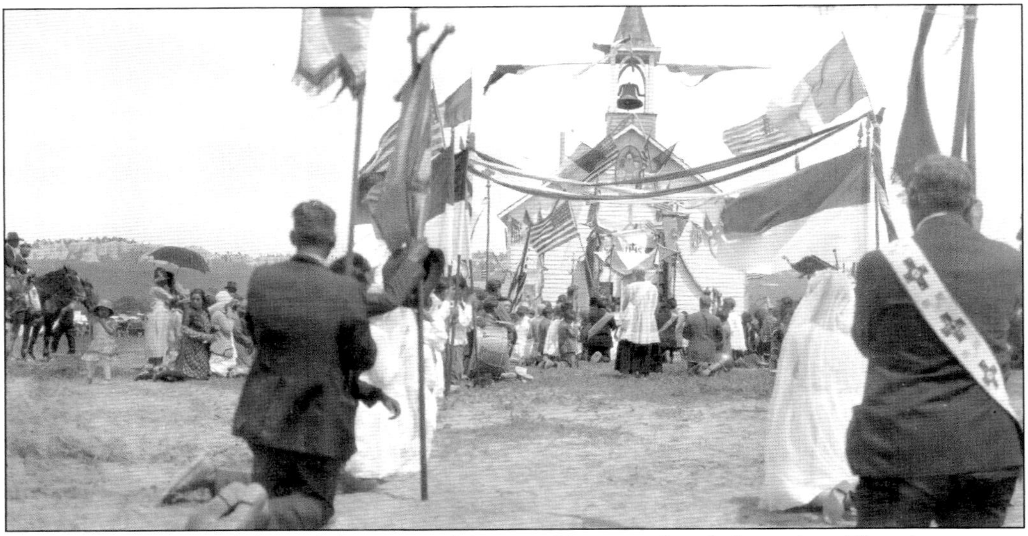

Jesuits and Lakota celebrated the Feast of Corpus Christi, a day dedicated to Christ's presence in the Eucharist, at Manderson Church. Those present at the procession and prayers wore their best attire. Children carried flags and banners. Girls dressed in white threw flowers. Since the Lakota felt comfortable with ceremonies, Jesuits carefully structured the Catholic ceremonies to appeal to them. (St. Francis Mission.)

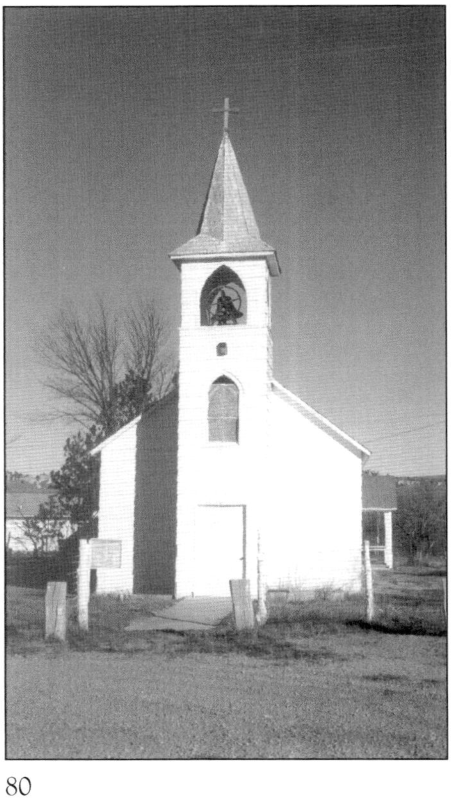

The first St. Agnes Church was built of logs soon after many converted to the Catholic faith. Catechists Nicholas Black Elk, Paul Catches, and Tom Yellow Bull served the present church, built in 1911. The first Native American ordained in the United States, Steven Red Elk, attended this church.

Elaine Goodale turned down Hobart Hare's offer to become an Episcopal missionary on the Pine Ridge. She had taught at Hampton Normal and Agricultural Institute in Virginia, before coming to the Great Sioux Reservation. She taught at White River Camp School on the Lower Brule, assisted by Laura Tileston, an Episcopal missionary. Then she was assigned to the duties of Superintendent of Education, which required her to travel throughout the reservations visiting government and religious schools. (South Dakota State Historical Society Archives.)

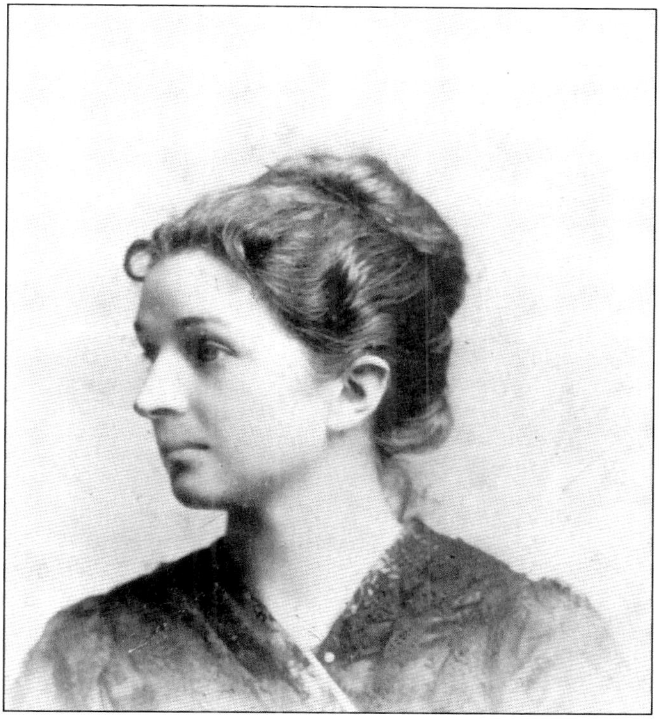

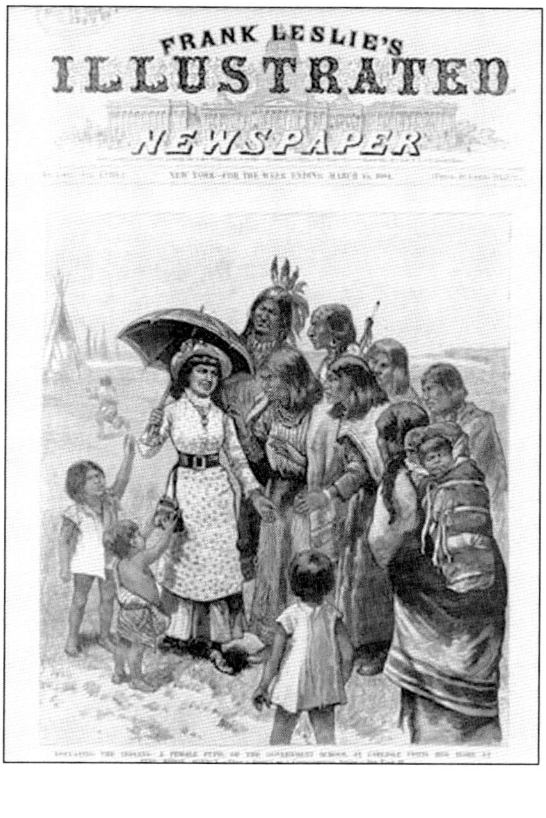

This 1884 cover illustration in Frank Leslies' *Illustrated Newspaper*'s March 15 edition reads: "Educating the Indians—a female pupil of the government school at Carlisle visits her home at Pine Ridge Agency." The image is a sketch done by an artist/correspondant. (Library of Congress Prints and Photographs Division. LC-USZ62-100543.)

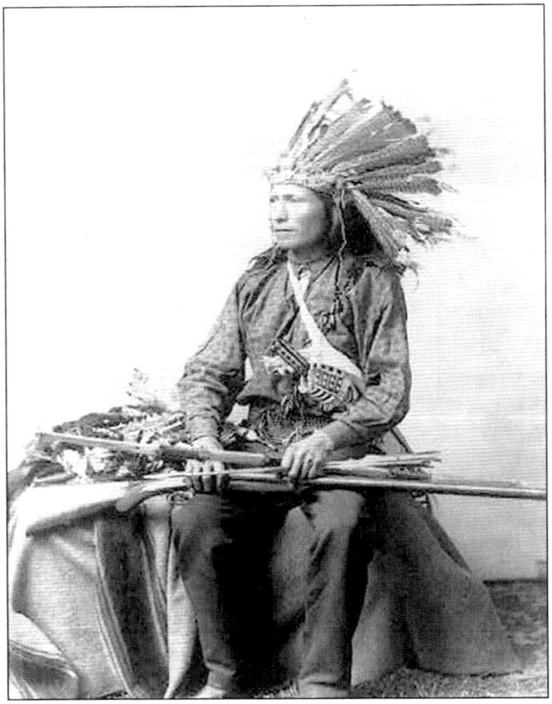

The photographer Grabill titled this photograph *"Little," The Instigation of Revolt at Pine Ridge, 1890*. Little was not the only agitator. Kicking Bird and Short Bull, distraught with the suffering of their people, believed that the Ghost Dance would restore their old way of life. Elaine Goodale was present at Pine Ridge when Little resisted arrest. American Horse intervened and prevented dangerous consequences. (Library of Congress Prints and Photographs Division; John C. Grabill Collection. LC-DIG-ppmsc-02532.)

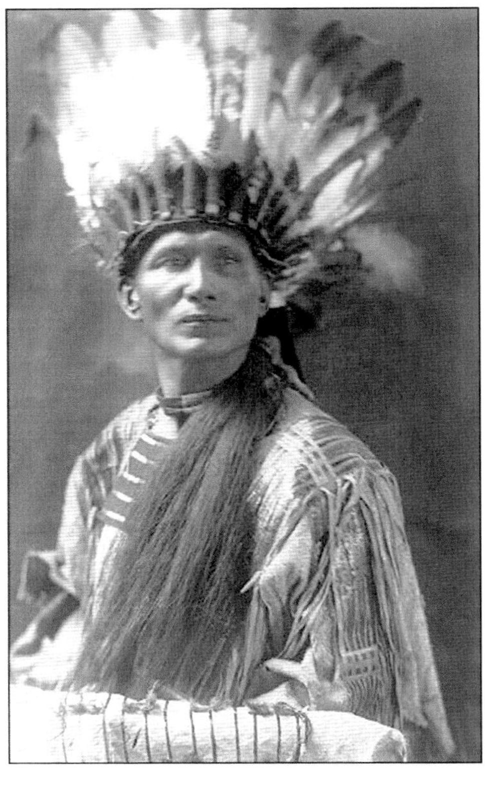

Encouraged by his father to adopt the white man's way, Charles Eastman, a Santee Sioux, attended Dartmouth College and Boston University, earning a medical degree. He came to Dakota as the United State's Physician at Pine Ridge. Eastman, along with Elaine Goodale, attended the Wounded Knee survivors at Holy Cross Chapel. Later, they would marry and write books on Sioux culture. (Library of Congress Prints and Photographs Division; Frank B. Fiske Collection. LC-USZ62-42187.)

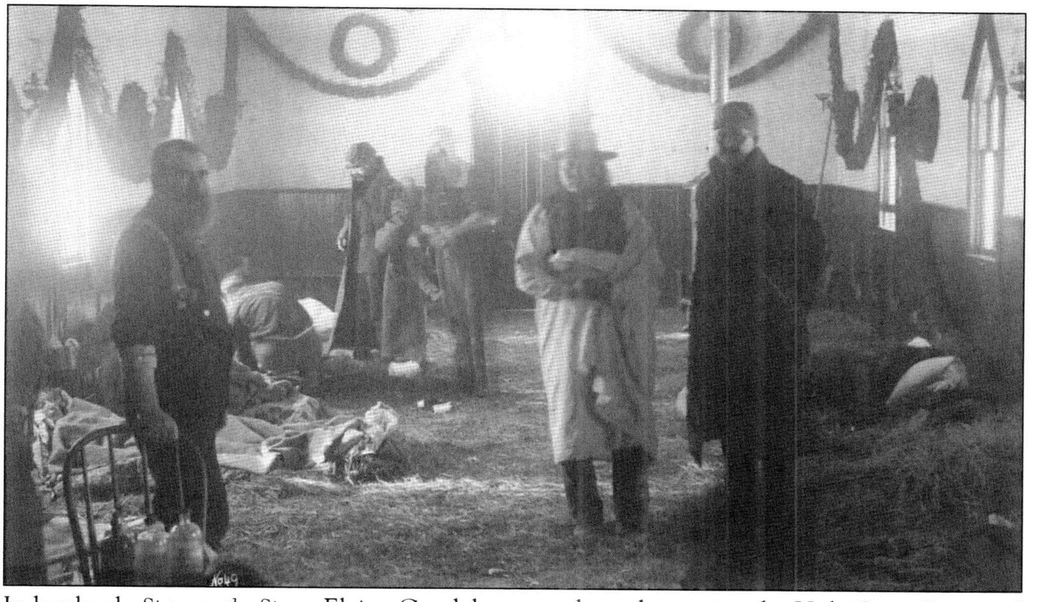

In her book, *Sister to the Sioux*, Elaine Goodale wrote about decorating the Holy Cross Episcopal Church for the Christmas season. On that fateful day, Elaine was present to help care for the wounded brought in from the Wounded Knee battle site. She assisted Dr. Eastman, army doctors, and Lakota women in the attempt to save lives. The Sioux pastor, Thomas Cook, removed the pews from the church and put down straw and blankets to better care for the injured. (Agate Fossil Beds National Monument.)

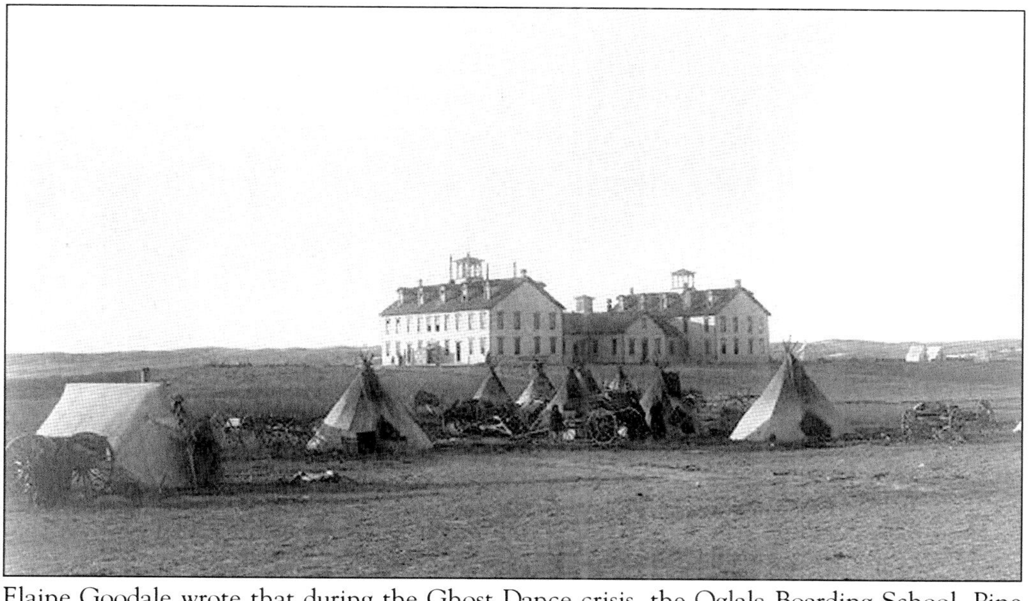

Elaine Goodale wrote that during the Ghost Dance crisis, the Oglala Boarding School, Pine Ridge, was locked down, surrounded by barbed wire and guarded. The students were held here to keep their parents on good behavior as well as to protect them, she said. This photograph is c. 1891. (Library of Congress Prints and Photographs Division; John C. Grabill Collection. LC-DIG-ppmsc-02511.)

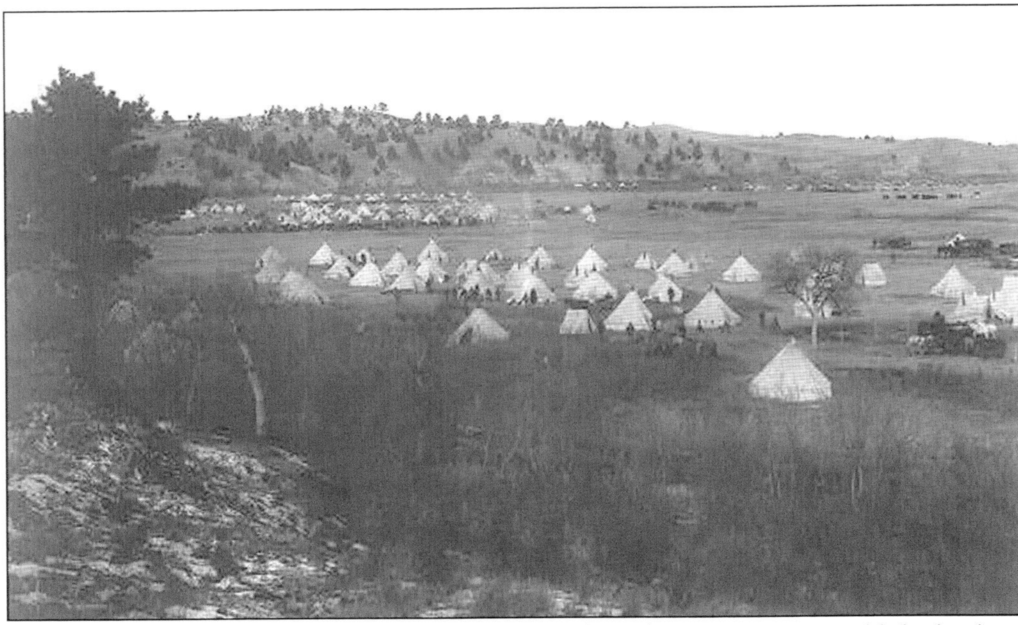

This January 17, 1891, photograph is of General Brook's military tent camp established to keep order on the Pine Ridge Reservation shortly after the Wounded Knee massacre. The Ghost Dance continued in secret. Fear and distrust were pervasive. (Library of Congress Prints and Photographs Division; John C. Grabill Collection. LC-DIG-ppmsc-02612.)

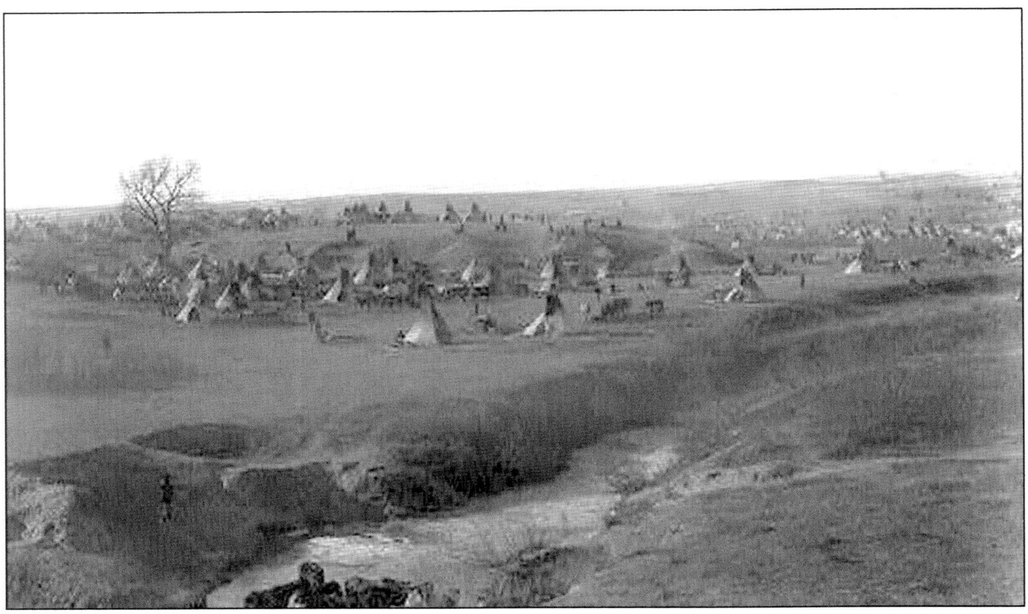

This 1891 photograph, entitled *Villa of Brule*, pictures an Indian camp on River Brule near Pine Ridge. The horses are watering at White Clay Creek. Beatrice Stocker, a Presbyterian missionary stationed at Porcupine wrote in an 1893 letter to her sister that the Native Americans and soldiers were still unsettled even after two years since Wounded Knee. (Library of Congress Prints and Photographs Division; John C. Grabill Collection. LC-DIG-ppmsc-02508.)

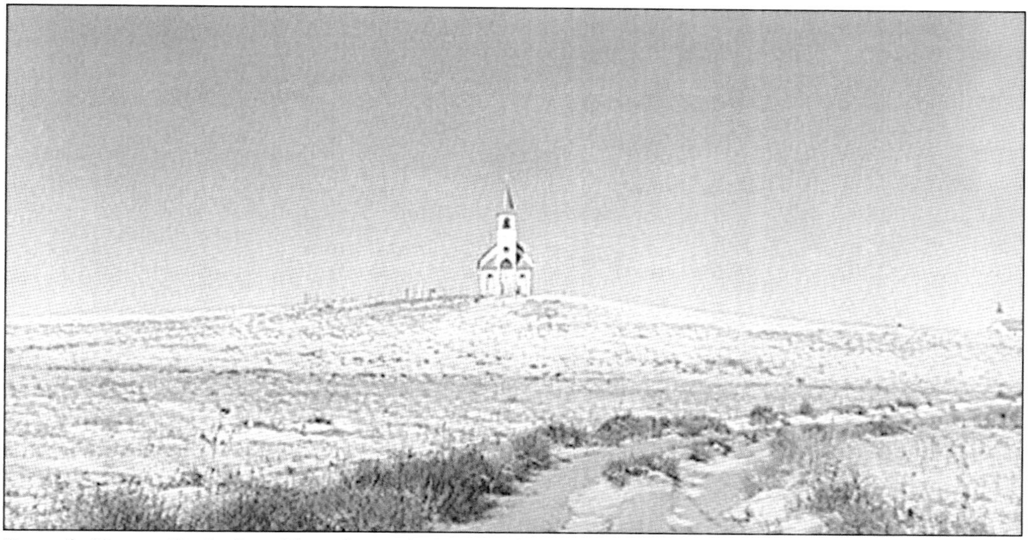

Sacred Heart Catholic Church and St. Andrew's Episcopal Church were both built at Wounded Knee. John Vachon photographed the two unidentified churches pictured in 1940 near Wounded Knee. (Library of Congress Prints and Photographs Division; John Vachon Collection. LC-USF34-061742-D.)

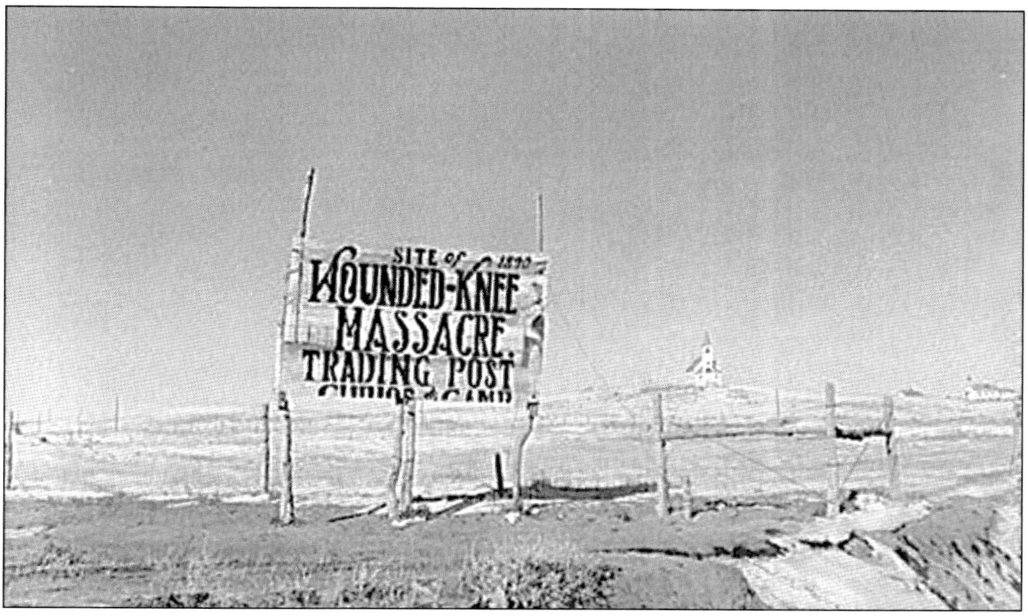

Two churches photographed in 1940 at Wounded Knee overlook the Wounded Knee Massacre site. The Sacred Heart Church was built in the early 1900s south of the mass gravesite. (Library of Congress Prints and Photographs Division; John Vachon Collection. LC-USF34-061741-D.)

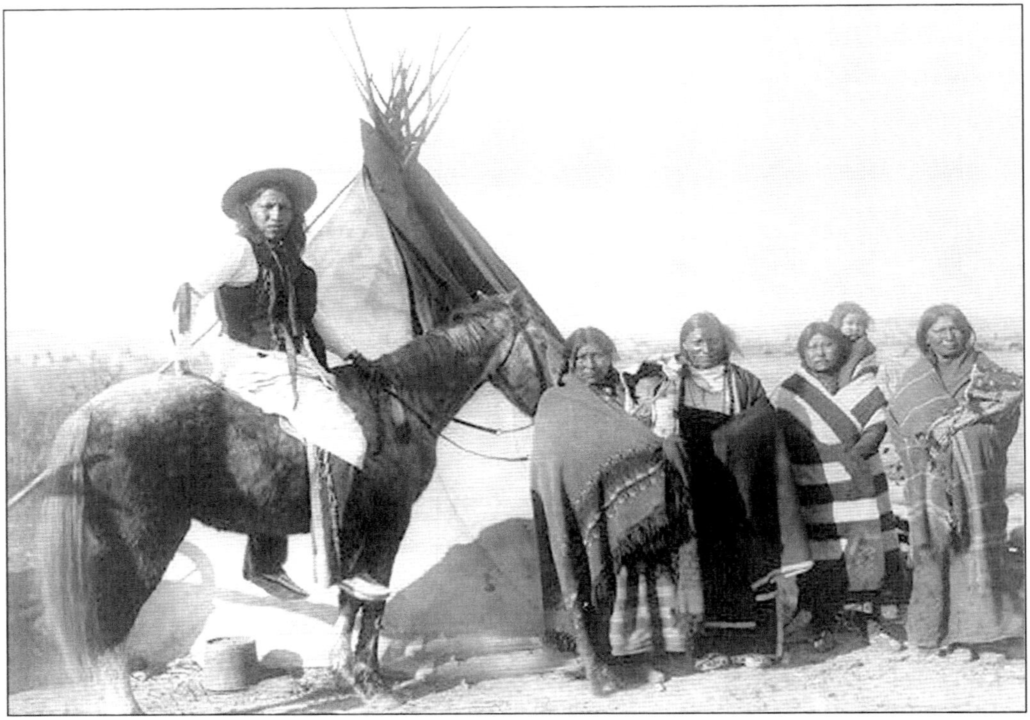

Three Lakota women stand beside a tepee holding infants in cradleboards in this 1891 Grabill photograph. Presbyterian missionary Beatrice Stocker received a letter from her sister inquiring how Native American women dressed. Stocker replied that they wore leggings and moccasins, a cotton dress, and shawl that covered most of their form. (Library of Congress Prints and Photographs Division; John C. Grabill Collection. LC-DIG-ppmsc-02419.)

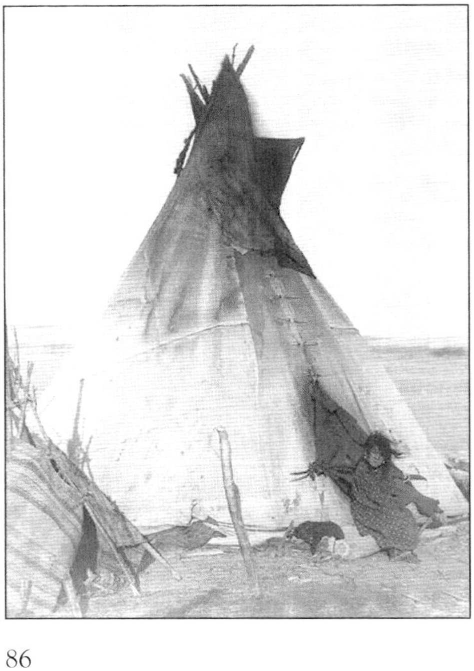

Grabill photographed an Oglala girl with a puppy in 1891. Beatrice Stocker desired to win over the Native American children, but found it a challenge because of her limited Lakota and their fear of white people. Some children did bring her a black cat that was good at catching mice. (Library of Congress Prints and Photographs Division; John C. Grabill Collection. LC-DIG-ppmsc-02515.)

Grabill photographed Red Cloud and American Horse in 1891. American Horse was noted for his eloquence and stood against the Ghost Dance craze. He, like Red Cloud, supported education for his people. His son, Samuel, was among the first students at Carlisle. (Library of Congress Prints and Photographs Division; John C. Grabill. LC-DIG-ppmsc-02522.)

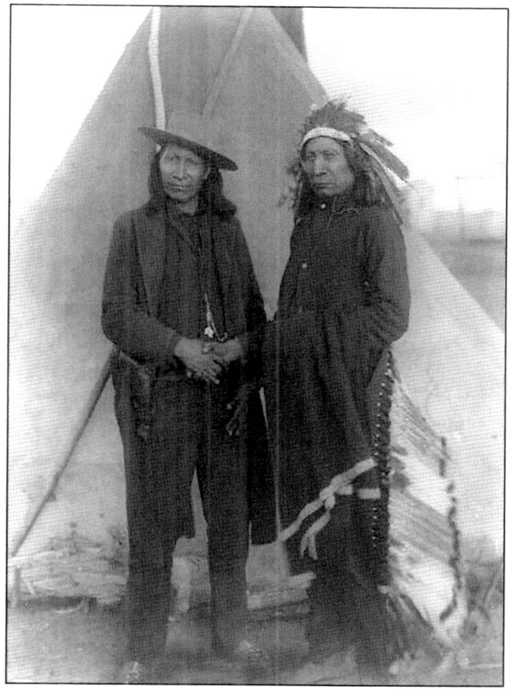

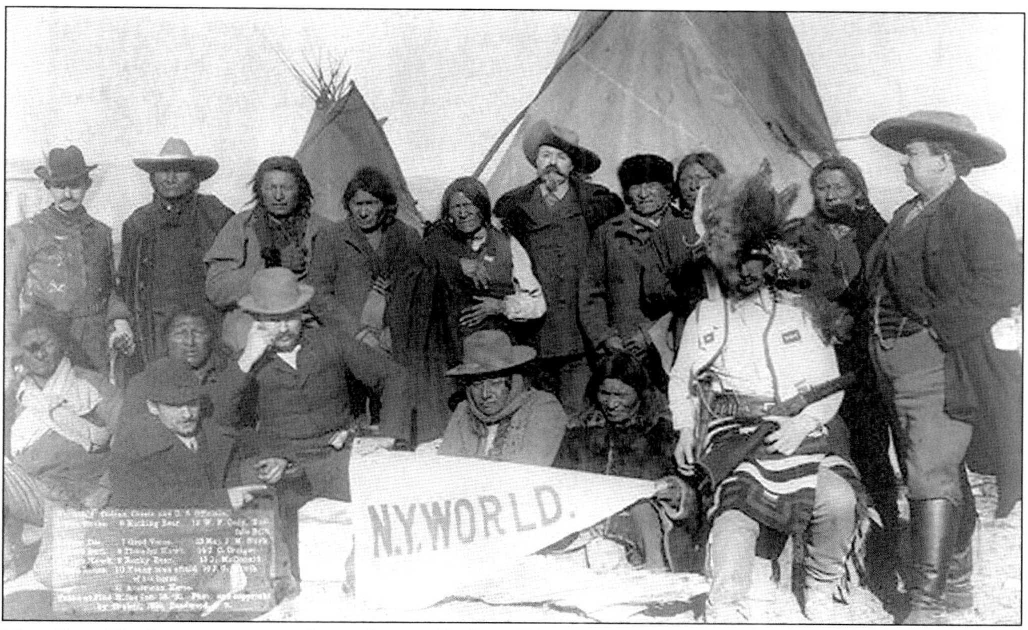

Not identified in any particular order are Indian Chiefs and U.S. officials who shaped the events on the reservations: Two Strike, Crow Dog, Short Bull, High Hawk, Two Lance, Kicking Bear, Good Voice, Thunder Hawk, Rocky Bear, Young Man Afraid of His Horse, American Horse, W. F. (Buffalo Bill) Cody, Major J.M. Burk, J.C. Craiger, J. McDonald, and J. G. Worth. This photograph is *c.* January 16, 1891. (Library of Congress Prints and Photographs Division; John C. Grabill. LC-DIG-ppmsc-02618.)

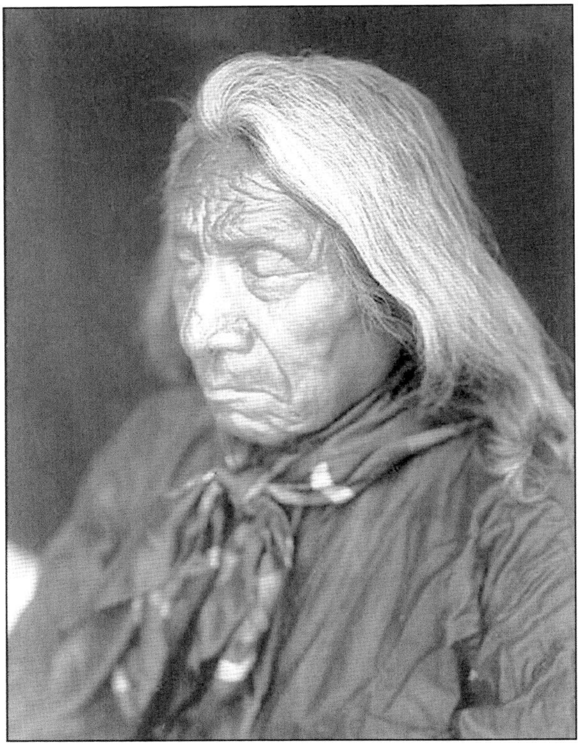

Red Cloud did not participate in the Indian Wars of 1876–1877, but he did continue to fight for his people's rights. Aware of the army's presence on the reservation, he did not support the Ghost Dance. He spoke against the allotment of Native American lands, which would divide the reservation into smaller units. In spite of his protests, the Dawes Act passed. (Library of Congress Prints and Photographs Division; Edward Curtis Collection. LC-USZ62-66856.)

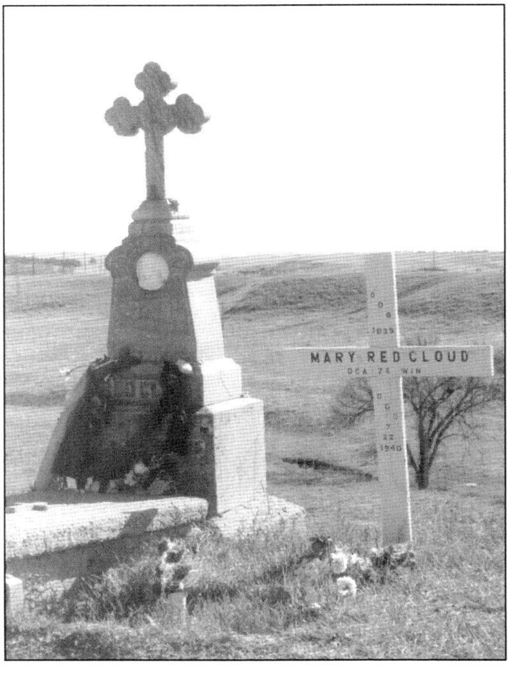

Red Cloud died in 1909 at the age of 87. He is buried in the Holy Rosary Cemetery on a hill overlooking the mission and surrounding country. The school at Holy Rosary Mission is named for him.

This stained glass window from Our Lady of the Sioux Chapel commemorates Native American clergymen Reno Richards of Allen and Steven Red Elk of Manderson, who were ordained in 1975 as deacons in the Rapid City Diocese. In 1985, Father Collins Jordan was ordained in the same diocese. (St. Joseph's Indian School, Chamberlain; David Meyers, photographer.)

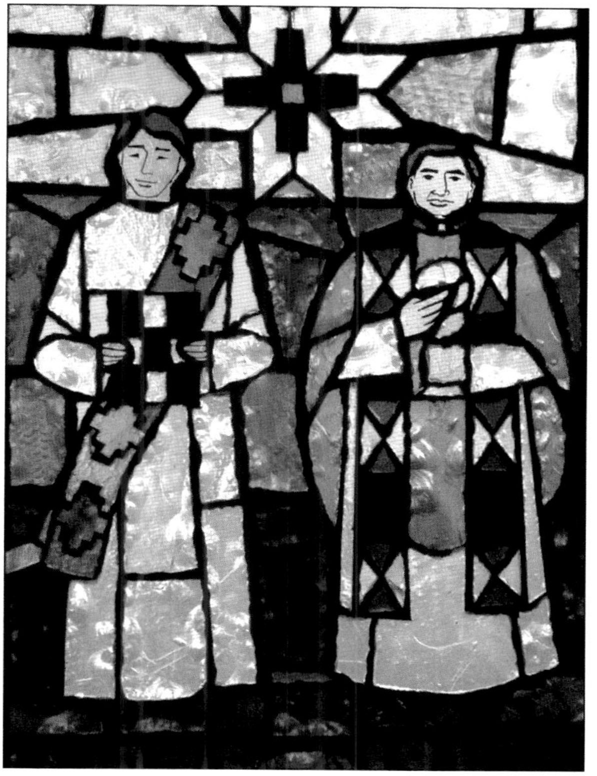

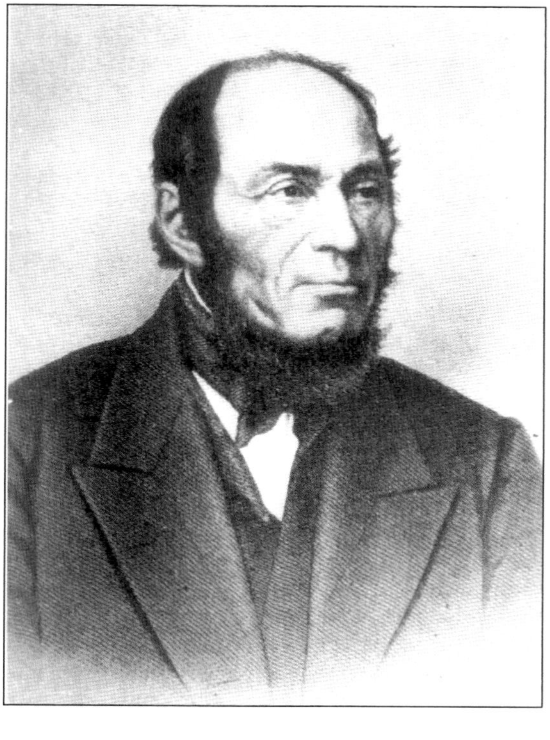

Pictured is the Presbyterian minister Rev. Thomas Williamson, who began his mission work in Minnesota with the Santee Sioux. His son, John, became a missionary too, and brought the Word farther west when he accompanied the Santee to the Crow Creek Reservation. John spent time on the Yankton Sioux Reservation where he established a mission. He also organized a mission on Pine Ridge near Porcupine Creek in 1886. Jennie Dickinson, Charlotte McCreight, and Beatrice Stocker were missionaries under his leadership. (South Dakota State Historical Society Archives.)

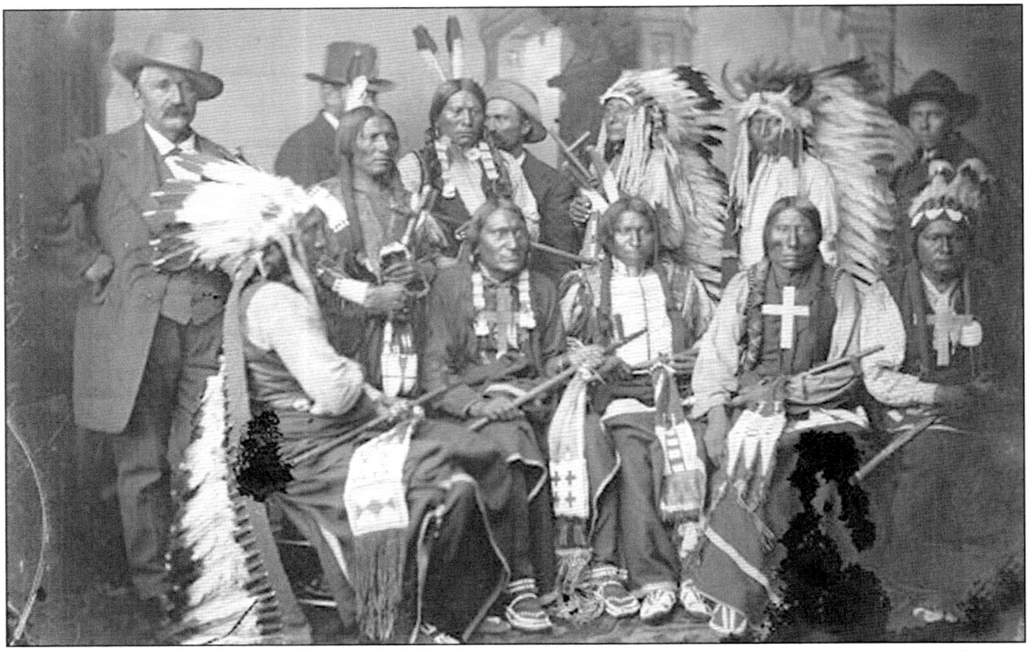

A delegation of Sioux and Arapahoe visit Washington, DC. From left to right, are: (seated) Red Cloud, Big Road, Yellow Bear, Young Man Afraid of his Horse, and Iron Crow; and (standing) Little Big Man, Little Wound, Three Bears, and He Dog. Young Man Afraid of His Horse wears the large cross. (Library of Congress Prints and Photographs Division; Matthew Brady Collection. LC-DIG-cwpbh-04474.)

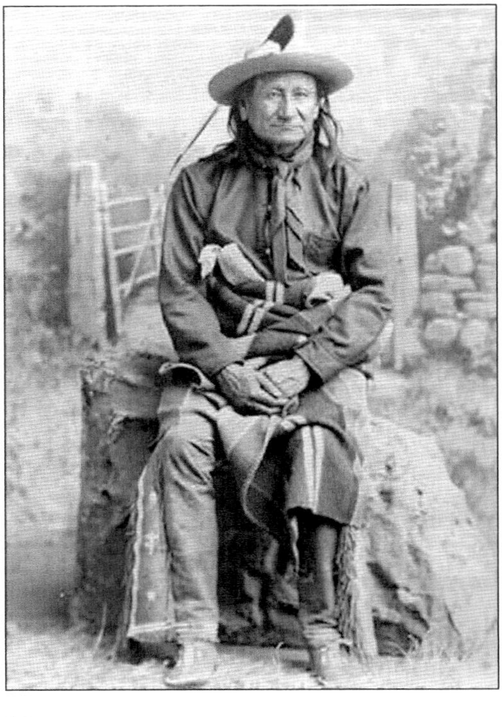

Young Man Afraid of His Horse was so named because he was so powerful in battle that his enemies were even afraid of his horses. Young Man participated in the Red Cloud War of the 1860s and eventually became a friend of the whites, realizing that the Sioux would never win their fight against white encroachment. As President of the Pine Ridge Indian Council, he made several trips to Washington. He is buried in the Makansan Presbyterian Cemetery near Oglala. (Library of Congress Prints and Photographs Division; Clarence Bell Collection. LC-USZ62-121245.)

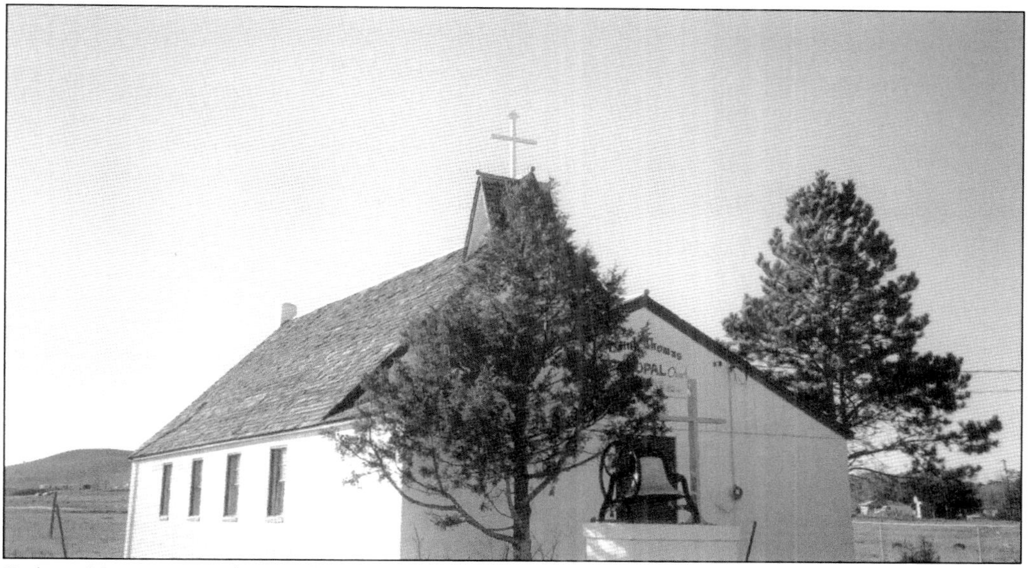

Bishop Hare sent Luke Walker and John Robinson to establish a mission at Pine Ridge in 1877. In 1879, Hare celebrated the first service of Holy Communion at Pine Ridge. By 1910, Rev. Neville Joyner and Rev. Amos Ross presided over approximately 26 mission churches. St. Thomas Episcopal Church in Manderson, pictured here, was served by Catechist Louis Shield in 1935 and by Rev. Stephen King and William Center as catechist in 1945.

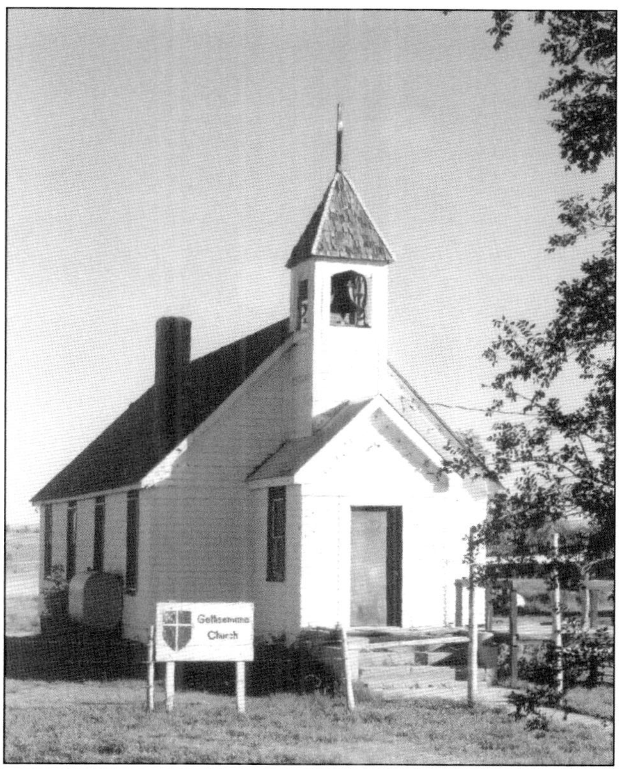

In 1910, Rev. Amos Ross, a Santee Sioux, oversaw the Pine Ridge Corn Creek Mission churches. Richard Lips was his helper at Gethsemane Chapel, Wanblee. Rev. W.H. Zephier ministered at Gethsemane in 1935.

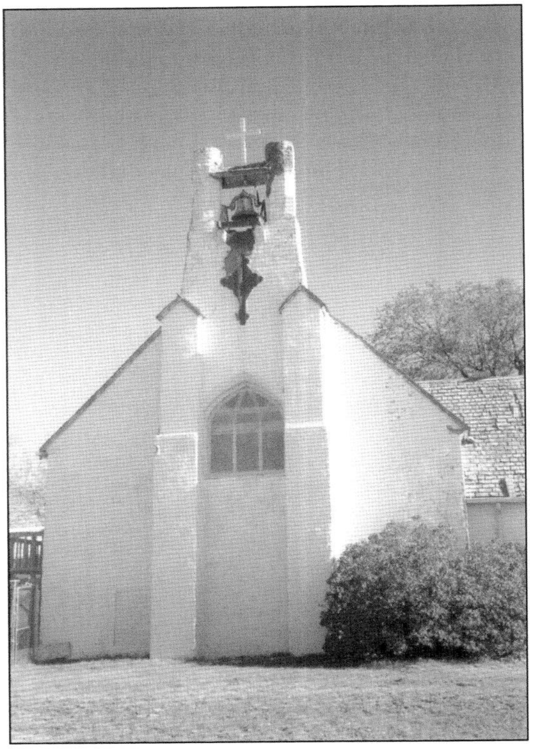

Rev. Neville Joyner became head of the Episcopal Pine Ridge Missions in 1910. This Spanish-style church, named Holy Cross after the original chapel built in 1881 was served by the catechist George Fire Thunder. Harry Little Soldier served as catechist in 1935 and Rev. Frank Thornburn and Sister Annie A. Horner ministered in 1945.

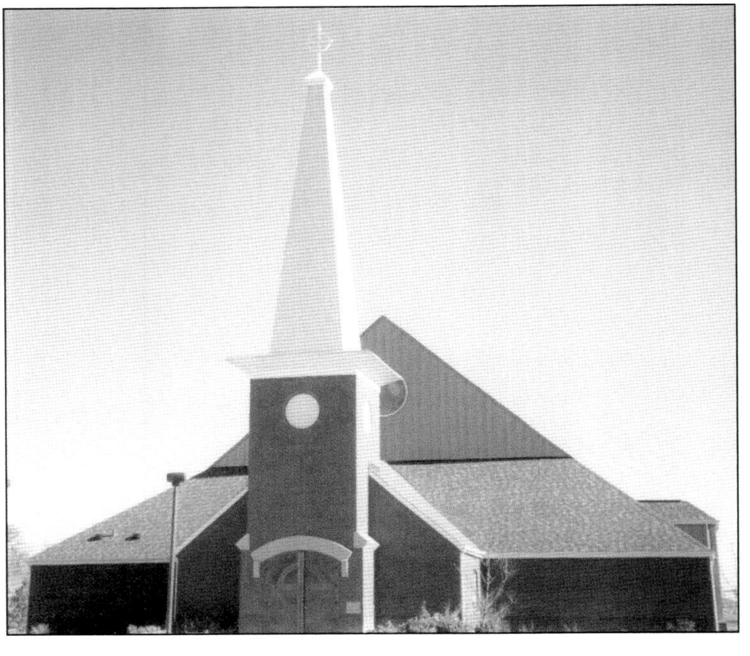

The original Holy Rosary Church burned down on Good Friday, April 5, 1996. A new church to serve the Red Cloud Indian School and neighboring families was dedicated by Bishop Blasé Cupich on October 7, 1998.

Five

St. Joseph's Indian School, Lower Brule

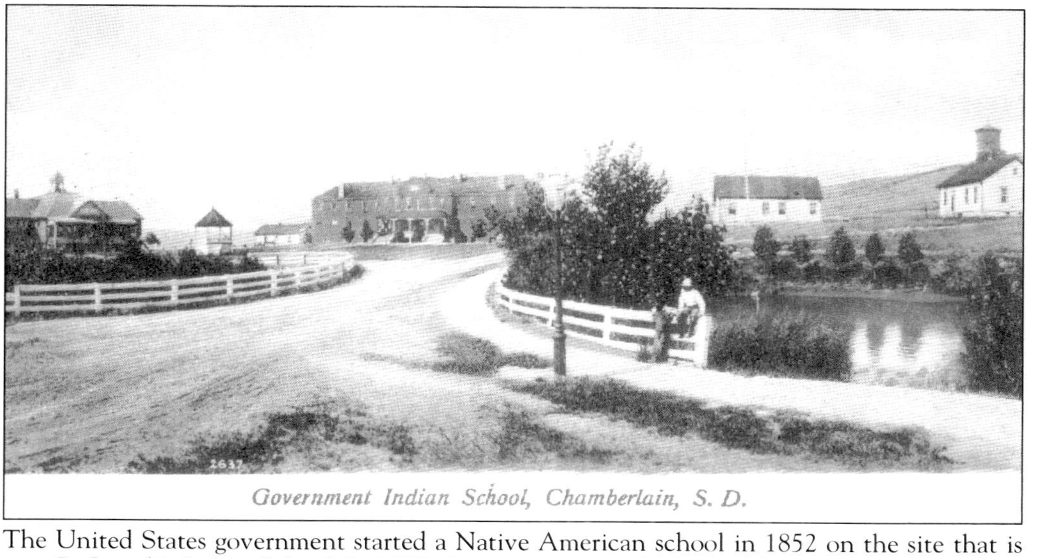

Government Indian School, Chamberlain, S. D.

The United States government started a Native American school in 1852 on the site that is now St. Joseph's Indian School. In 1909, the government sold the buildings to Rt. Rev. Thomas O'Gorman. (St. Joseph's Indian School, Chamberlain.)

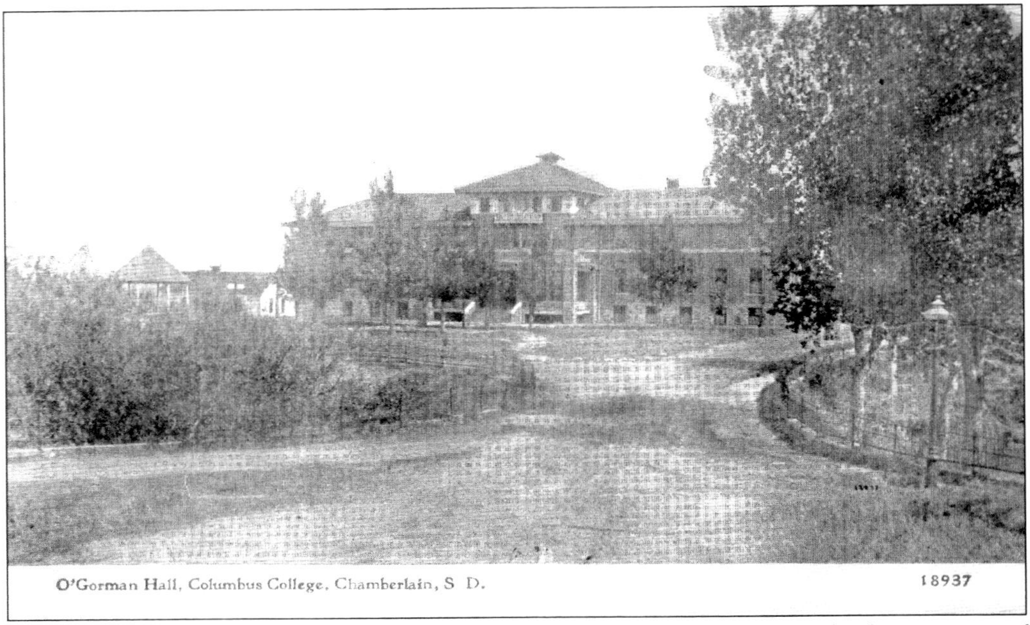

Bishop O'Gorman of Sioux Falls bought the government buildings with the purpose of establishing a men's college for his diocese. The Clerics of St. Viator took charge of the institution, which was to be named Columbus College. When a new college was opened in Sioux Falls, the old Columbus College closed in 1923 because it was no longer needed. (St. Joseph's Indian School, Chamberlain.)

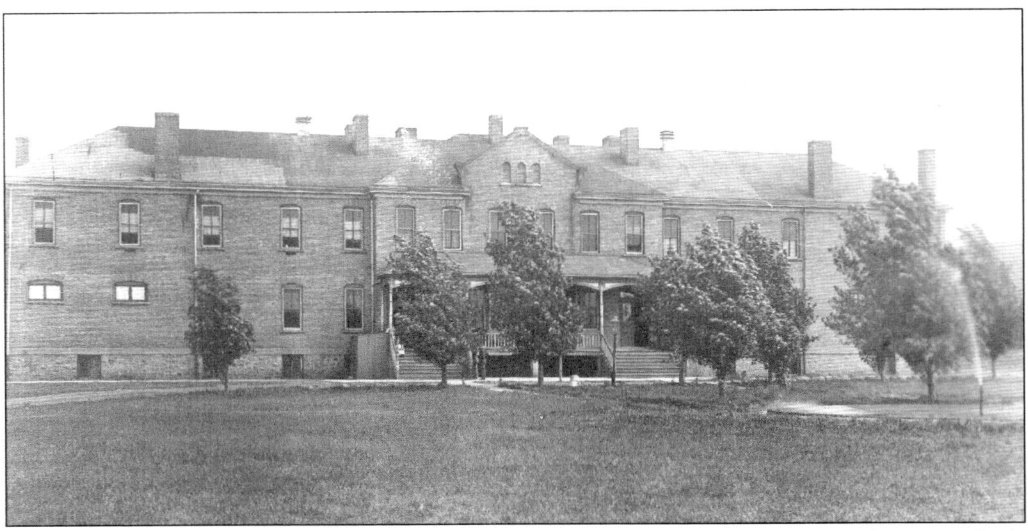

All the buildings still remained from the original government purchase except for one, which burned in 1910. The Viatorians erected another building on the same site. When Columbus College ceased to be, the Priests of the Sacred Heart purchased the buildings in 1927. (St. Joseph's Indian School, Chamberlain.)

Born in France, Father Dehon founded the Congregation of the Priests of the Sacred Heart in 1888. Members of the Sacred Heart came to Lower Brule in 1923 to minister to the Sioux and founded St. Joseph's Indian School in 1927. (St. Joseph's Indian School, Chamberlain.)

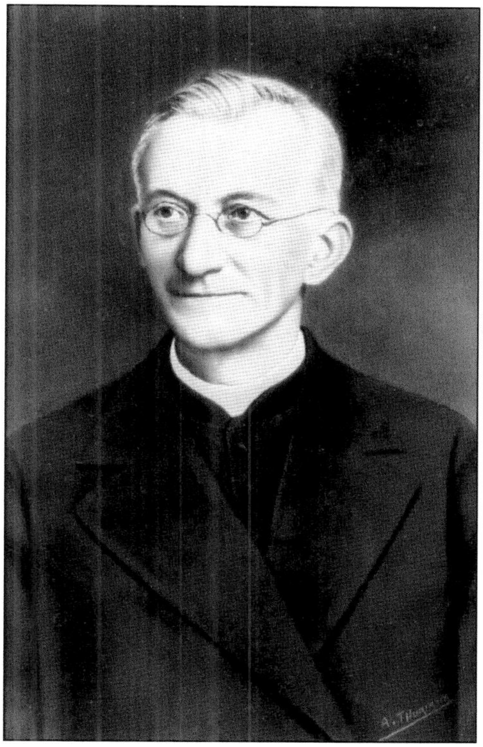

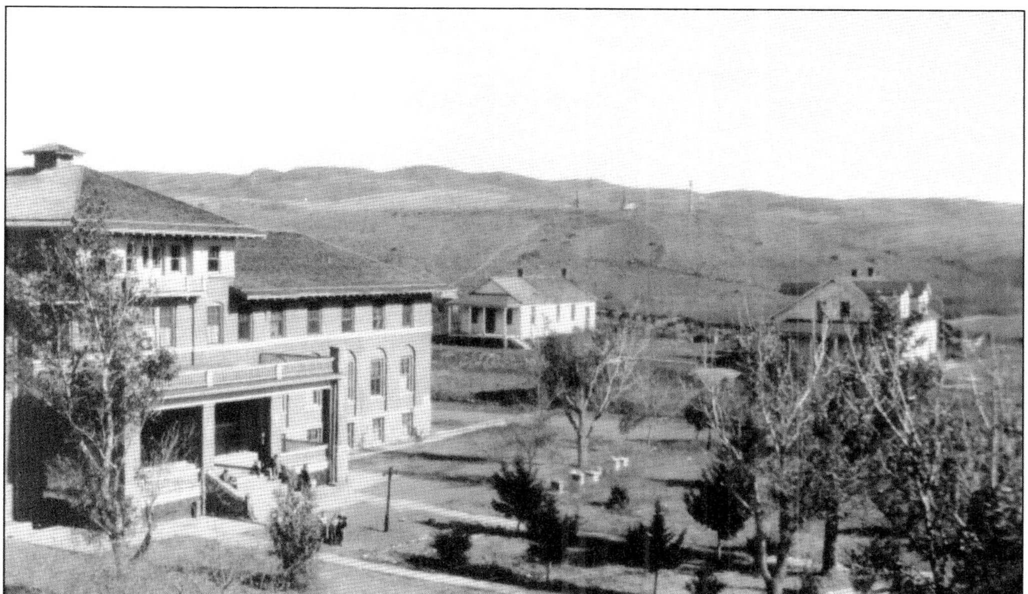

Father Henry Hogebach opened the school in September 1927 with 53 children from the Cheyenne River Reservation in attendance. Father Henry faced the challenge of converting a college facility into a school for children as well as operating with limited staff. Two years later, Franciscan Sisters came to assist him and brought a homier atmosphere to the school. (St. Joseph's Indian School, Chamberlain.)

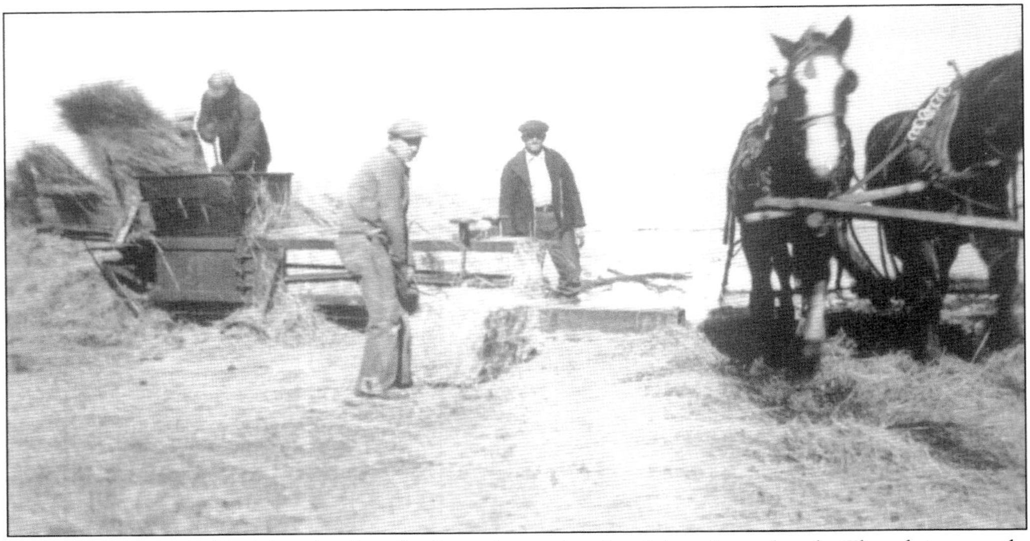

The men put up hay for the herd of cattle maintained by the school. The dairy cattle provided milk for the children. The Sisters and children tended the garden and fowl as well. The boys hunted rabbits with snares and fished in the Missouri River. Supplying enough food for the school was always a challenge, especially during the lean years. (St. Joseph's Indian School, Chamberlain.)

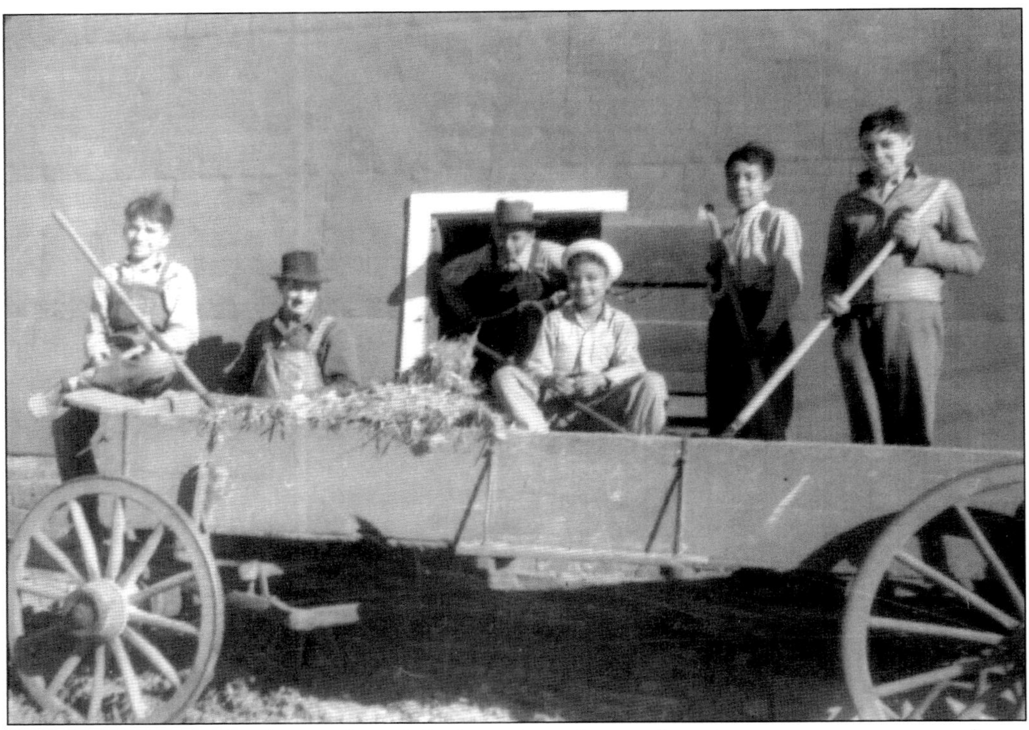

Putting up hay for the livestock and feeding them during the winter were a constant chore. Sometimes in the summer the boys would herd cattle along the banks of the Missouri River, especially during dry years when grass was scant. (St. Joseph's Indian School, Chamberlain.)

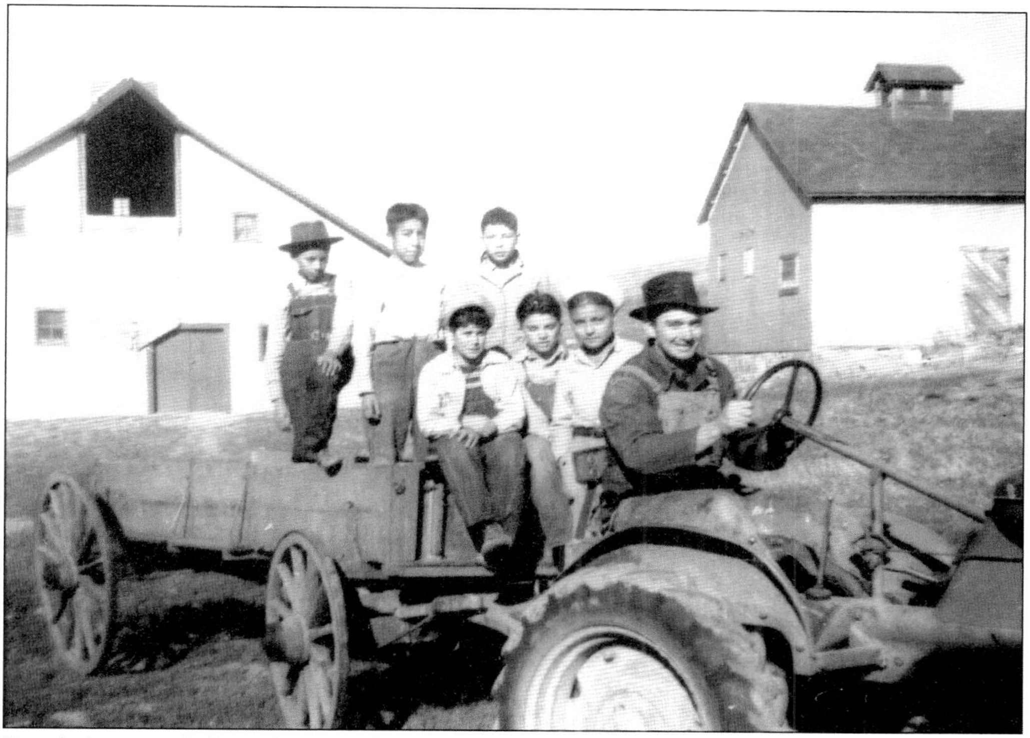

Boys help out with farm chores in this 1954 photograph. The boys took care of the livestock and milked the cows. They also planted corn, potatoes, and vegetables, and tended to the garden. (St. Joseph's Indian School, Chamberlain.)

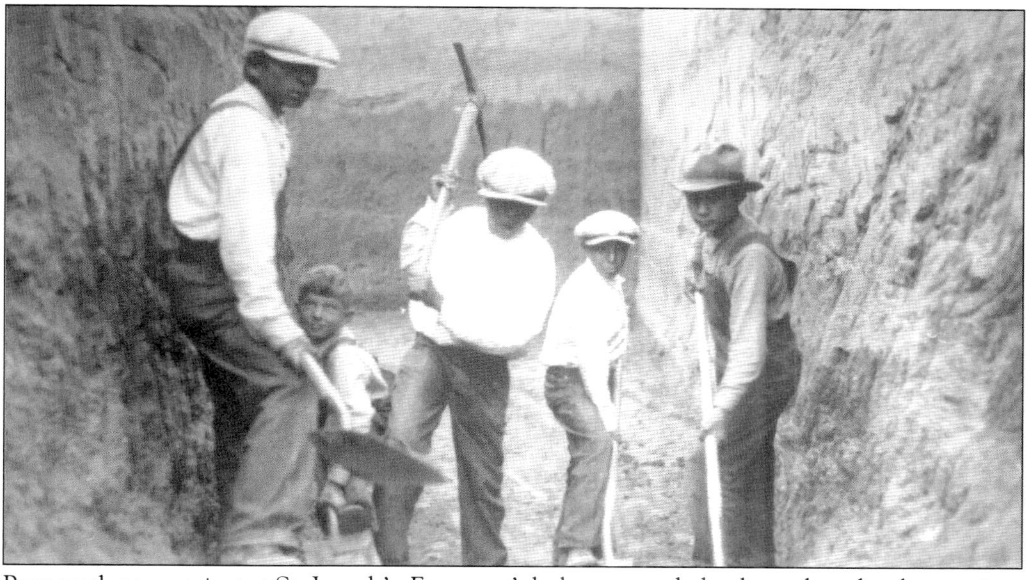

Boys work on a project at St. Joseph's. Everyone's help was needed to keep the school operating. One half of the day was spent on academics, the other half in vocational training. When the boys found free time, they would play horseshoes, run relay races, and fish. (St. Joseph's Indian School, Chamberlain.)

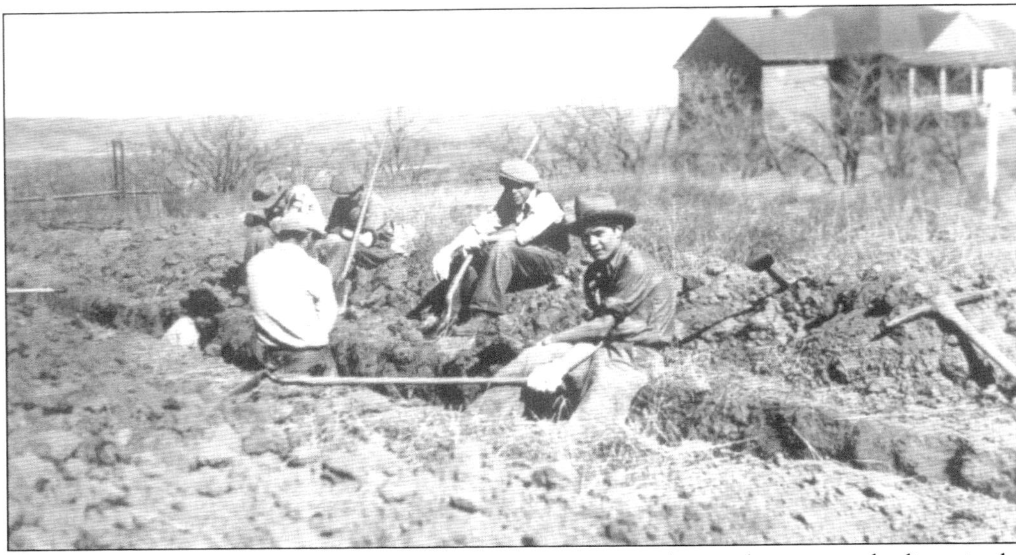

Schoolboys appear to be working on water lines. Sometimes during the winter, the lines in the inadequately heated buildings froze and broke. Keeping a furnace in running order presented problems. In the early years, the school used coal to provide heat. When coal shipments on the trains were delayed on account of winter storms, the school was forced to conserve on heat. (St. Joseph's Indian School, Chamberlain.)

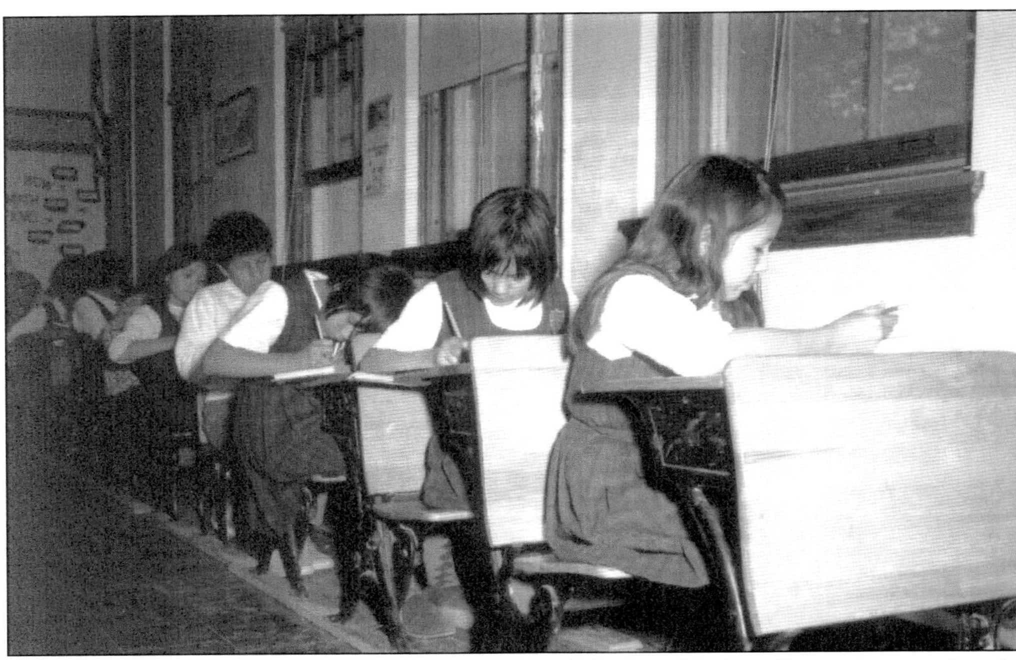

Children from the surrounding reservations attended St. Joseph's. Enrollment increased as the years wore on. Enough space and shortage of funds were a continual problem. By 1935, the number of children in attendance increased to 145 boys and girls, 187 youngsters in 1943, 221 in 1947, and steadily increased. (St. Joseph's Indian School, Chamberlain.)

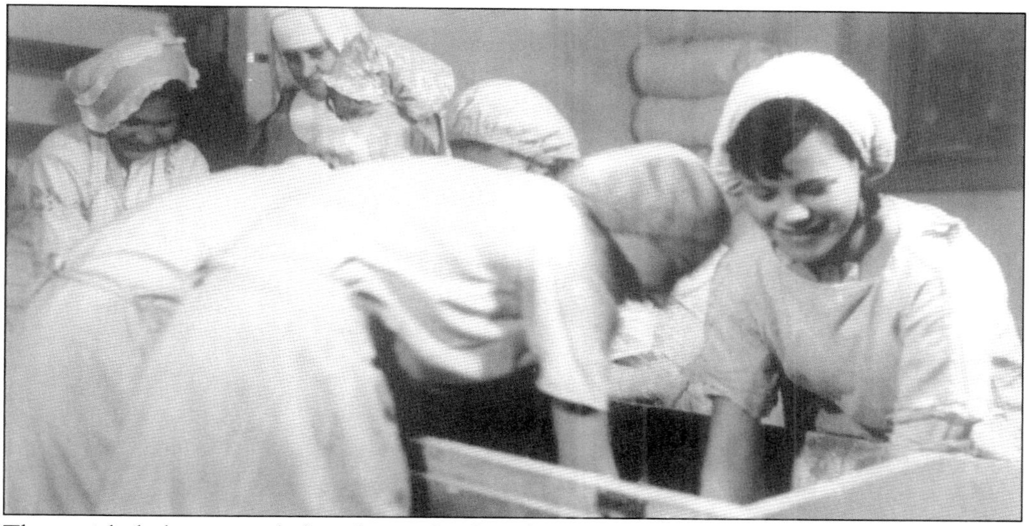

These girls help out with laundry at St. Joseph's. Water for the school's use was pumped out of the Missouri River into holding tanks. When the river was low, this method became ineffective, and buckets of water had to be carried to the school. Eventually, the school hooked in to Chamberlain's water system. Compounding these difficulties, the laundry facility burned two times in 1930–1931. (St. Joseph's Indian School, Chamberlain.)

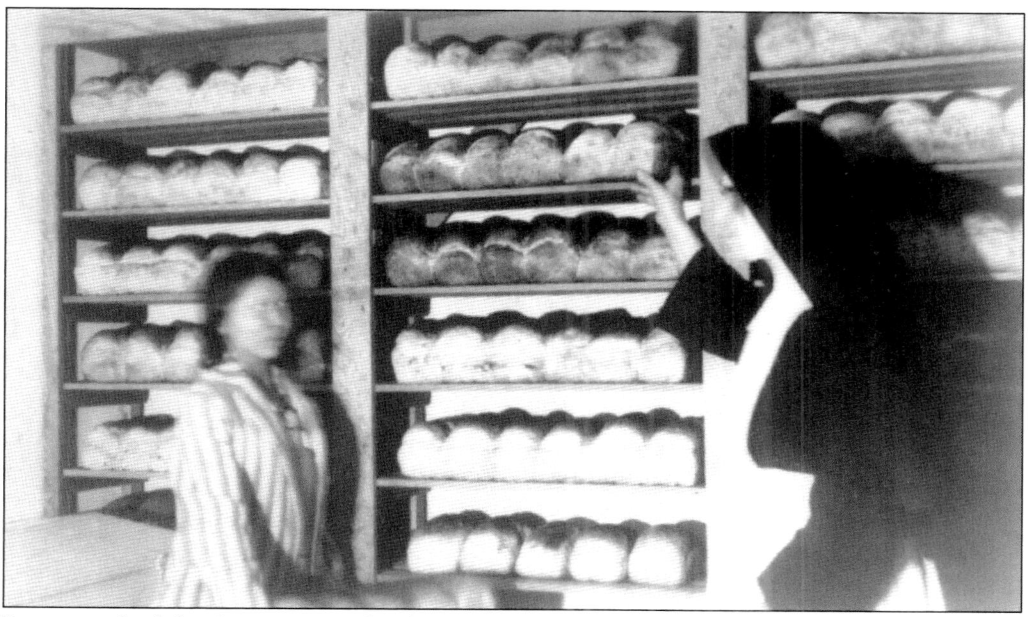

Preparing food for the mission school presented an incredible task. The drought years of the 1930s and the war of the 1940s increased the difficulty of keeping everyone fed. (St. Joseph's Indian School, Chamberlain.)

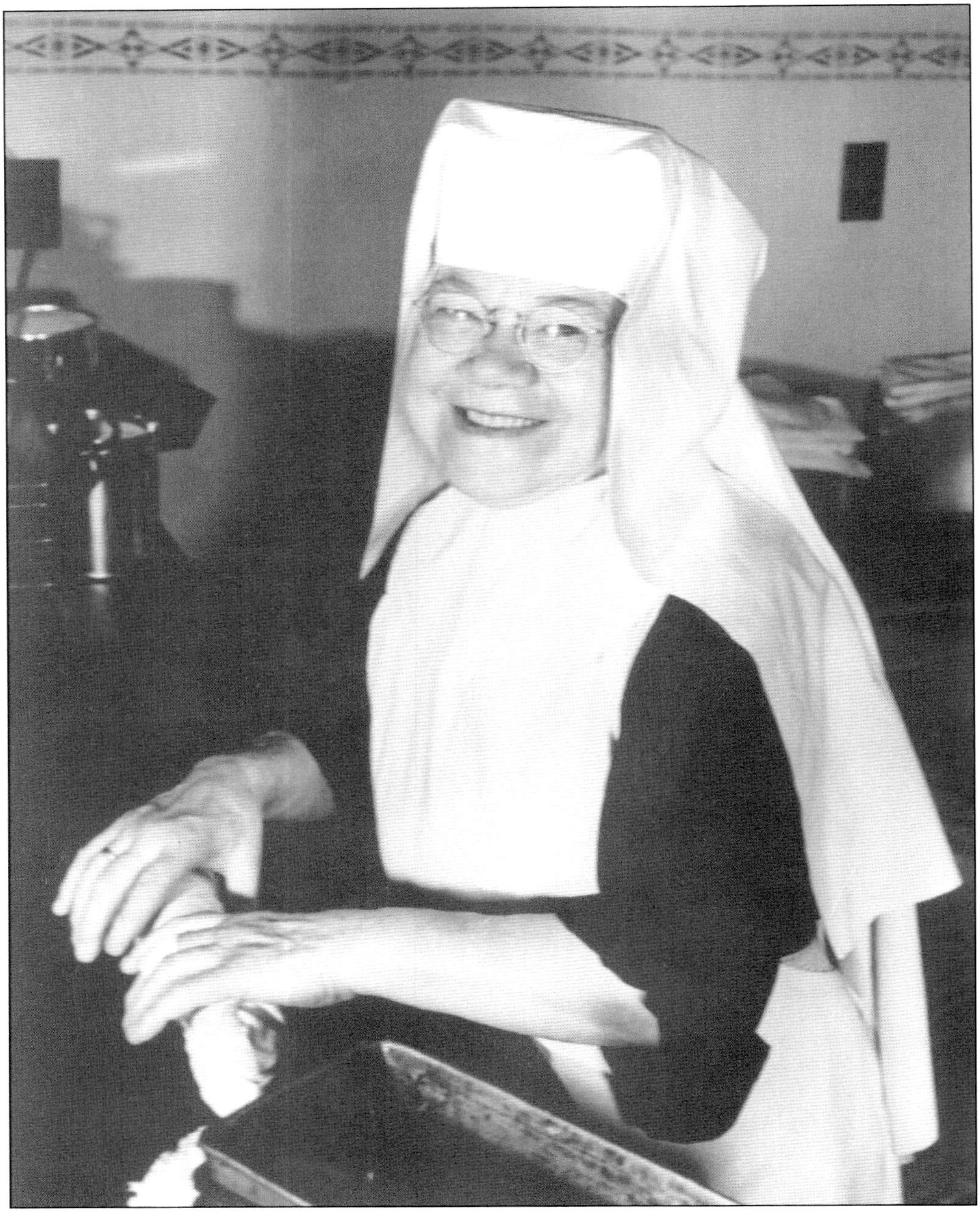

Each Sister served in various capacities. Cooking and baking was a full time job for this unidentified Sister. (St. Joseph's Indian School, Chamberlain.)

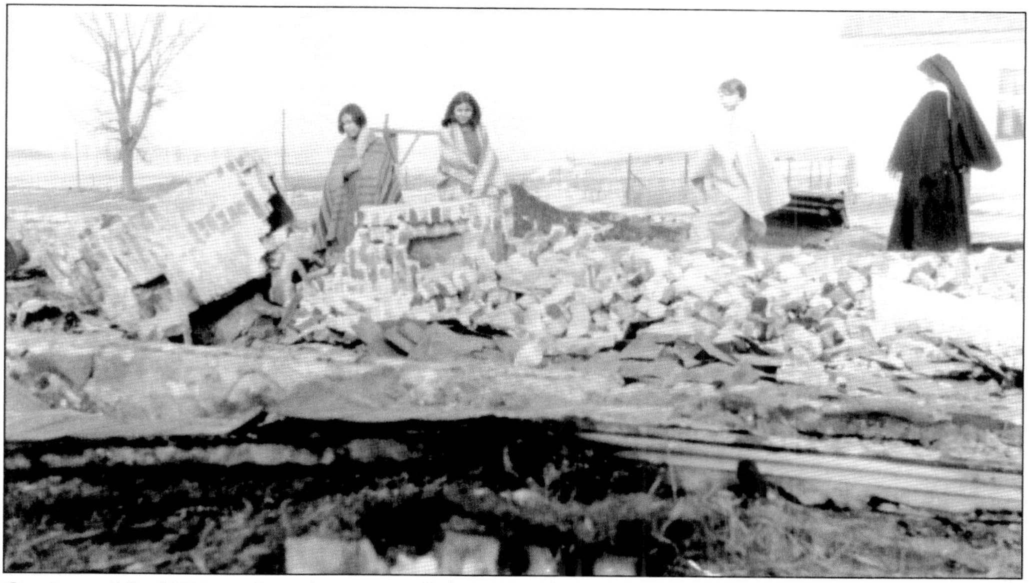

On June 17, 1931, a fire that started from sparks in the kitchen chimney destroyed the kitchen, dormitory, laundry, classrooms, boiler house, garage, and implement shed. (St. Joseph's Indian School, Chamberlain.)

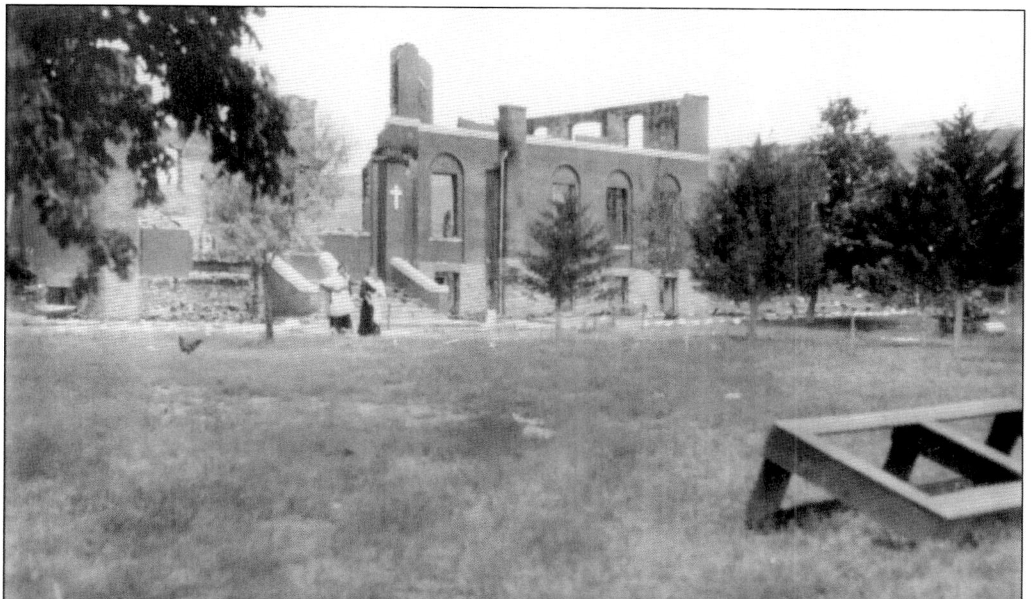

No one had been hurt in the disastrous fire. The next day, a heavy rain collapsed what of the structure remained standing. Sisters directed a salvage operation of what was left of furniture and clothing. The Sisters used a freshly scrubbed chicken coop for their temporary quarters. (Joseph's Indian School.)

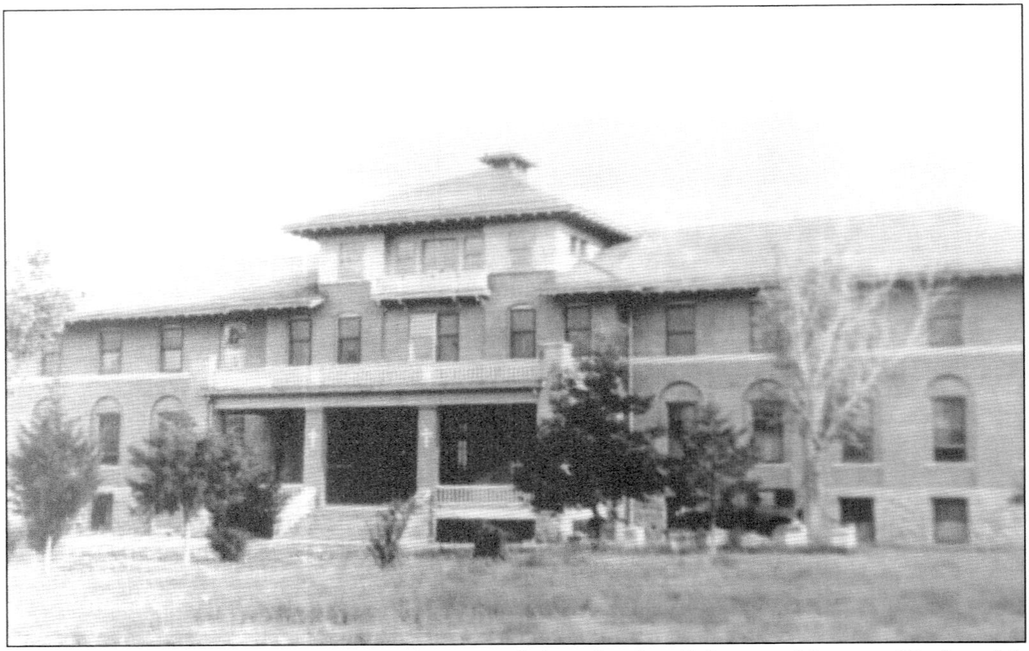

This building, destroyed by the 1931 fire, served the school well for over 30 years. (St. Joseph's Indian School, Chamberlain.)

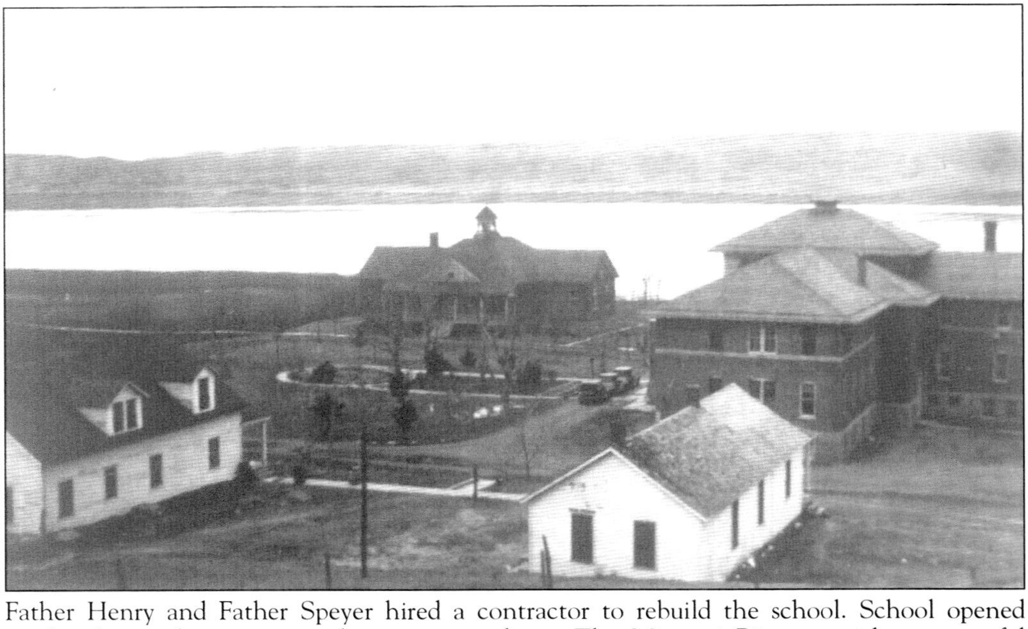

Father Henry and Father Speyer hired a contractor to rebuild the school. School opened in October with approximately seventy students. The Missouri River provides a peaceful background for the school. (St. Joseph's Indian School, Chamberlain.)

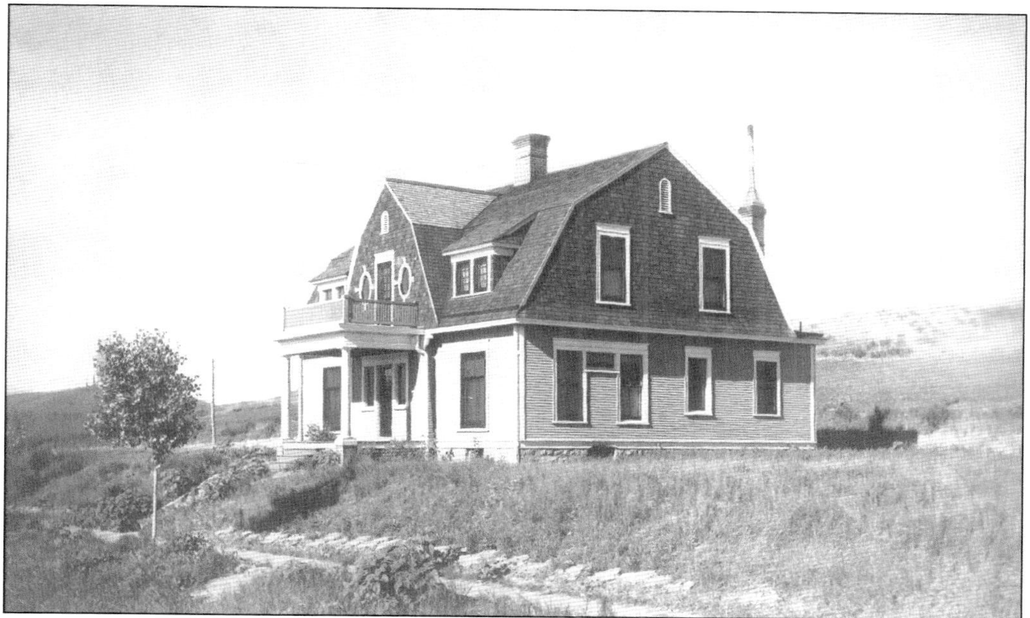

This house, which no longer stands, has provided a home for many people over the years since its beginning as a government school. The priests lived here in the early years. Then families occupied it, and finally high school girls used it as a dorm. The school was forced to demolish the building due to black mold. (St. Joseph's Indian School, Chamberlain.)

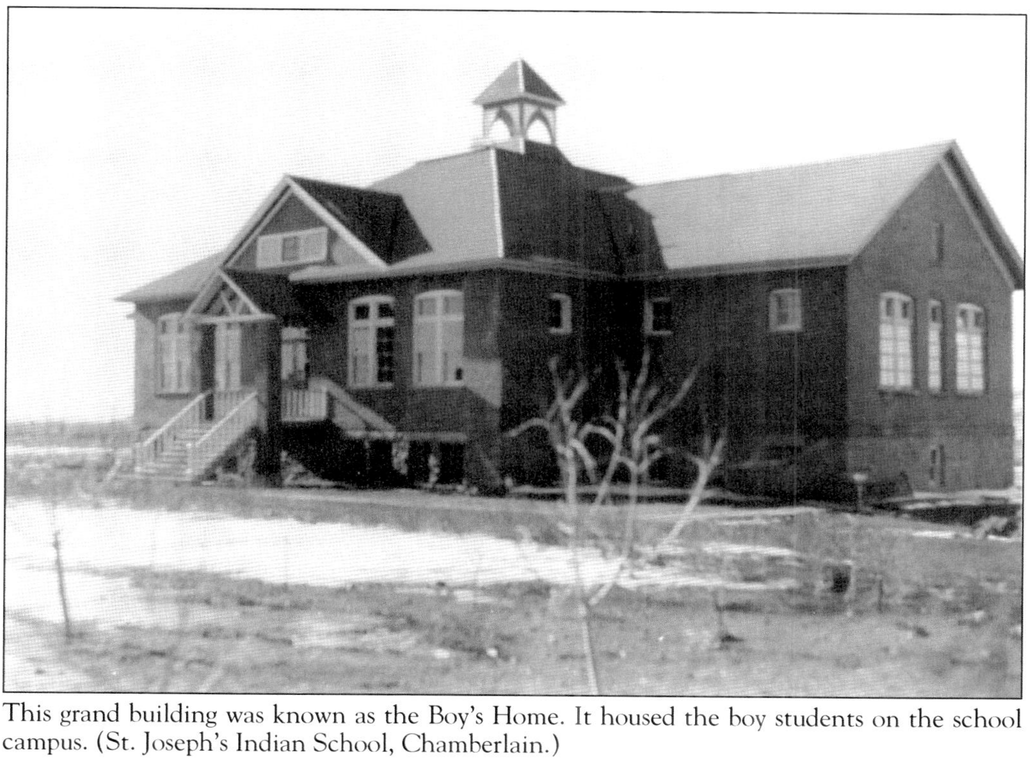

This grand building was known as the Boy's Home. It housed the boy students on the school campus. (St. Joseph's Indian School, Chamberlain.)

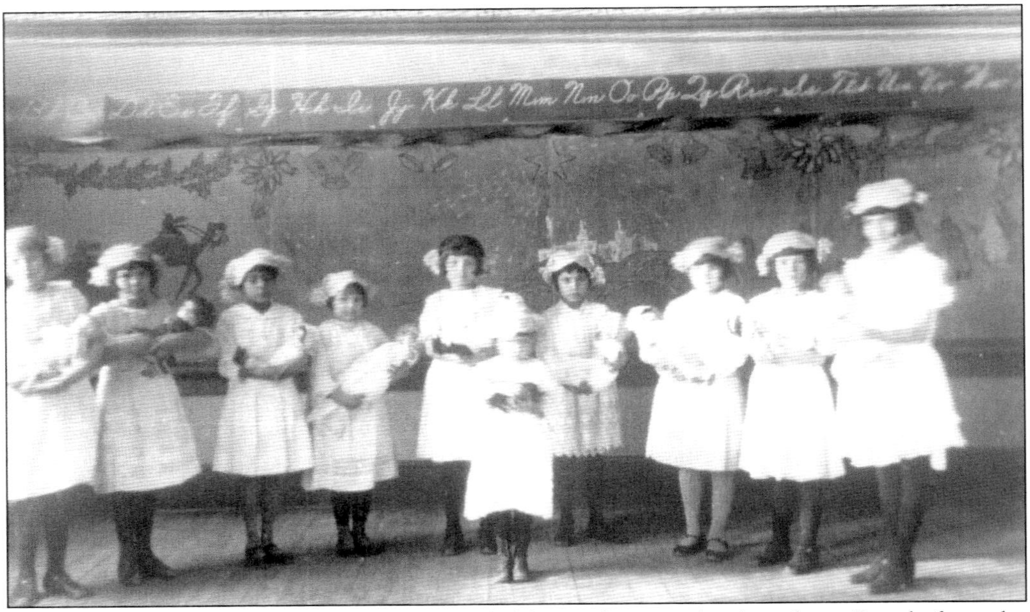

The girls in this early photograph are dressed alike, perhaps a school uniform. People from the East often sent a gift of dolls to the Indian School. The girls are showing off their dolls in this classroom photo. (St. Joseph's Indian School, Chamberlain.)

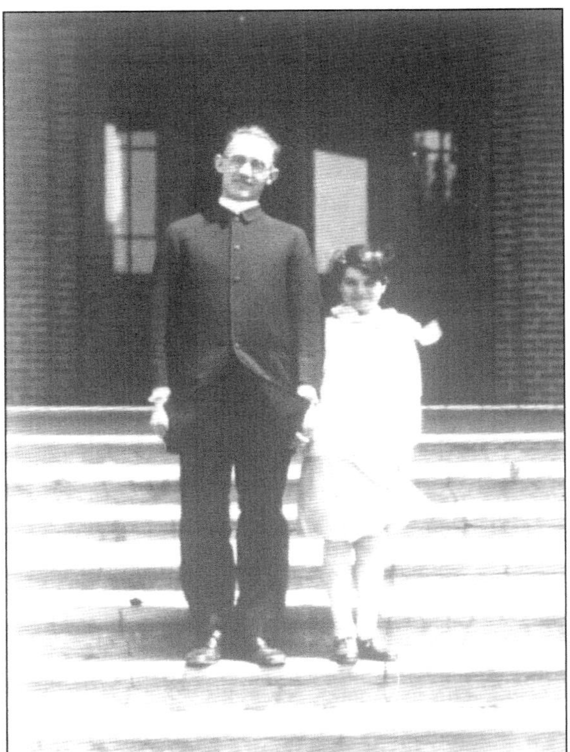

Father Henry spent many years at St. Joseph's and was a well-loved priest. Father Henry takes time from his busy schedule for a photograph. (St. Joseph's Indian School, Chamberlain.)

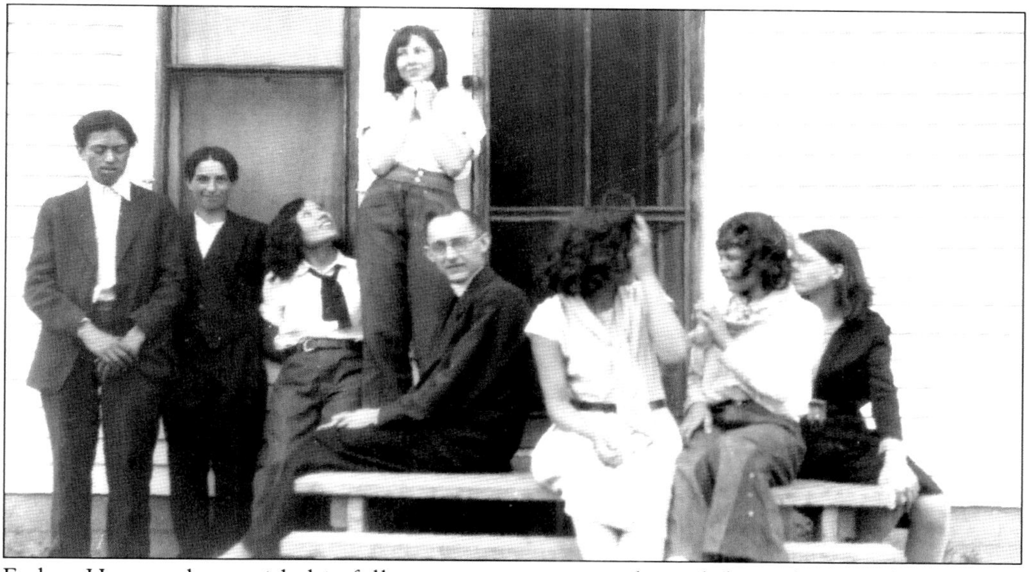

Father Henry, along with his followers, engages in a chat while a photographer snaps a picture. Father Henry ministered on both the Lower Brule and Cheyenne River Reservations. By 1924, six Sacred Heart priests were working on both reservations. (St. Joseph's Indian School, Chamberlain.)

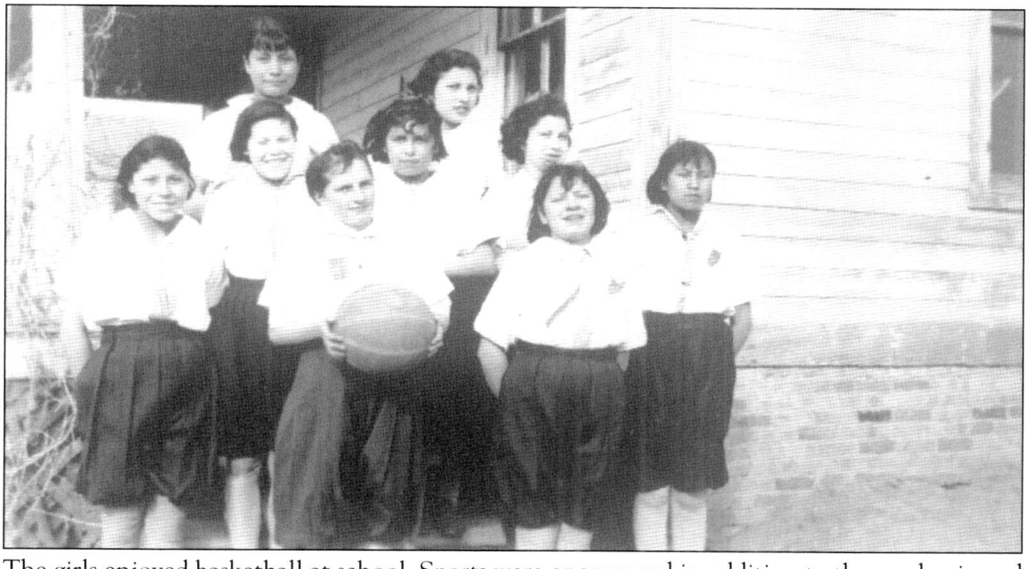

The girls enjoyed basketball at school. Sports were encouraged in addition to the academic and religious instruction. (St. Joseph's Indian School, Chamberlain.)

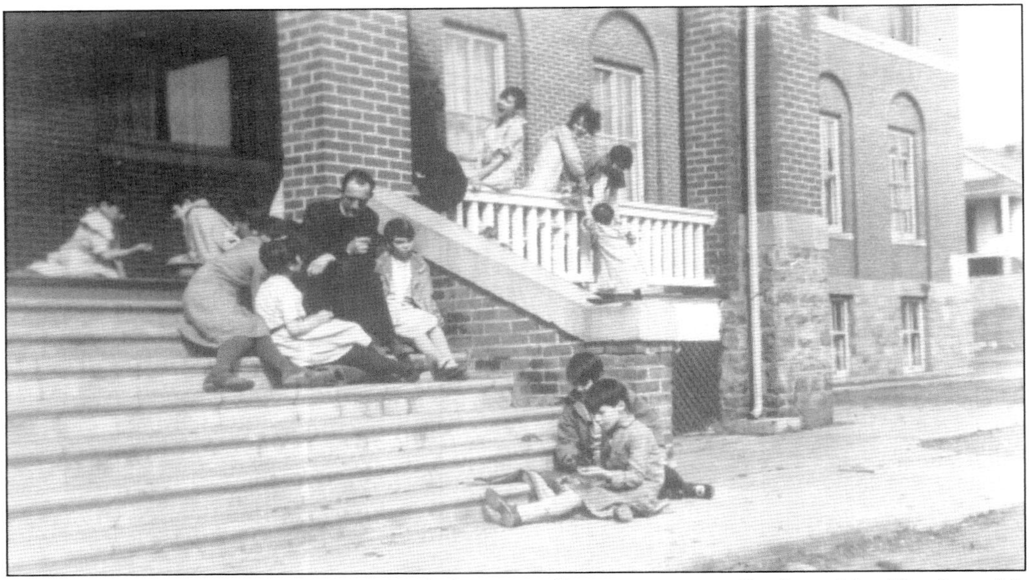

Students visit with the priest and relish some idle moments at St. Joseph's. (St. Joseph's Indian School, Chamberlain.)

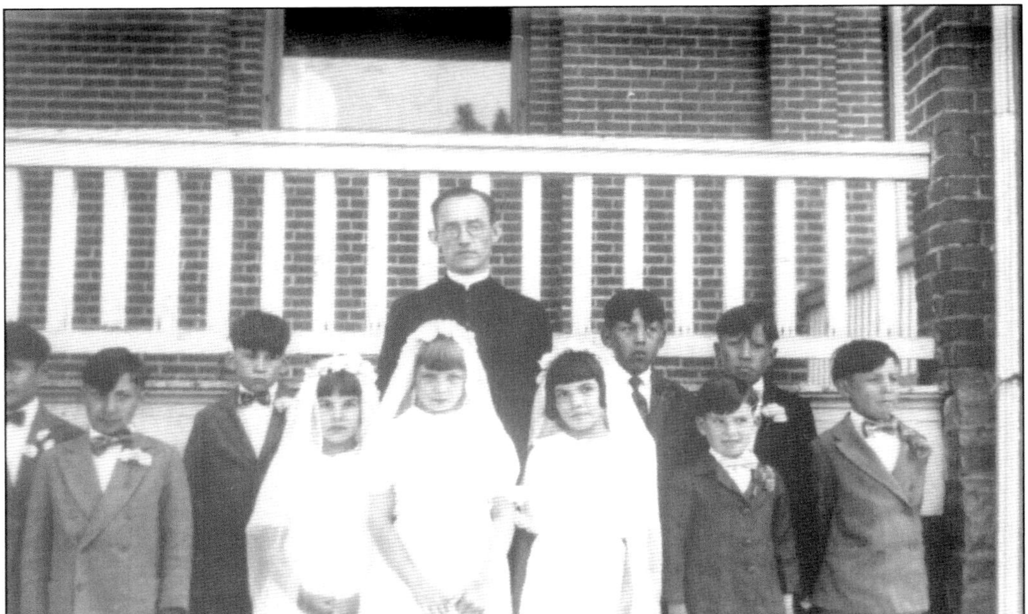

Father Henry is pictured with students ready for their First Holy Communion. Months of preparation took place for this big event. In addition to religious instruction, Sisters searched for the needed dresses, suits, and accessories for the occasion. (St. Joseph's Indian School, Chamberlain.)

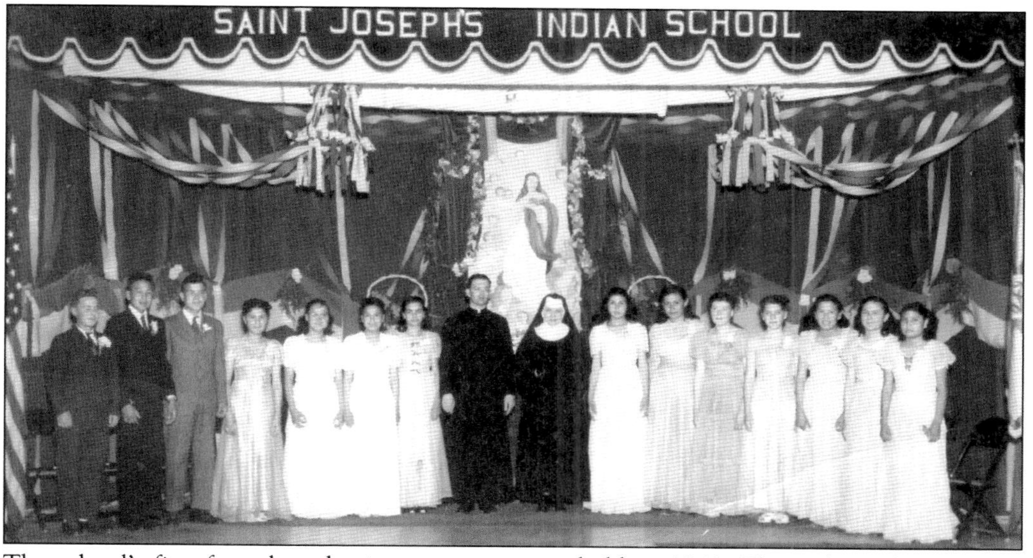

The school's first formal graduation ceremony was held in 1948. The girls in this undated photograph wear formals altered or redesigned by the girls themselves. (St. Joseph's Indian School, Chamberlain.)

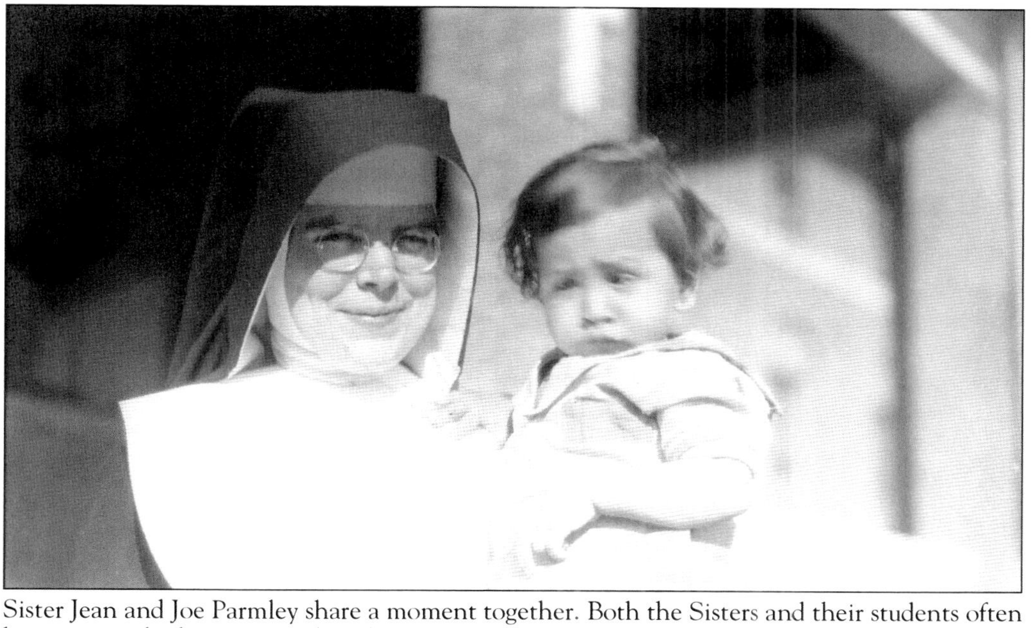

Sister Jean and Joe Parmley share a moment together. Both the Sisters and their students often became attached to one another. (St. Joseph's Indian School, Chamberlain.)

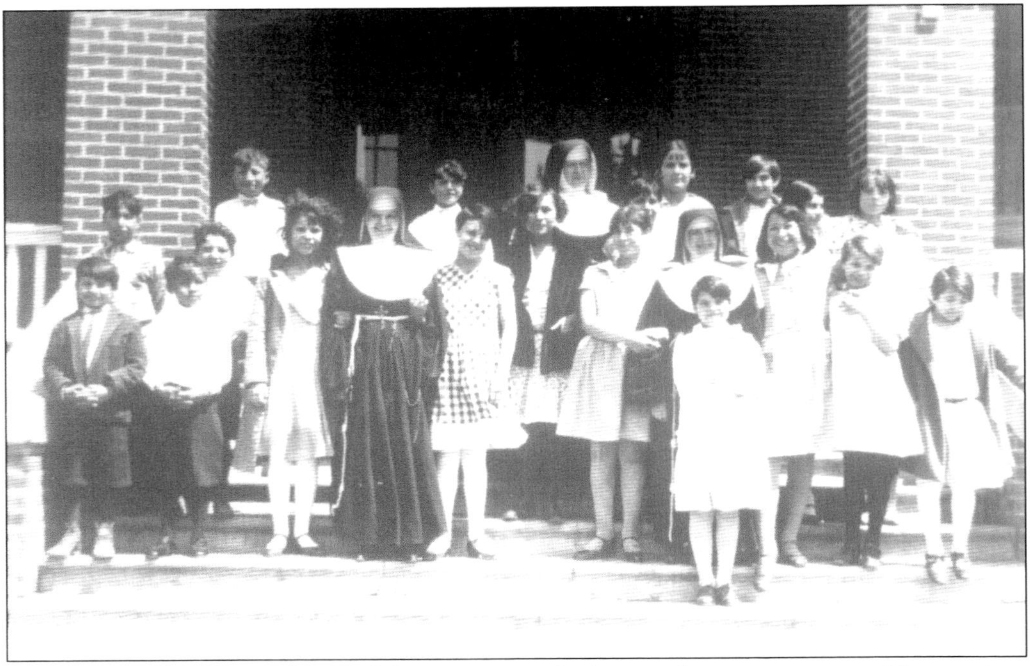

Sister Jean and other unidentified Sisters pose with their students on a memorable occasion. (St. Joseph's Indian School, Chamberlain.)

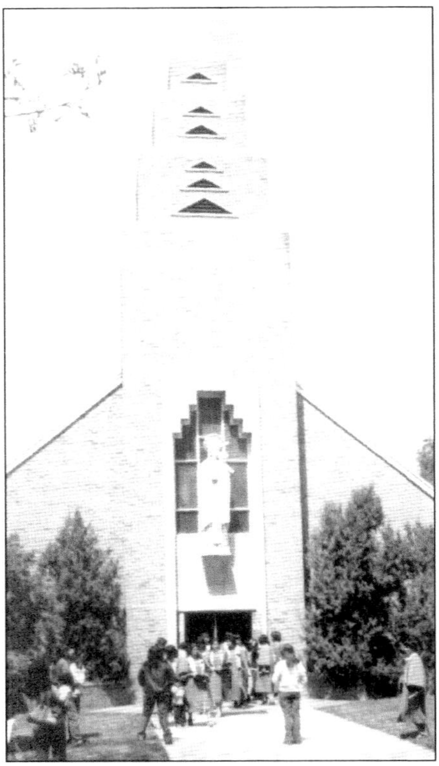

Our Lady of the Sioux Chapel, pictured here, was built in 1956 and remodeled in 1985. The original chapel, Blessed Sacrament, escaped the 1931 fire and is still used on campus for daily Mass. (St. Joseph's Indian School, Chamberlain.)

A stained glass window in Our Lady of the Sioux Chapel, honors Saint Kateri, the first Native American nominated for Sainthood. She devoted her short life to teaching children prayers, and helping the aged and sick. She led a virtuous life and performed extraordinary penances. (St. Joseph's Indian School, Chamberlain; David Meyer, photographer.)

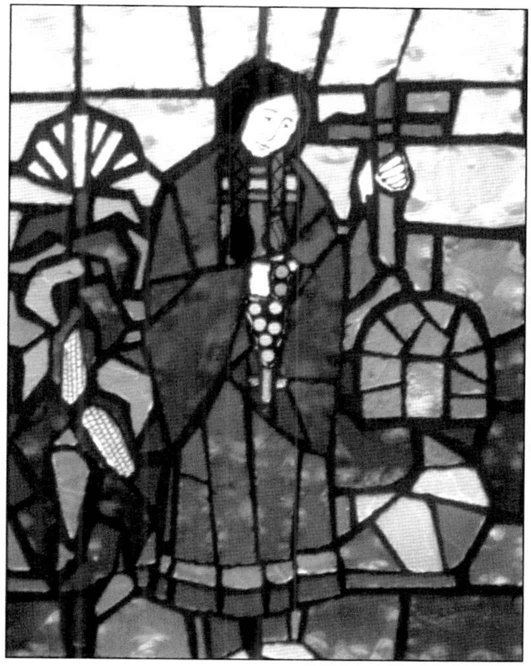

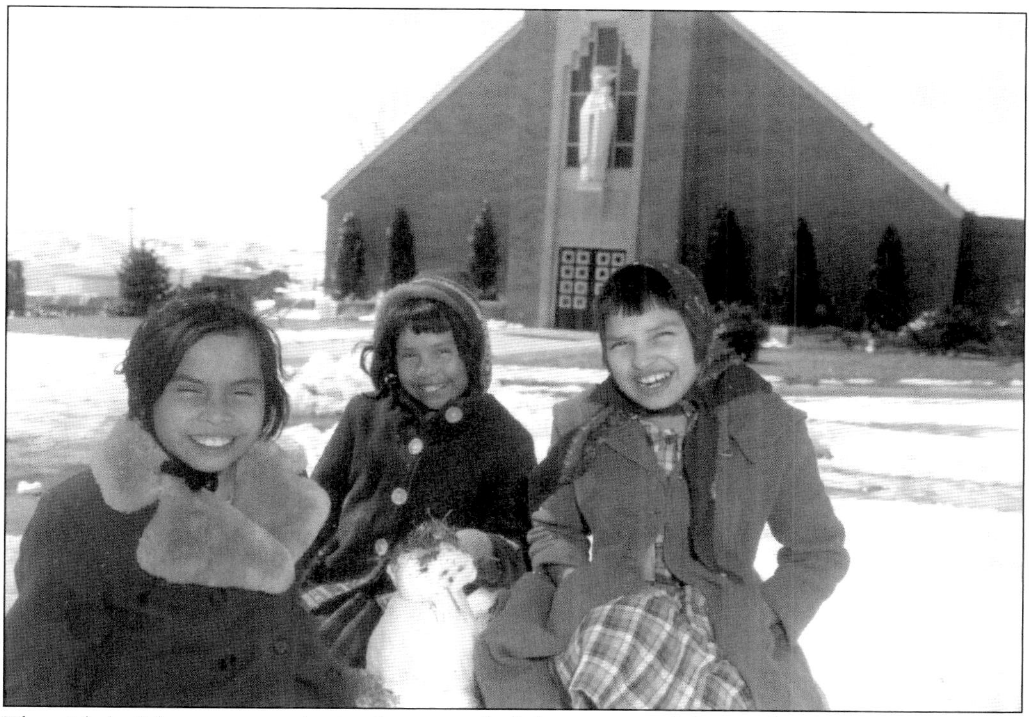

The girls build a snowman in the foreground of this picture of Our Lady of the Sioux Chapel. (St. Joseph's Indian School, Chamberlain.)

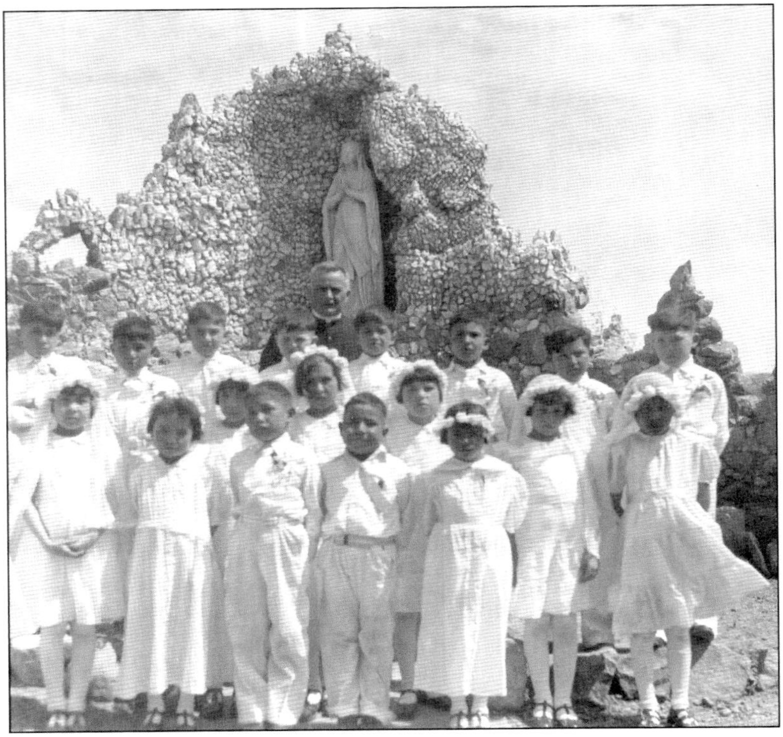

This Holy Communion picture was taken in front of a grotto with the Statue of Mary looking on. (St. Joseph's Indian School, Chamberlain.)

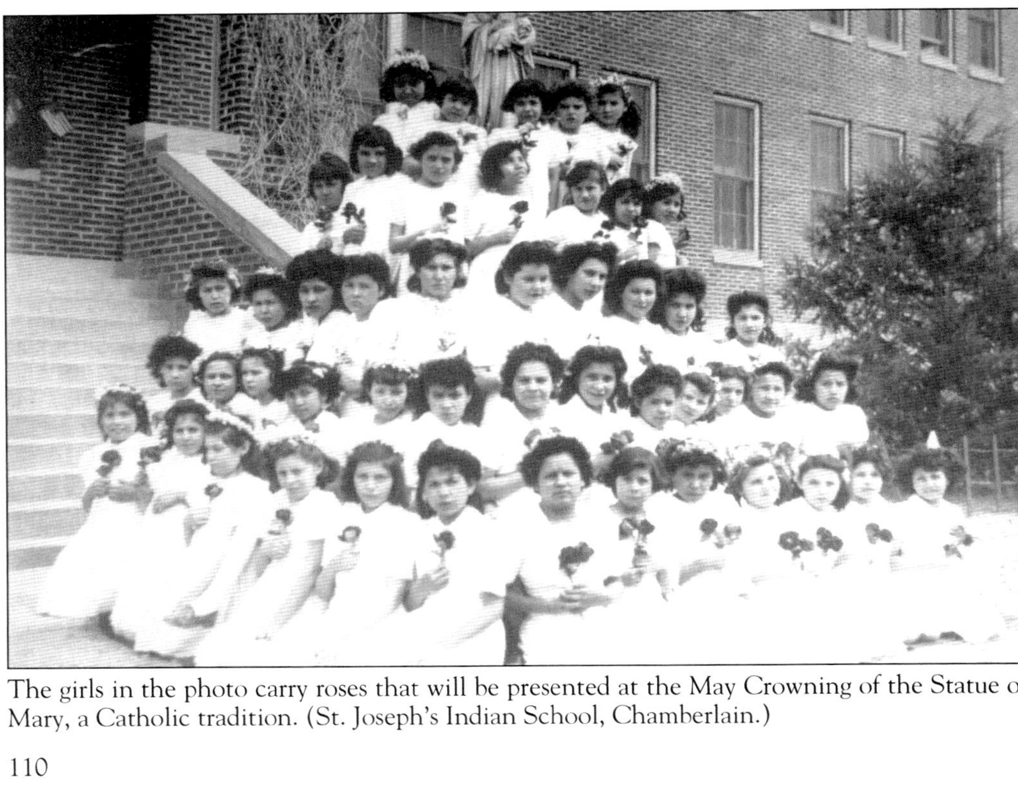

The girls in the photo carry roses that will be presented at the May Crowning of the Statue of Mary, a Catholic tradition. (St. Joseph's Indian School, Chamberlain.)

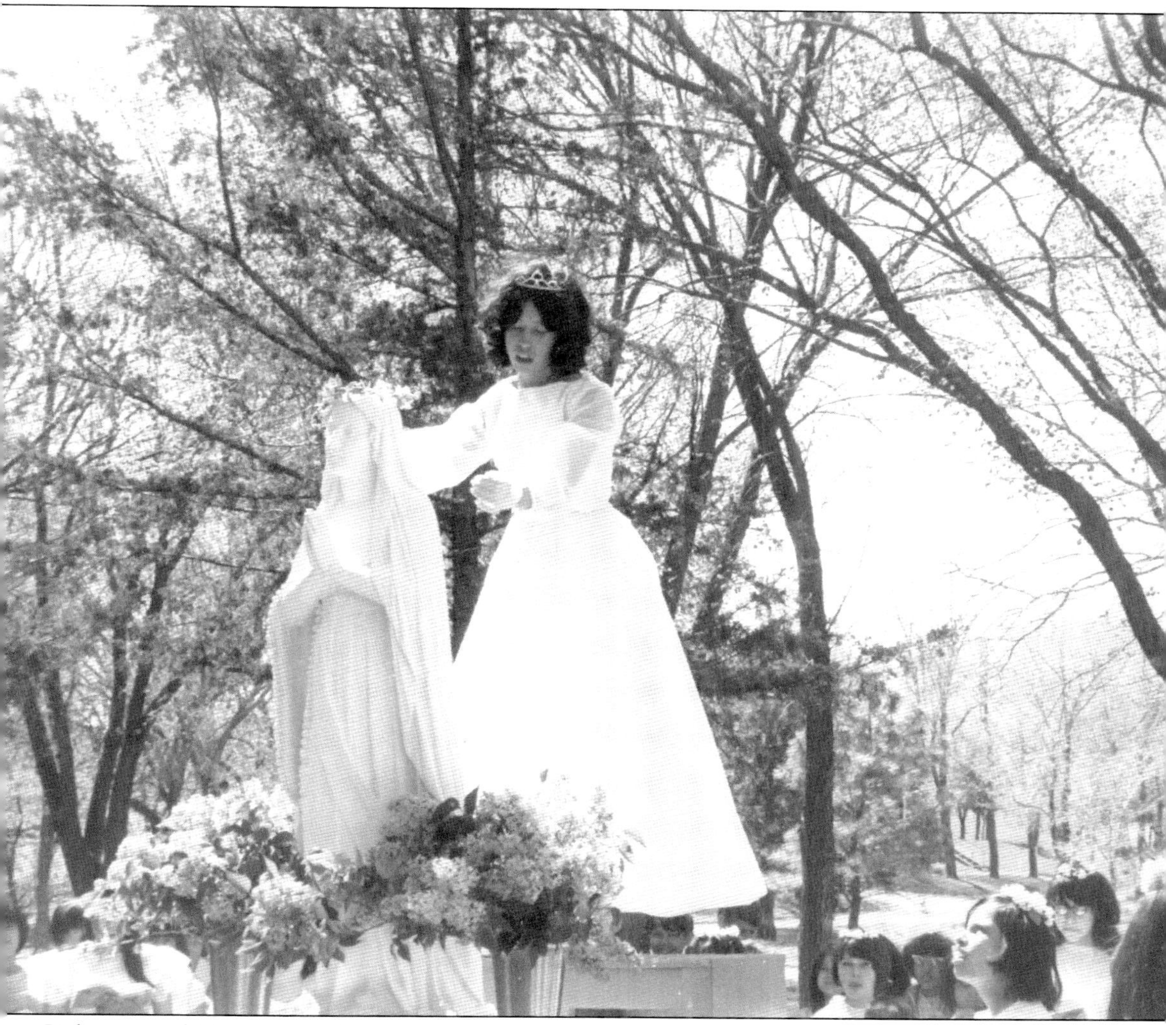

Girls crowned Mary every May as part of a Catholic tradition. The Statue of Mary resided in the grotto sometime before 1946 and then was moved to the circle in front of Benedictine homes, as shown in this photo. The Statue is now in front of the business office. (St. Joseph's Indian School, Chamberlain.)

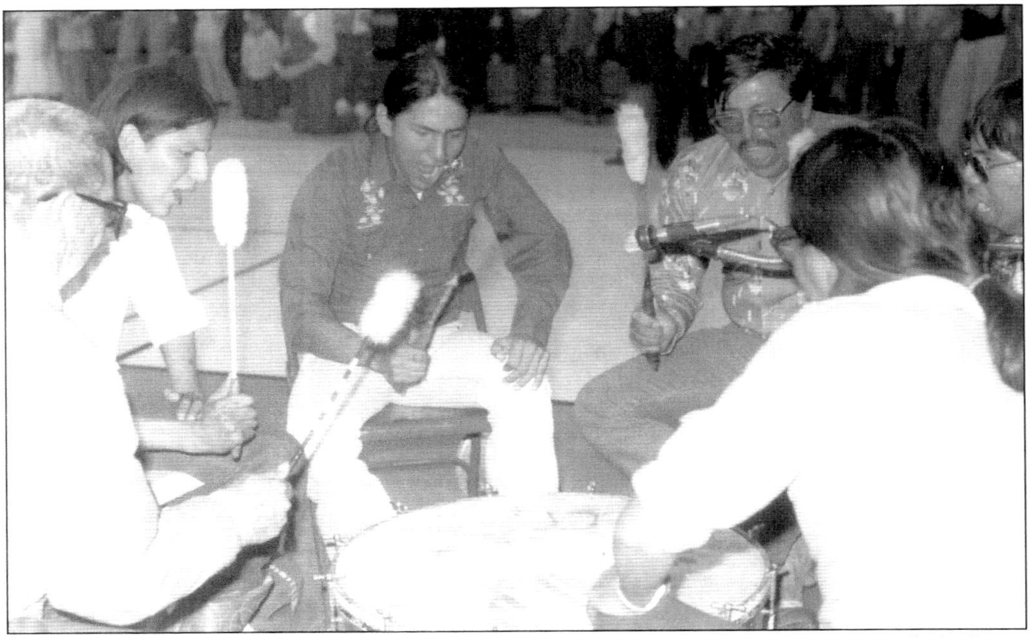

Powwows are a part of St. Joseph's School tradition. Singers strike the beat on a rawhide drum. The dancers dance according to the change in drumbeat and must stop when the beat ceases with both feet on the ground. (St. Joseph's Indian School, Chamberlain.)

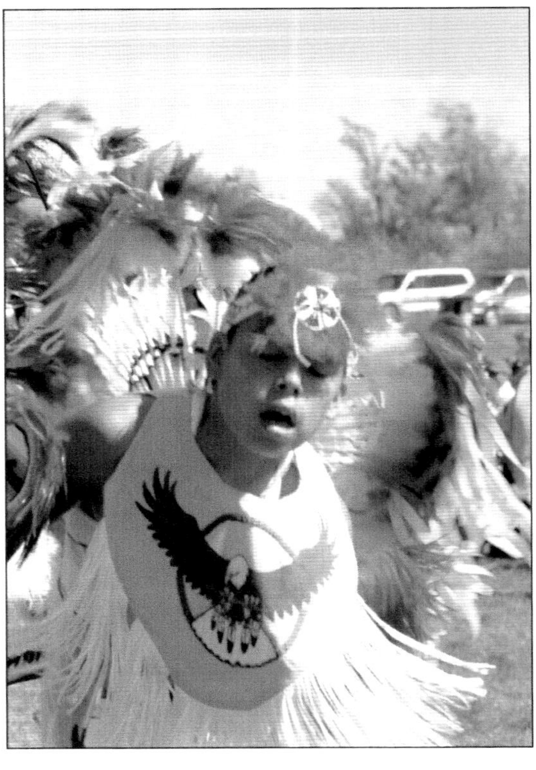

Children from all nine South Dakota reservations and neighboring states attend the school. All children are instructed in their traditions, culture, and language. Of those attending, 61% are Catholic, 25% are Episcopal, and 14% practice other religions. (St. Joseph's Indian School, Chamberlain; David Meyer, photographer.)

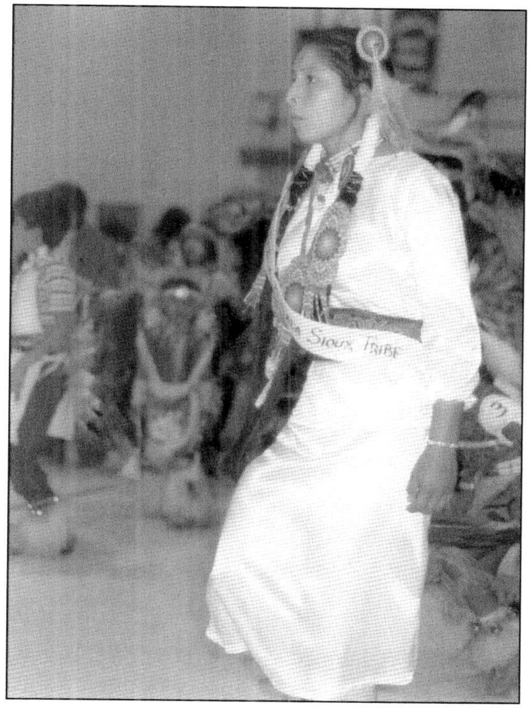

This young lady performs the traditional dance where the women bend at the knees with a graceful up and down movement of their body. Originally, their dresses were made of buckskin, decorated with shells and elk's teeth. Later, cloth dresses were worn. (St. Joseph's Indian School, Chamberlain.)

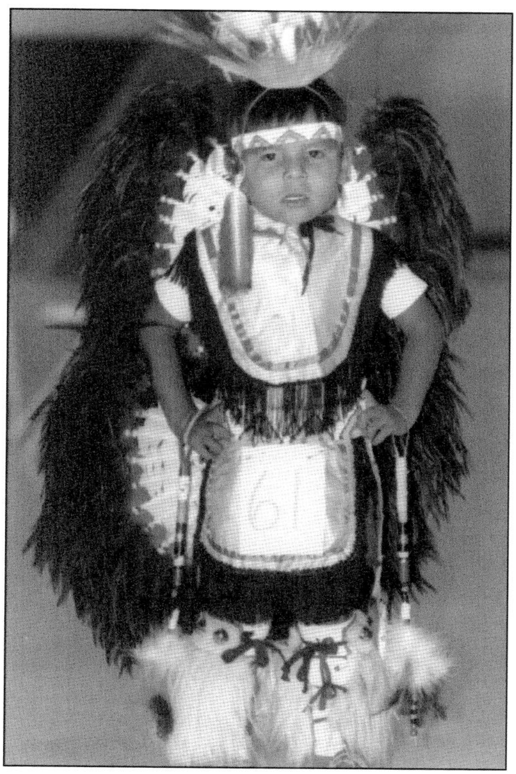

The students at St. Joseph's have participated in competitive dancing. This young man has the number 61 on his regalia. (St. Joseph's Indian School, Chamberlain.)

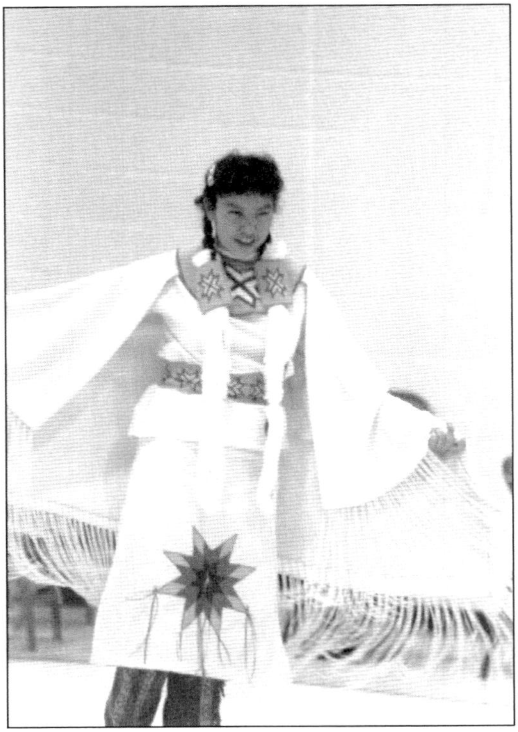

This young girl dances the Fancy Shawl Dance. The dress is knee length with a fancy shawl, matching leggings, and beaded jewelry. (St. Joseph's Indian School, Chamberlain.)

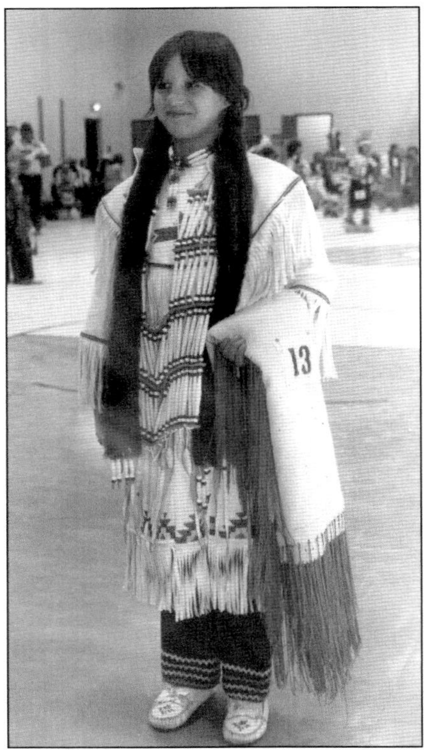

Dancers in the Traditional Women's Dance usually carry a shawl and an eagle or hawk feather fan. Beaded moccasins and assorted beaded jewelry complete their regalia. (St. Joseph's Indian School, Chamberlain.)

Originally a dance to honor the story of battle or return from the hunt, the dancer in the Traditional Men's Dance often carries a shield, honor staff, or medicine wheel. The dancer's movements often replicate those of animals or birds. The dancer's regalia is subdued in color, and he often wears a circular bustle of eagle feathers. (St. Joseph's Indian School, Chamberlain.)

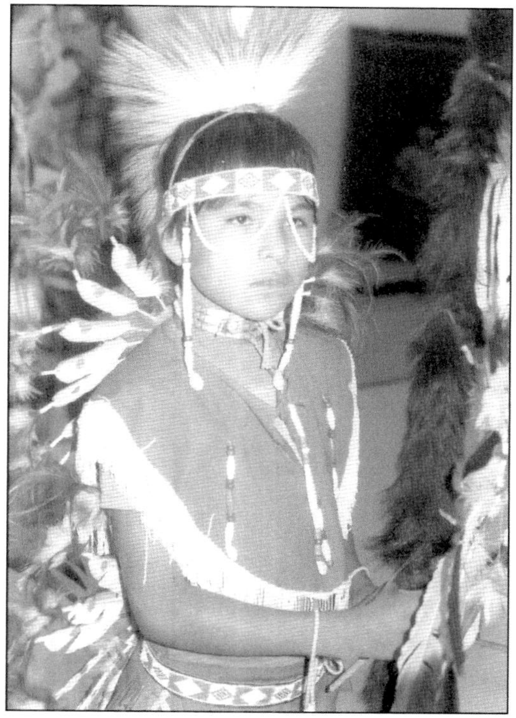

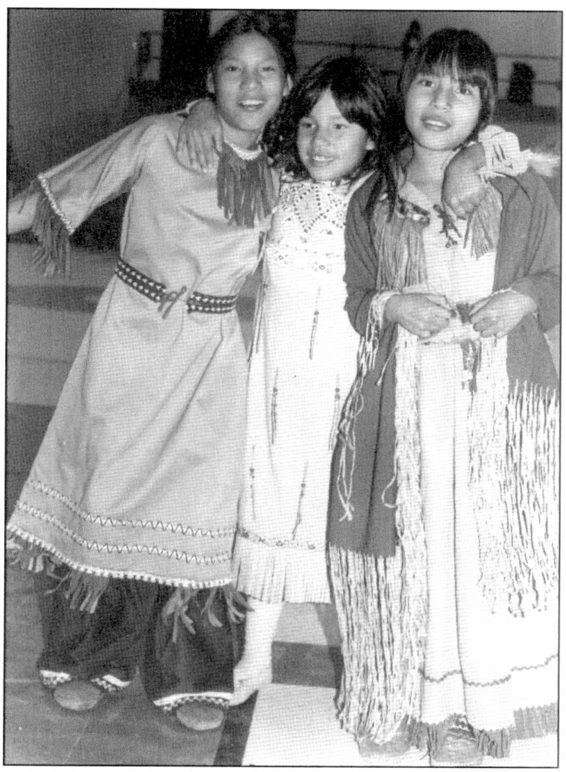

Three young ladies, apparently enjoying themselves at the dance competition, pause for the photographer. (St. Joseph's Indian School, Chamberlain.)

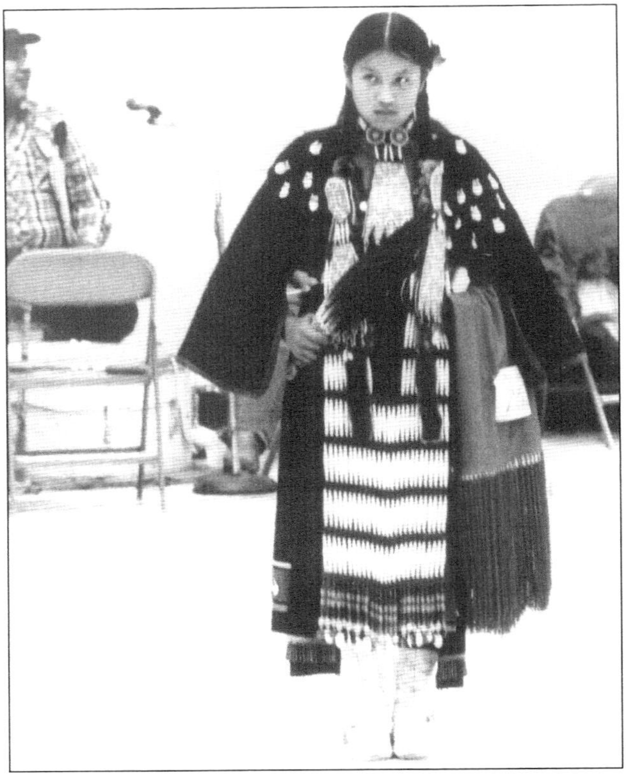

This young lady dressed for the Women's Traditional Dance will dance with subtle movements. Traditionally, women only danced at certain occasions and usually remained in the background. (St. Joseph's Indian School, Chamberlain.)

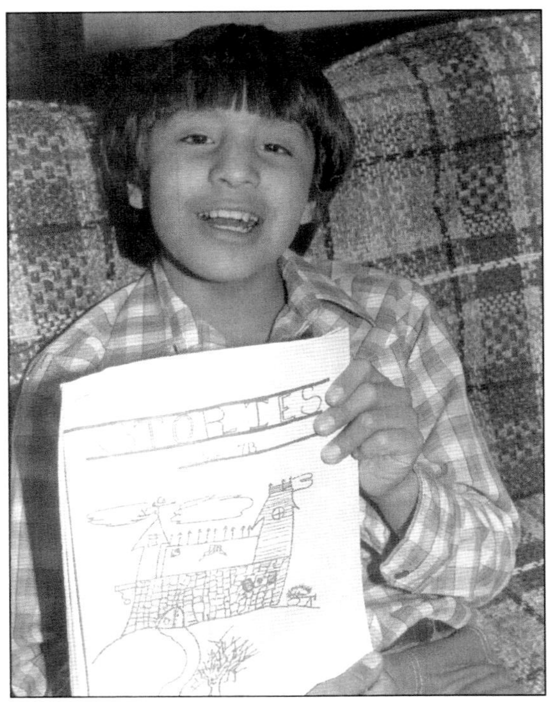

This boy appears to be proud of his illustrated storybook. Currently, St. Joseph's provides education for grades one through eight on campus. High school students attend the Chamberlain Public School. (St. Joseph's Indian School, Chamberlain.)

This boy explores the library and its books in this undated photo. A library was started in 1936 with regular scheduled student visits. (St. Joseph's Indian School, Chamberlain.)

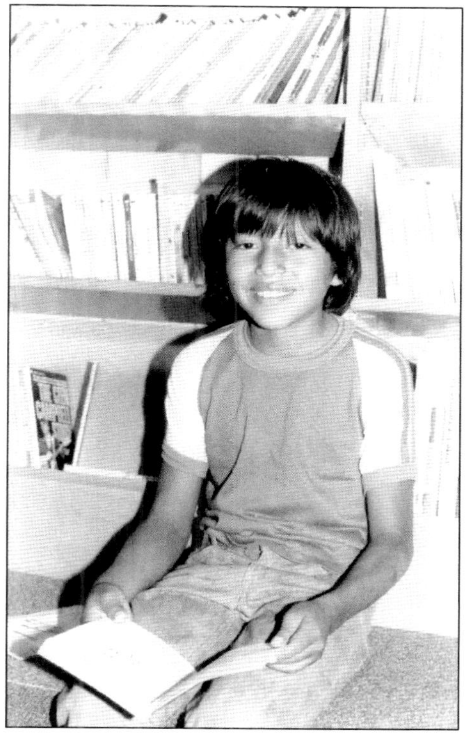

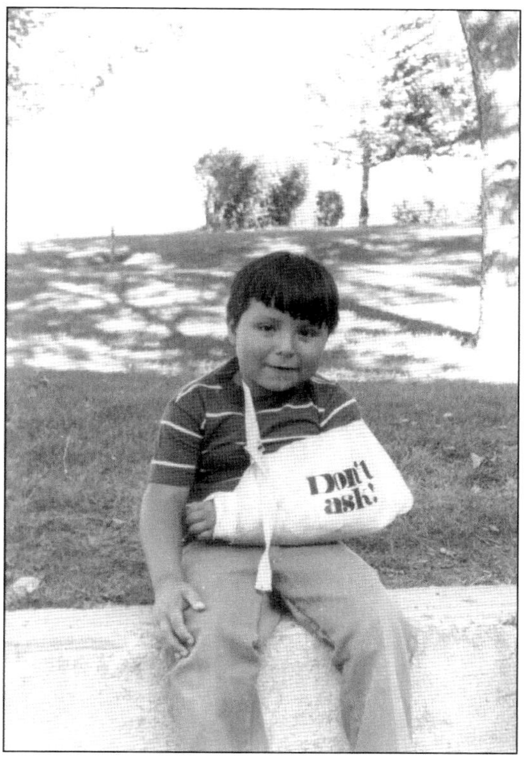

This lad is typical of many students who experience the ups and downs of school life. O.K., we won't ask! (St. Joseph's Indian School, Chamberlain.)

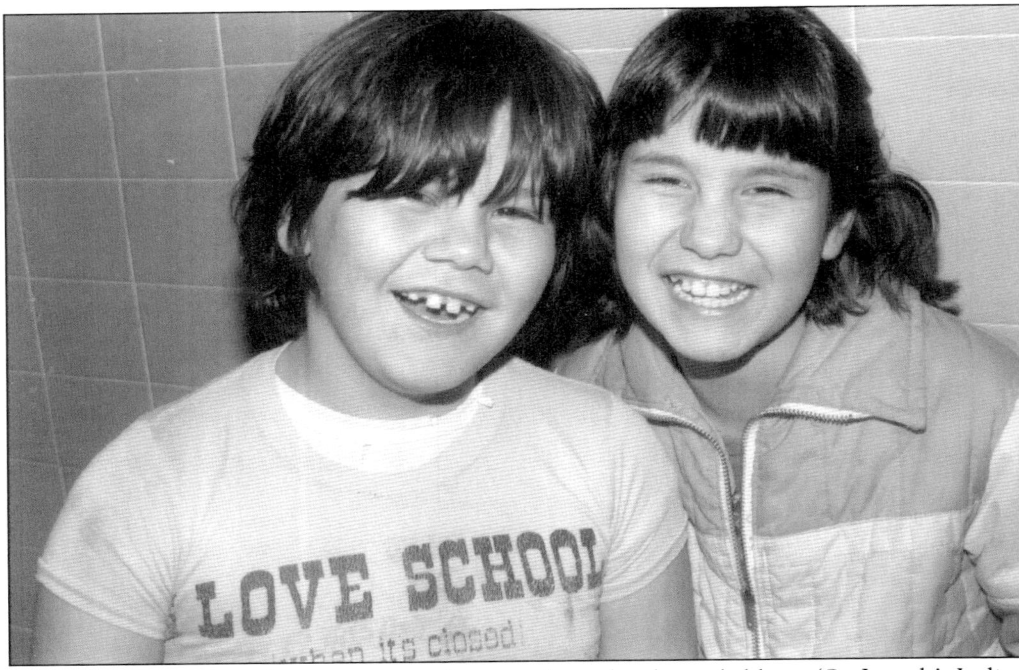

This student expresses the sentiments of many other school age children. (St. Joseph's Indian School, Chamberlain.)

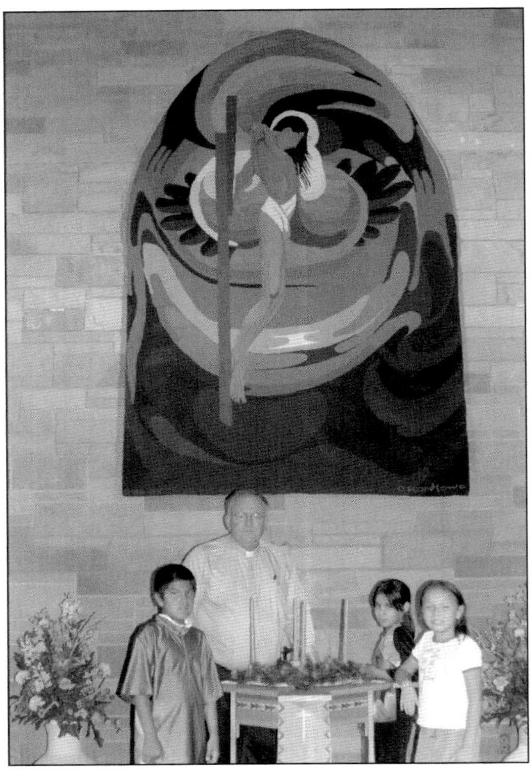

Deacon David Nogel, SCJ, has been at St. Joseph's for 25 years. He has served as Executive Director for eight years. Deacon Dave and three children are observing Advent in Our Lady of the Sioux Chapel. (St. Joseph's Indian School, Chamberlain.)

Six

Lower Brule

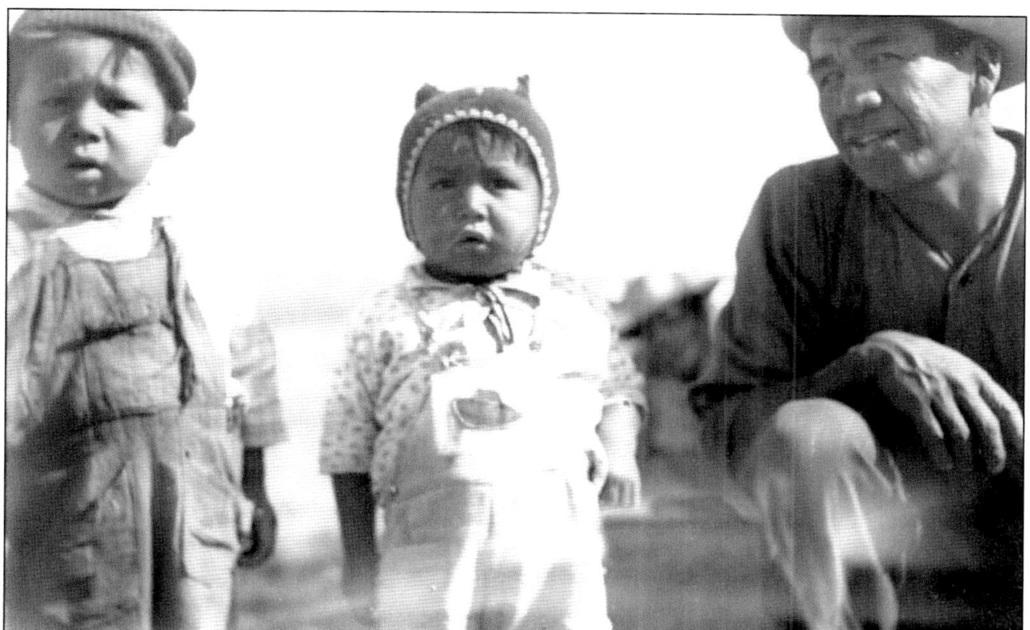

The missionaries from Lower Brule not only served Lower Brule, the smallest of the reservations, but the Cheyenne River Reservation as well. Missionaries traveled numerous miles visiting the many families scattered throughout the isolated region. (St. Joseph's Indian School, Chamberberlain.)

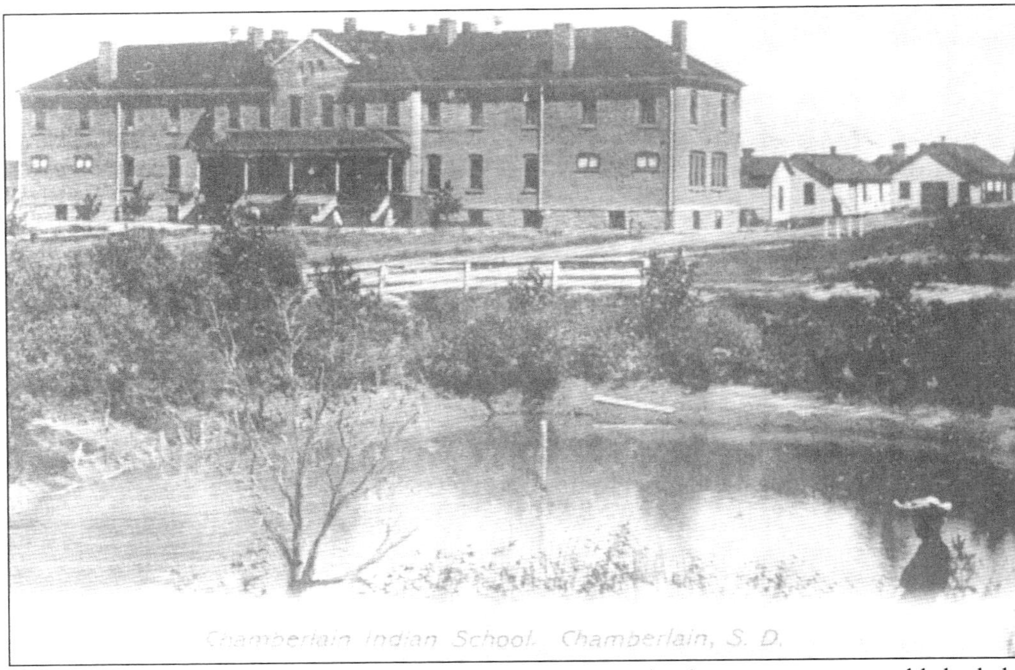

An early postcard depicts the Chamberlain Indian School. The government established the Indian School in 1852 to educate the Sioux. In 1909, the buildings were sold to Rev. Thomas O'Gorman. (St. Joseph's Indian School, Chamberlain.)

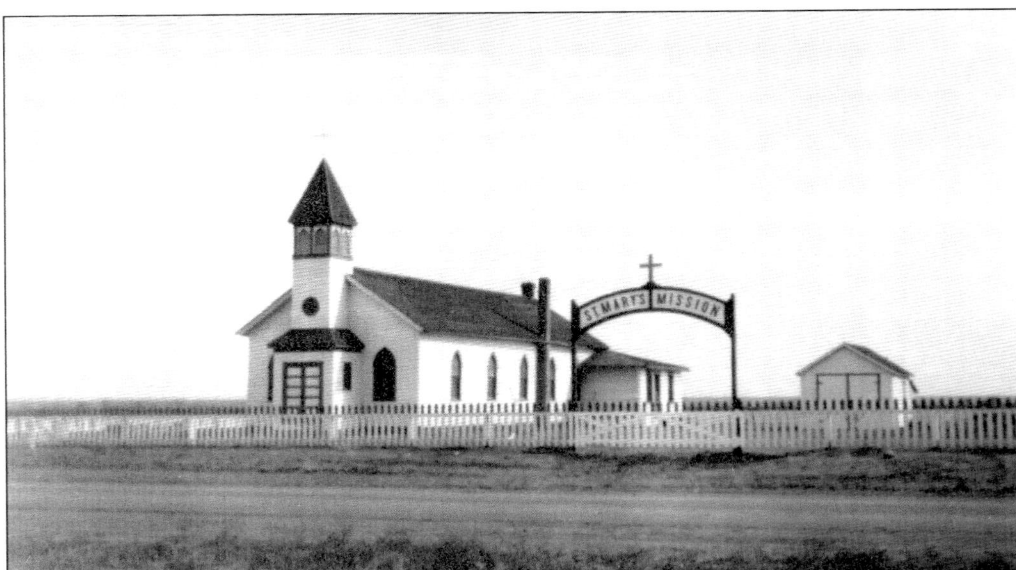

St. Mary's Mission is located in Lower Brule and is administered by St. Joseph's Indian School. In 1887, the Benedictines of Crow Creek at Stephan Indian School began to work with the Brule Sioux on the Lower Brule Indian Reservation. The Priests of the Sacred Heart carried on the work of the original mission when a fire destroyed the original church. Bishop John Lawler dedicated the newly erected church in 1944. (St. Joseph's Indian School, Chamberlain.)

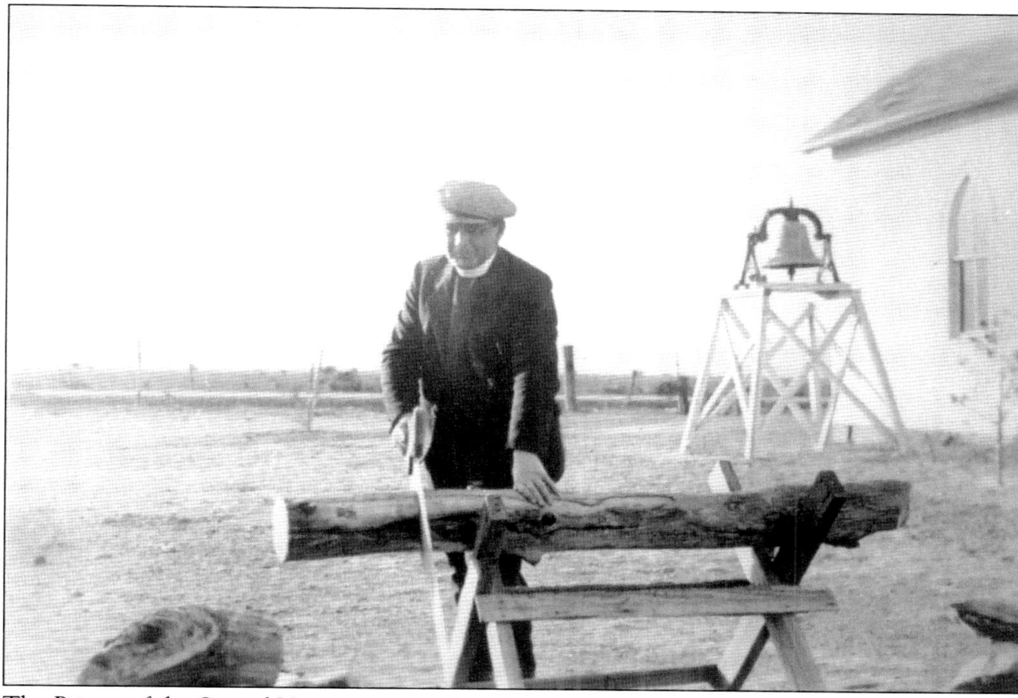

The Priests of the Sacred Heart ministered to churches throughout the reservations. The clergy served in many capacities, as shown in this photo. (St. Joseph's Indian School, Chamberlain.)

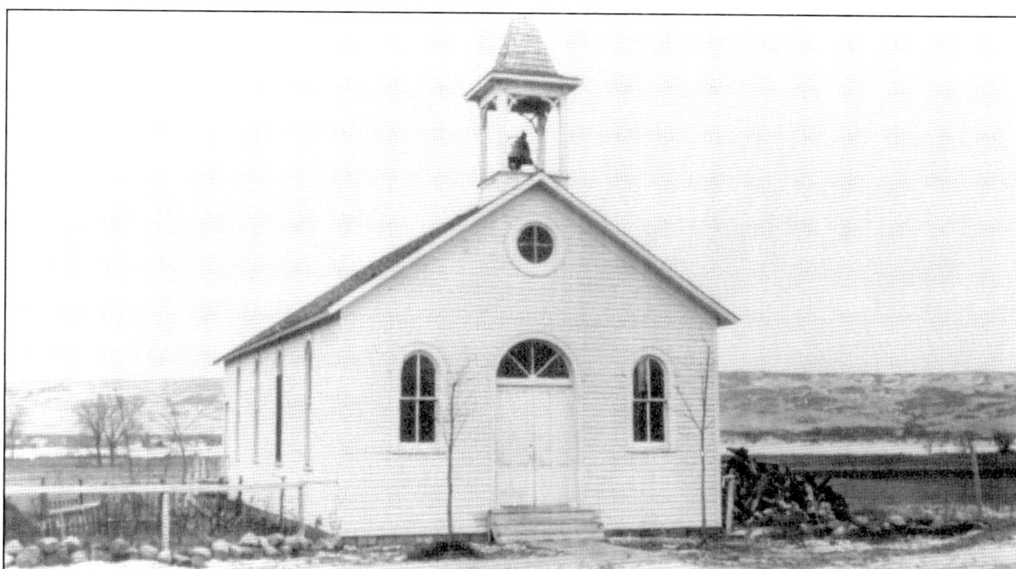

Many churches have disappeared over the years. This unidentified church was located near the Missouri River. (St. Joseph's Indian School, Chamberlain.)

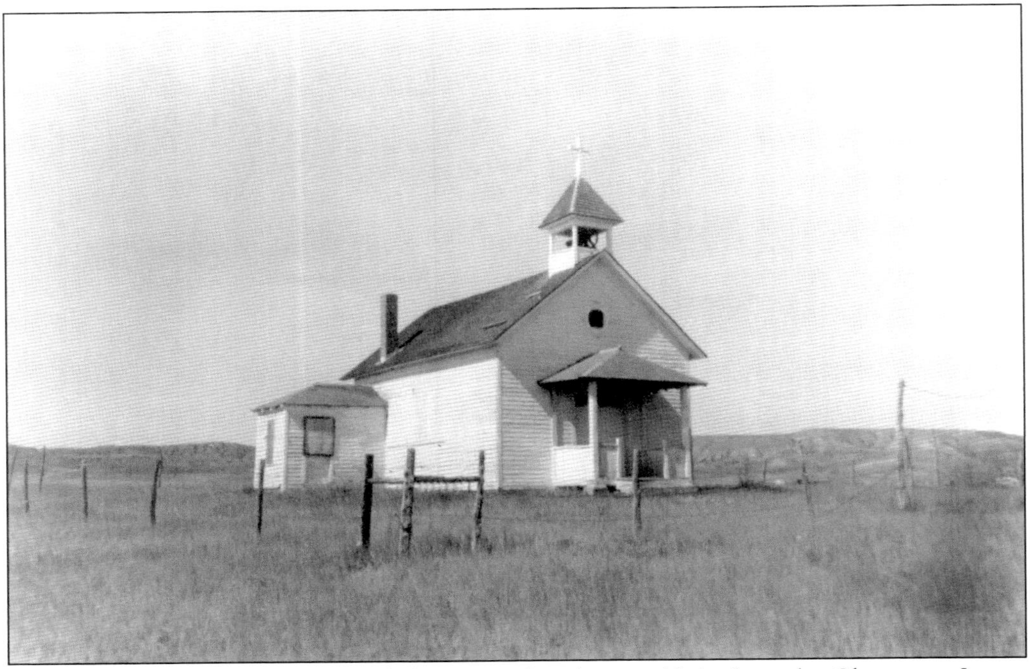

This unidentified church is one of the many churches established on the Cheyenne, Lower Brule, and Crow Creek reservations. (St. Joseph's Indian School, Chamberlain.)

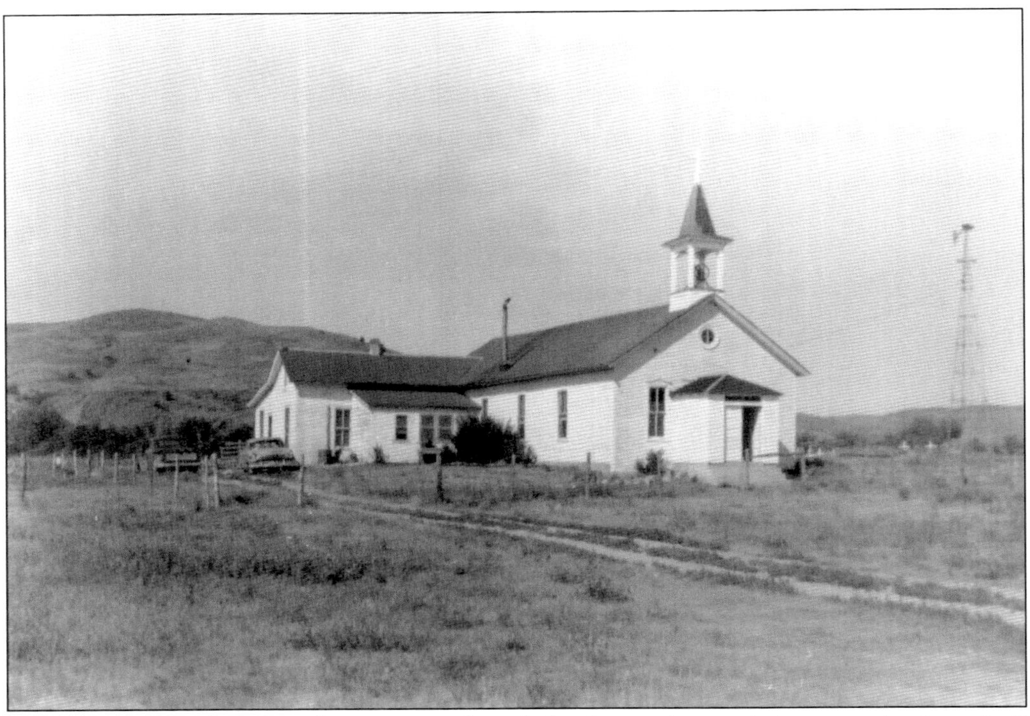

Another unidentified church is a reminder of the far-reaching mission organization of all denominations in the late 1800s and early 1900s. (St. Joseph's Indian School, Chamberlain.)

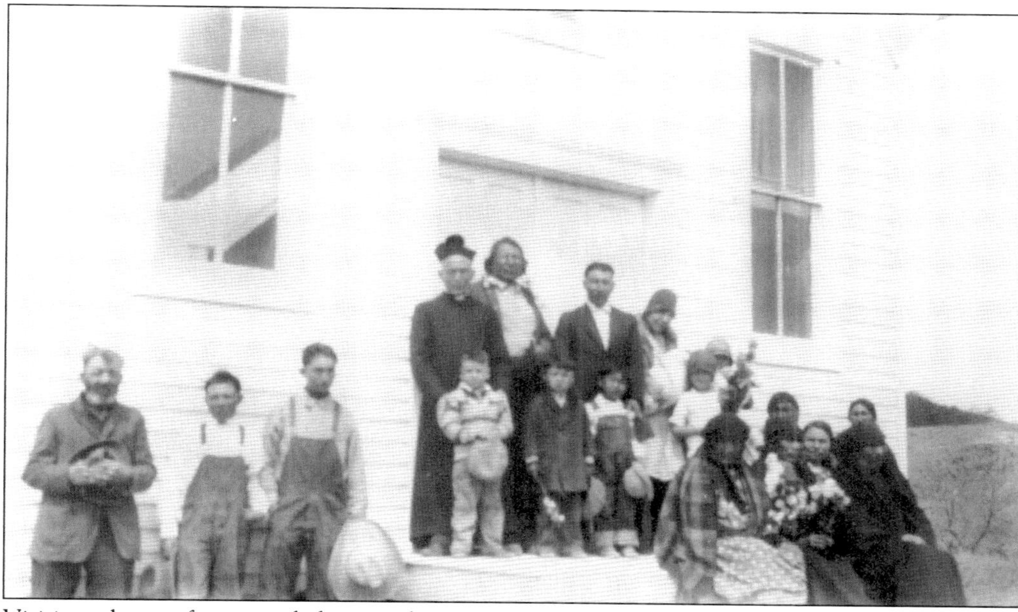

Visiting clergy often traveled great distances to outlying churches. Catechists or lay people conducted the services when a priest was unavailable. (St. Joseph's Indian School, Chamberlain.)

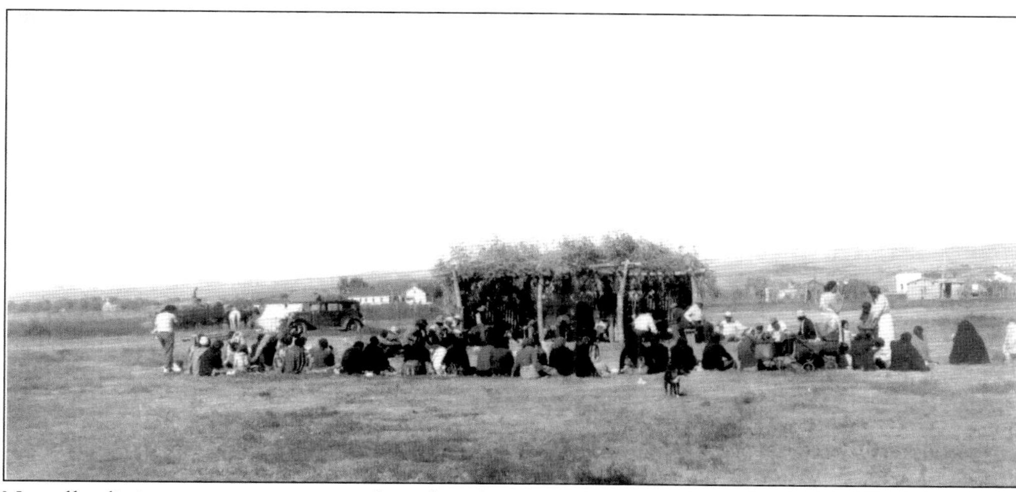

Not all religious activities occurred in churches. Many events on the reservations were held in brush-covered arbors, as shown in this photograph. The clergy traveled many miles to visit the native people. (St. Joseph's Indian School, Chamberlain.)

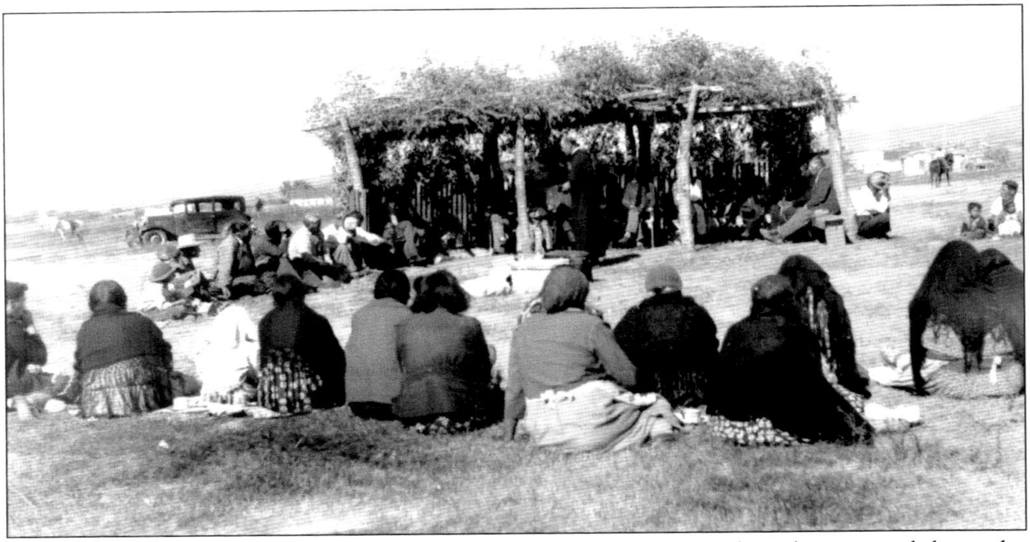

Women gather to listen to a traveling priest who probably arrived in the automobile to the left. Not all priests who came to St. Joseph's knew how to drive. They had to learn in order to conduct visitations in the mission fields. (St. Joseph's Indian School, Chamberlain.)

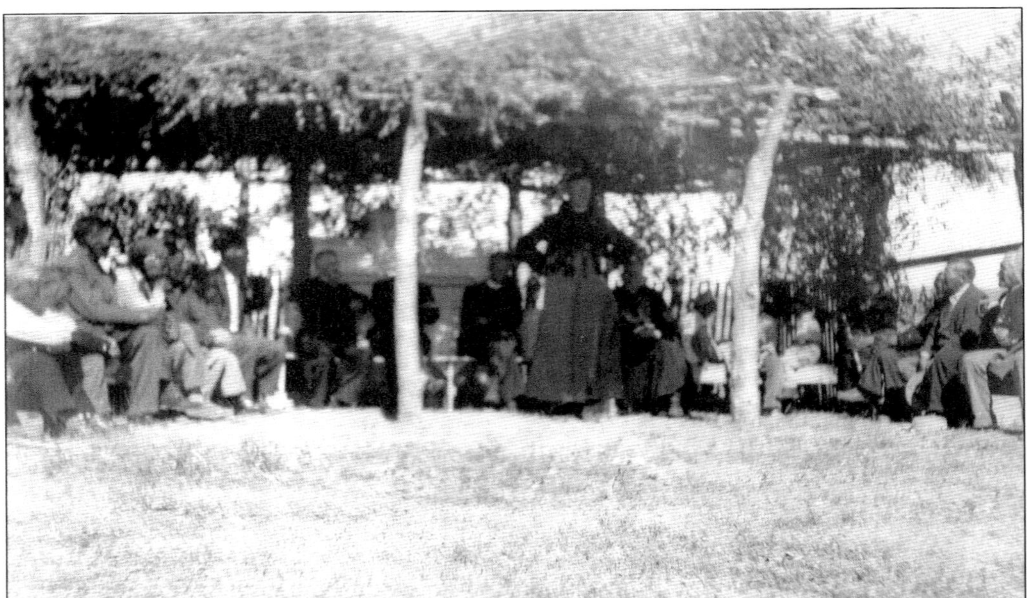

A priest speaks to his flock in the mission field. Many Lakota people lived miles away from a church, and could not attend on a regular basis. During the Great Depression, many of their horses died due to starvation conditions attributed to a drought. They depended on horses as their primary means of transportation. (St. Joseph's Indian School, Chamberlain.)

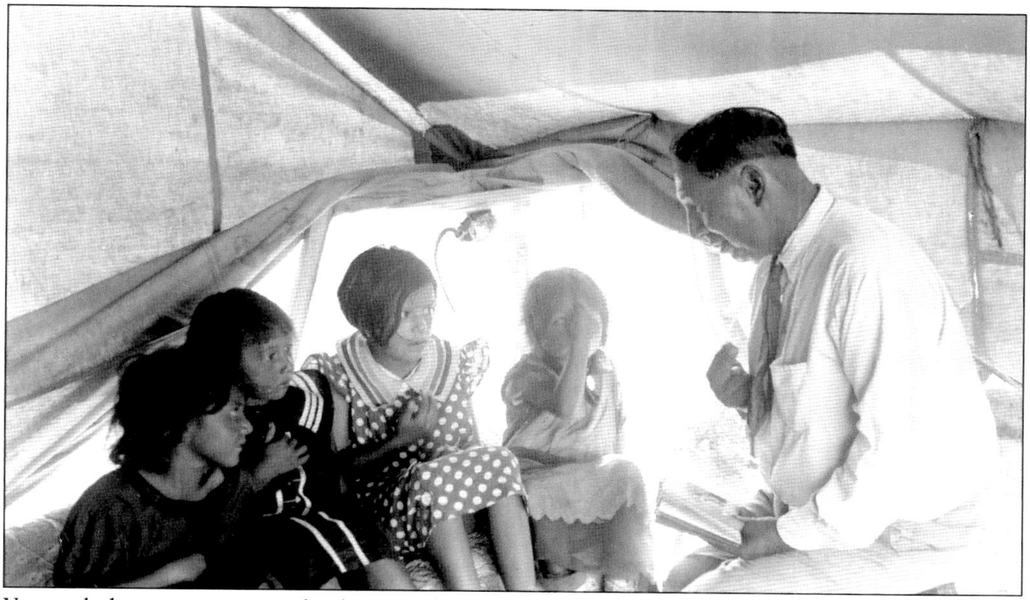

Young ladies in a tent study the catechist intently as they learn the sign of the cross. (St. Joseph's Indian School, Chamberlain.)

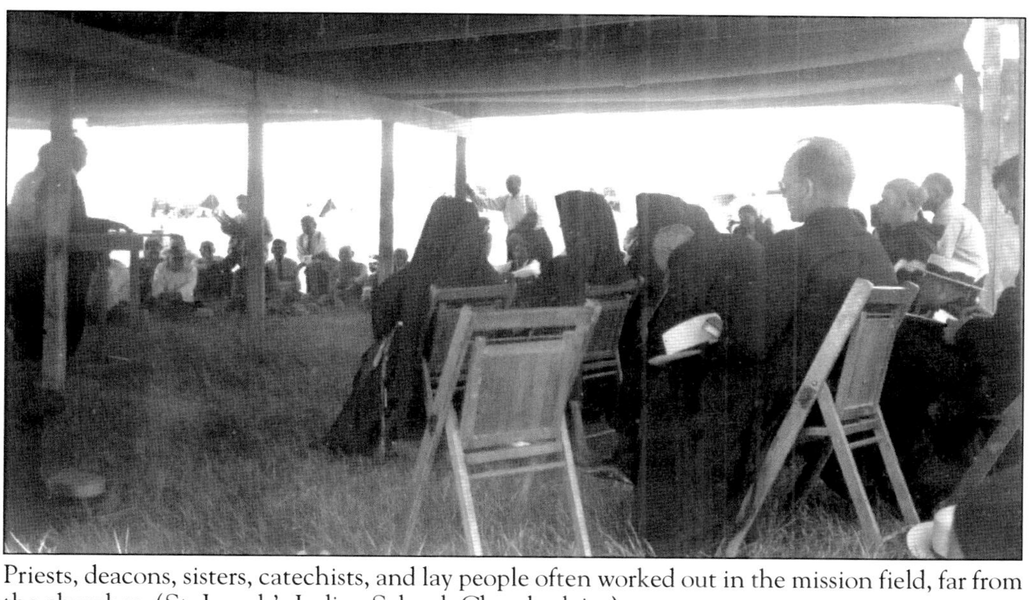

Priests, deacons, sisters, catechists, and lay people often worked out in the mission field, far from the churches. (St. Joseph's Indian School, Chamberlain.)

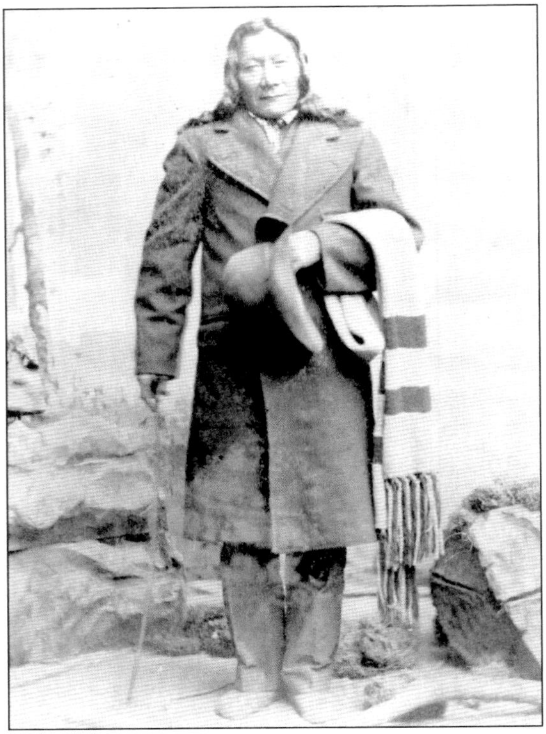

Chief Medicine Bull established his camp near the mouth of the White River. He sent his two children to the Hampton Institute in Virginia to be educated. Elaine Goodale worked at his camp where she set up a school. In her book, she referred to Medicine Bull's kindly face. Chief Medicine Bull became an Episcopalian and is buried in an Episcopal Cemetery. Medicine Bull's son, Sam, was trained to become a catechist, farmer, and carpenter on the Lower Brule. (South Dakota Historical Society Archives.)

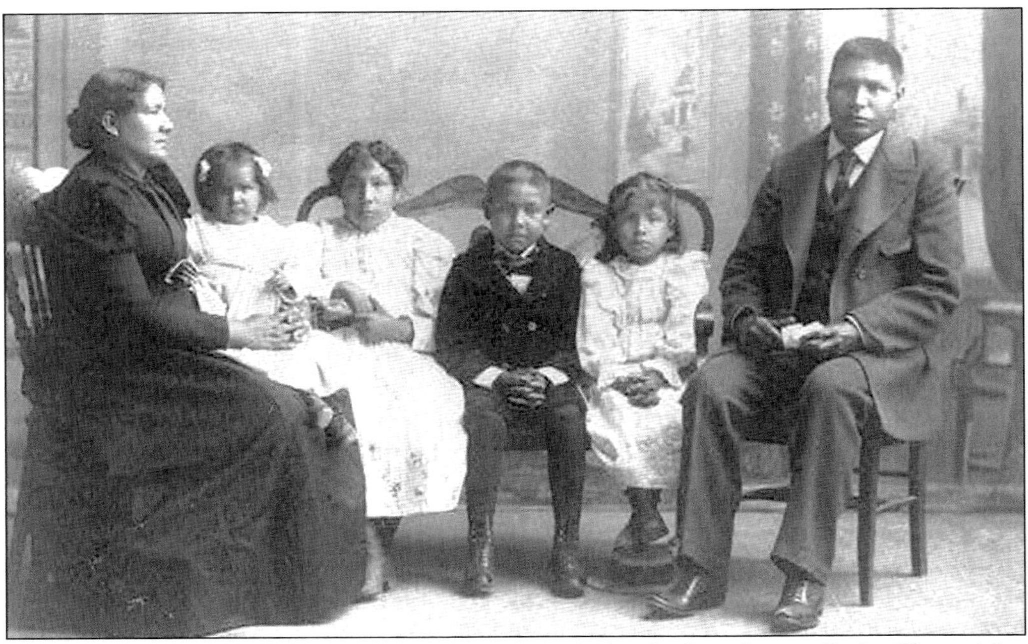

This 1899–1900 photograph is of Benjamin Brave's family from Lower Brule. He and his wife were both educated at Hampton Institute. (Library of Congress Prints and Photographs Division; Frances Benjamin Johnston Collection. LC-USZ62-78701.)

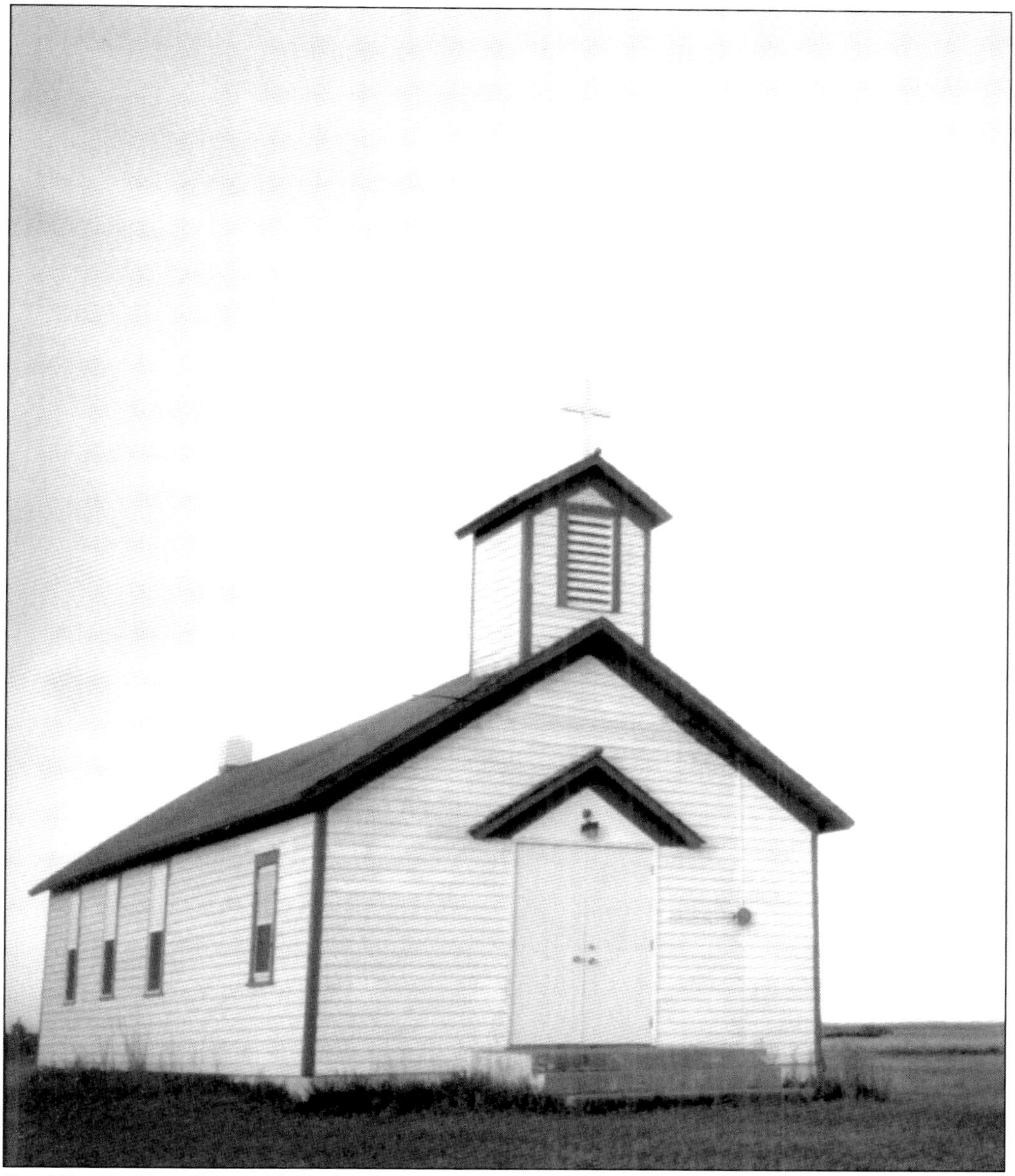

St. Alban's Church, established around 1884 in Standing Cloud's jurisdiction, is located near old Fort Hale, north of Chamberlain. Fort Hale was established in 1878 and abandoned in 1884. Chief Medicine Bull's son, Samuel Medicine Bull, became the Episcopal catechist several years afterward. Other clergy who have served St. Alban's include Rev. Thomas Heminger, Rev. T.J. Rouilland, Rev. Ronald Hennies, and the Rev. John B. Lurvey. By 1892, the Episcopal Church had established eight stations on the Lower Brule under the leadership of Rev. Luke Walker, a native priest. The names of these churches were: Church of the Holy Comforter, St. Alban's Chapel, Chapel of the Messiah, Chapel of the Holy Faith, Chapel of the Holy Name, Chapel of the Savior, and St. Peter's Station. Tornadoes struck both the Crow Creek and Lower Brule Reservations on June 14, 1924, destroying six of ten chapels on both reservations. Plans were made to rebuild soon after.

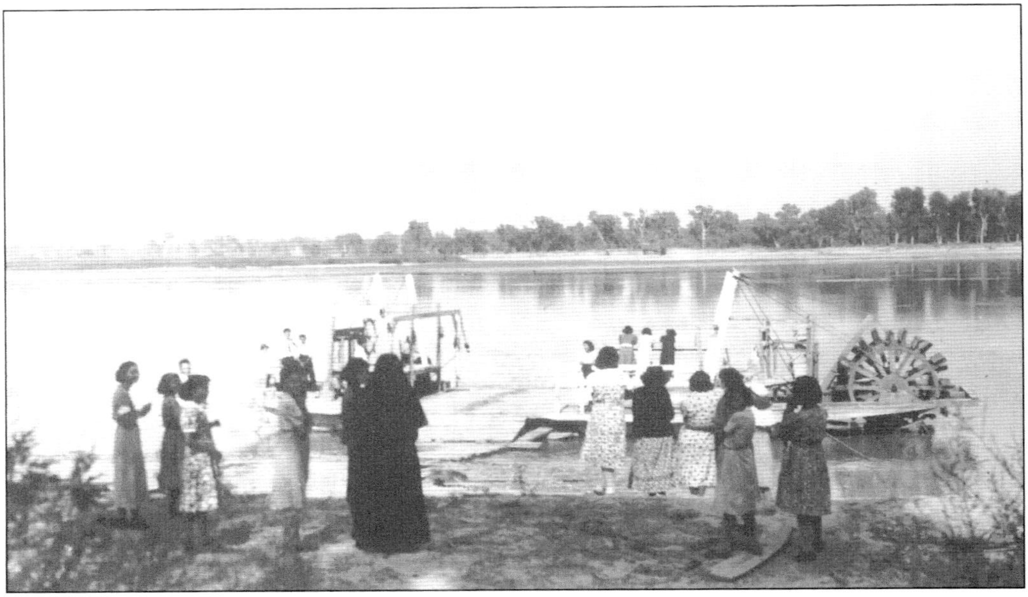

Ferry boats were used to transport passengers across the Missouri River from St. Joseph's on the east side to the reservations on the west bank of the river.

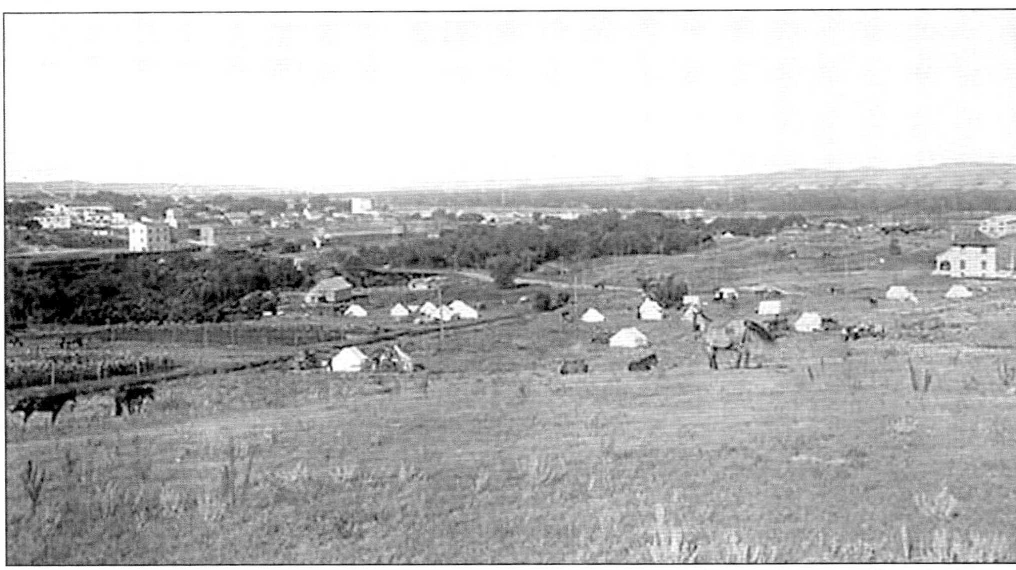

This undated postcard is of a Native American encampment on the outskirts of Chamberlain, a historic area, beginning with Lewis and Clark's expedition in 1804 when they camped near the area. The Columbia Fur Company organized Fort Lookout in 1822, which was later absorbed by the American Fur Company. Ft. Kiowa had been built nearby. In 1840, Father Christian Hoecken baptized children near here. The treaty of 1865, signed by Medicine Bull, Iron Nation, and 13 other chiefs, created the Lower Brule Reservation. Lower Brule agency was moved to Oacoma near Chamberlain in 1876.